Turnaround

Turnaround

THE UNTOLD STORY
OF BEAR BRYANT'S FIRST YEAR
AS HEAD COACH AT ALABAMA

◆

TOM STODDARD

Black Belt Press
Montgomery

The Black Belt Press

P.O. Box 551

Montgomery, AL 36101

Excerpts from *The Legend of Bear Bryant* © 1987 by Mickey Herskowitz reprinted by permission of Mr. Herskowitz. Excerpt from *Memoir from Ant Proof Case: A Novel* © 1995 by Mark Helprin, reprinted by permission of Harcourt, Brace & Company.

Library of Congress Cataloging-in-Publication Data
Stoddard, Tom. 1939–
    Turnaround : the untold story of Bear Bryant's first year as head coach at Alabama / by Tom Stoddard.
      p. cm.
    Includes index.
    ISBN 1-881320-70-7
    1. Bryant, Paul W. 2. Football coaches—United States—Biography.
3. University of Alabama—Football—History. I. Title.
GV939.B785S86 1996
796.332'092—dc20
[B]   96-32533
                                                  CIP

Design by Randall Williams
Printed in the United States of America
by the Maple-Vail Book Manufacturing Group
96 97 98   5 4 3 2 1

The Black Belt, defined by its dark, rich soil, stretches across central Alabama. It was the heart of the cotton belt. It was and is a place of great beauty, of extreme wealth and grinding poverty, of pain and joy. Here we take our stand, listening to the past, looking to the future.

For my mother,

Doris Rich,

who got me started

Contents

ACKNOWLEDGMENTS
and AUTHOR'S NOTE

I am grateful to the players and coaches from the Alabama Crimson Tide team in 1958 for their willingness to talk about their experiences in 1958. Fred Sington Jr. was the first player I interviewed and I owe him thanks for starting me off with an excellent overview and for providing many leads to other players. A Club president Harry Lee was always willing to help with a telephone number or an address. Morris Childers read the manuscript and offered many useful suggestions.

Much of the research for this book was done at the Paul W. Bryant Museum at the University of Alabama and I am indebted to the cooperative staff there for many favors and kindnesses. In particular Director Ken Gaddy, Jan Adams, and Taylor Watson were willing and able at any time to search out a file or answer a question. Marvin Whiting and others at the Birmingham Public Library Archives also provided help and advice.

ALTHOUGH I WAS at the University of Alabama in 1958, and worked in the athletic department, I began this book with only a sketchy knowledge of the events described, and without personal acquaintance with any of the players or coaches I later interviewed. I felt certain, however, that there would be some interesting stories about Bear Bryant's first year at Alabama.

The stories were not only interesting, but poignant. As I began to interview the men who were on the team upon his arrival in 1958, it soon became clear that what happened to them then has profoundly affected their views of the stories of their lives. Placed at a young age under tremendous physical and mental pressure, some failed and some survived. They would agree that nothing they did then was as important as building a career or raising a family. But to a great degree they still define and even judge themselves today on their success as football players then.

Virtually everyone I interviewed had a sense of Bryant's tremendous personal force, and the great majority of the men who played football under him feel they were privileged to have done so. Most say they learned valuable lessons that have served them well in life. But among many there is some ambivalence, too. One can also learn lessons from being in a hurricane.

This book is based on hundreds of hours of interviews with players, coaches and others who knew Bryant in 1958. But the arrangement and interpretations are mine, not the players'. The following passage from Mark Helprin's novel, *Memoir from Ant Proof Case*, says it better than I can:

> "Anchored though you are in fact and document, to write a history is to write a novel with checkpoints, for you must subject the real and absolute truth, too wide and varied for any but God to comprehend, to the idiosyncratic constraints of your own understanding. A 'definitive' history is only one in which someone has succeeded not in recreating the past but in casting it according to his own lights . . . ."

"There is little difference between man and man,

but superiority lies with him

who is reared in the severest school."

King Archidamus of Sparta,
quoted by Thucydides

PROLOGUE

Incredibly, it was Alabama 3, LSU 0.

It was halftime. As the team filed into the grubby dressing room at Ladd Stadium in Mobile, sweating and muddy, they felt a sense of exhilaration. Each of them felt a strong sense of accomplishment from just being there. Now it appeared that they had a chance to defeat Paul Dietzel's powerful, deep and incredibly fast Bengal Tigers.

Seated in front of their lockers, sipping Coca-Cola, the young men from Alabama were also seeing another side to their complex, charismatic new coach, Paul (Bear) Bryant.

Up to now the young men had experienced Bryant as a demanding taskmaster, relentless and judgmental. Some of their most talented teammates, pushed beyond the limits of their endurance, had left the team. Those who had endured through the grueling days of practice were still struggling to learn Bryant's system and how to meet his expectations. But now Bryant was visibly excited, and he urged his players to continue to battle.

"Everybody listen now," Bryant said. "It's the most important 30 minutes of your lives. You are headed for one of the greatest victories in the history of Alabama football. Everybody needs to decide what he's going to do. If we fumble the first play, are you going to give up? Or are you going to hold?

"You've come this far — give it your best. Give it your very best. Let's go."

Bryant's young coaches made very few changes at halftime. Alabama would have the wind in the fourth quarter. If they could keep the lead until then, if they could get a break — who could tell?

A win over LSU would have been a remarkable accomplishment. The team the new coach had inherited from former Alabama Coach J. B. (Ears) Whitworth, had won only four games, and tied two, in three previous years. Alabama had lost to the Tigers 28-0 the previous year. But less than ten months after his return to the campus where he had played the "other end" from Don Hutson in 1935, Bryant had brought the team to a peak of physical conditioning and had begun to restore his players' belief in themselves and their ability to win.

But there had been a price to pay — a high price.

CHAPTER ONE

Disarray & Defeat

T o understand what the return of Paul Bryant meant to Alabama football in 1958, one needs to know the depths to which the program had fallen before his arrival. Everyone knows that under Coach J. B. (Ears) Whitworth, the team had won only four games in three years. But the rot went far beyond Whitworth. There was a lack of leadership and vision throughout the athletic department and even in the University itself.

The decline in Alabama's football program began slowly in 1947, after the retirement of the legendary Frank Thomas, who won 115 games in 15 years. Forced to step down from active coaching because of high blood pressure, Thomas offered the job to Bryant, then coaching at Kentucky, and Bryant had informally accepted. But when Kentucky President Dr. Herman Donovan got wind of the move, he forbade Bryant to leave and rewrote Bryant's contract. "You've got a contract here. You're not going anywhere," he said. So Bryant backed out, and Thomas then chose Harold (Red) Drew, head coach at Ole Miss, who had been an assistant coach at Alabama from 1931 to 1942.

Drew's teams were competitive in his early years. He scrapped the single wing, put in the split-T offense, and oversaw the renewal of the series with Auburn in 1948. Alabama pounded the cross-state Tigers five years out of six.

In 1954, with most of its starters back after a 6-3-3 season, Alabama won four of its first five but then sagged, scoring only two touchdowns in six games and failing to win again. By the time of the final loss, to Auburn 28-0, it was clear to knowledgeable observers that the program was falling behind. Sophisticated young coaches like Darryl Royal at Mississippi State and Bud Wilkinson at Oklahoma were building strong programs by applying modern organizational techniques to football. Practitioners of the old game were becoming outmoded.

Bryant, in his book *Bear,* says he was approached again by Alabama and offered the head coaching job. But Drew had been his end coach, and "I wouldn't be a party to replacing him," he said. Another problem was that Hank Crisp, who had recruited Bryant, had just been named athletic director in March 1954. Crisp had been at Alabama since 1921, had coached virtually every sport, and had already served one tour as AD between 1931 and 1939. Crisp liked to exercise authority, and would sometimes contradict Drew about football matters. Bryant knew that, and he was smart enough to know that kind of divided authority was poison.

Under the uncertain leadership of Dr. O. C. Carmichael, Alabama was unable to sign Bryant and dropped the quest for a top-notch coach. While denying for weeks it had any plans to replace Drew, the athletic committee of the Board of Trustees was still looking, and in a secret meeting early in December 1954 finally settled on Whitworth, a former Alabama lineman then head coach at Oklahoma A&M. Whitworth was flown to Tuscaloosa, and after a bargaining session was offered a three-year contract at $11,000 a year. Drew was farmed out to the track team.

Whitworth was an amiable, good-hearted man with close ties to Alabama alumni. He had played alongside Fred Sington, Sr., on the Alabama line for three years. Following his graduation, he had coached linemen at Alabama, LSU, and Georgia. When summoned home, he had been head coach at Oklahoma A&M for five years.

Whitworth's record as a head coach at Oklahoma A&M was 22-27-2. In a friendly column the day Coach Whit was hired, Benny Marshall of the *Birmingham News* reported that coaches in the Southwest Conference attributed Whitworth's failure to build a winner at Oklahoma

University of Alabama Sports Information

Coach J.B. (Ears) Whitworth

A&M to the difficulty of recruiting against Oklahoma's Wilkinson. Quoting an unnamed source from out west, Marshall wrote that Whitworth was a "disciplinarian" and a "fundamentalist" whose teams "may not beat you, but, brother, they'll fight you to the end."

In Marshall's column, Whitworth sounded almost like Bear Bryant. "About half of [Whitworth's] first squad had quit before the first spring training was over," Marshall said, quoting an "Oklahoma admirer."

"Only those who were willing to pay the price in hard work . . . the guys who could really take it . . . stayed on."

Athletic Director Crisp, who knew Whitworth from his playing and coaching days at Alabama, said, "The coaches I talked to agreed that Whit was a sound football coach, a hard worker, and a man well-liked by the public and his players."

That was true, but Alabama football did not need a nice guy. Whitworth had neither the temperament nor the experience to bring Alabama into the increasingly sophisticated world of modern college football. Neither was he given the administrative clout. He was allowed to hire only two coaches, and required to retain the rest from Drew's staff. That meant divided loyalties to begin with. "He didn't have a whore's chance," said Finus C. Gaston, who worked as sports information director for both Whitworth and Bryant.

To make it worse, Whitworth's boss, Crisp, was still on his coaching staff, ostensibly in charge of the defense. This muddled line of authority, a problem under Coach Drew as well, was a continued source of confusion and a sense of helpless lunacy around the football program. Crisp was notoriously tight with a dollar, and vetoed Whitworth's plans for improvements such as providing traveling uniforms for the team. Near the end of Whitworth's tenure, the two men got into an unseemly dispute about socks — socks! — while the players watched in amazement.

The Whitworth approach to practice did little to teach players the kind of skills they would need to compete in the Southeastern Conference. There was virtually no plan except in his head. On some days drills would last for hours. On others, Whitworth and Crisp might disagree, Whitworth would become tearful, and the athletes would be told to go in early. In his memoirs, Bart Starr, who was benched by Whitworth, said the coach preceded nearly every statement with, "Here's what they are doing at Oklahoma."

It wasn't that the practices were soft or easy. Crisp, who had lost a hand as a youth, could be especially fierce. Constantly gnawing on a piece of foam rubber as a replacement for cigarettes during practice, Crisp had a surefire way to get players' attention. "I'd love to have a nickel for every time Coach Hank would take that nub and hit you in the ribs," said Dave Sington, who played under Whitworth in 1956 and 1957.

But many athletes did not get any significant work during practice, and the coaches were inconsistent in their approach. Running sprints one day under the direction of Moose Johnson, one of the coaches Whitworth had brought with him from Oklahoma, the players became fatigued. Sammy Smith, who lettered as a lineman for two years under Whitworth, remembers that one of the players spoke up.

"Damn, coach, I'm tired," the player said, "we've run enough of these wind sprints."

Johnson said, "Well, golly, guys, I wanted to get you in shape." But when someone else said "I think we've run enough" Johnson sent the team in. Smith thought to himself, "I'm tired, but gosh this is no way to run a football team."

Johnson himself resembled Babe Ruth; he was a porcine prototype of the intellectually limited lineman. Johnson was a good recruiter — instrumental in courting and signing a number of good athletes — but as a coach he had limitations. Once, a player relates, Coach Whitworth told Johnson to demonstrate a 45-degree pass pattern. Johnson didn't know what it was.

In most practices, after working out for an hour or so, most of the players, as many as 80 or 90 boys, would stand around watching the first and second teams scrimmage. Roy Holsomback, a freshman lineman in the fall of 1957, remembers standing for what seemed like hours. Then finally a coach would grab him, and say, "get in there."

"You couldn't hardly move, after . . . all that time," he said.

Charlie Gray, an All-State end from Pell City, starting as a sophomore in 1956, remembers how poorly prepared the team was in his first game at Alabama. Alabama was playing Rice in Houston. On defense, Gray was awaiting a linebacker's decision on who would cover Buddy Dial, an All-American end. The linebacker was confused.

"Gray, you get him," he called. "No, I'll get him. Oh, blankety blank, let the blankety blank go."

Gray rushed the passer, and the uncovered Dial caught a long touchdown pass. "My goodness," Gray thought, "this thing has to get better than this." But under Whitworth it never did.

The lack of oneness on the team was compounded by cultural gulf between the athletes at Alabama at the time. In the dorm during the Whitworth years were a number of older boys, men really, who had served in the military during the Korean War. Drinking and carousing were common. Gary O'Steen, an innocent 17-year-old freshman in 1956, remembers a group that demanded he drive them around while they went on a toot. "I would try to hide in my room and they'd just tear the door down . . . kick it in . . . if you didn't open it they'd put lighter fluid under it and set the door on fire. So I had to get up and drive them around while they drank all night." An athlete found guilty of tearing down a door would be punished by having his $15 laundry money docked for restitution. But some of the rougher veterans would have to have played until they were middle-aged to pay everything back, one observer recalled.

The atmosphere was destructive and a bad influence on the younger players. Upon his arrival on campus as a freshman, Sammy Smith brought his new school books into the dorm and was putting them away when an upperclassman stopped by.

"What are you going to do with those books?" the upperclassman asked. Smith said, "I'm going to go to school."

"Hell, man, I'll show you what to do with those books," the upperclassman said.

"Well, I was a kid, a freshman," Smith said. " . . . he was an upperclassman . . . he took me down to some black market store that they knew of, and we sold my books. He said, 'That's what you do with your books. Now you know what you're going to do with your money? Drink some beer, man. Football players drink beer.' And we drank the money away."

One of the toughest of the military veterans was Don Kinderknecht, from Hays, Kansas. Whatever his virtues as a player, Kinderknecht when drinking was not a peaceful man. A number of players remember an epic fight between Kinderknecht and another veteran, Carl Valletto, after Kinderknecht pulled a knife on Valletto's roommate, Richard Strum from Biloxi, Mississippi.

Strum was talking on the telephone to his girl friend, and apparently Kinderknecht was bitter from a recent romantic experience that had not turned out to his satisfaction. He made some lewd remarks that were intended, Strum thought, to embarrass him and his girl friend. When Strum objected, Kinderknecht — he was drunk — backed him into the phone booth, pulled a knife and cut him on the arm.

At about that point, Valletto, who was Strum's roommate, intervened. Valletto was a big ex-Marine and he liked Strum. He bludgeoned Kinderknecht with his huge hands — as big as dinner plates — until the Kansan was whipped. Neither Valletto nor Kinderknecht was disciplined as a result. On another night, Kinderknecht picked up manager James Beall and threw him out a window. Fortunately, they were on the first floor at the time.

Dorm visits by the police and fire departments were common. On one memorable occasion, the athletes set fire to wastebaskets filled with paper, and blew the smoke out the windows with fans. Arriving firemen were pelted unmercifully with water balloons.

By 1957, freshmen who were tough enough and not yet spoiled by the losing attitude would dominate the older players in practice. "We'd just manhandle them," remembers Don Cochran, later a Bryant favorite. "They were out of shape, they'd lunge at you one time, and that was about all if they were on offense. And on defense they sure weren't going to pursue long, [because that would give] you . . . a chance to knock 'em down two or three times." But players less prepossessing than Cochran might face retaliation in the dorm.

The first floor of Friedman Hall was senior territory. One day freshman Duff Morrison, an all-American high school halfback from Memphis, strayed into a senior party in the first floor commons. "Someone yells, 'Freshman what are you doing in here?' I took off running back down that hall, and just as I made that turn a can of beer, a full can of beer, took the plaster out of the ceiling . . ."

Whitworth's first team lost ten straight. The defense allowed at least 20 points in every game, and the least lopsided loss was by 15 points, 6-21, to Vanderbilt.

When Whitworth — often overruled by Crisp — attempted to impose stricter discipline in the spring of 1956, athletes in the Alabama athletic dorm staged what amounted to a strike. About 100 athletes from the track, football and basketball teams moved out of the dorm and a spokesman said they would "go elsewhere" if their demands were not met.

The trigger for the walkout was the suspension of a football player, Roy Vickery, who had been involved in an automobile accident in Tuscaloosa. But the athletes were also unhappy with required study halls, early curfews, and a requirement that they get a signed slip from the coach who was in charge of the dormitory if they wished to go home for the weekend.

Crisp met immediately with a delegation of athletes and cleared up a misunderstanding about Vickery's status. He had been put on probation, not expelled. Crisp quickly agreed to almost all of the players' other demands, and the mini-crisis was over.

That may have been a signal to Alabama athletes that they, not the coaches, could run the show. For whatever reason, conditions in Friedman Hall got even worse. Friedman Hall became known as the "ape dorm," and the reputation of athletes among students and faculty was low. Seeing athletes approaching, "real" students would cross to the other side of the street.

Pedestrians and motorists passing the dorm were often pelted with water balloons, and freshmen were hazed unmercifully and sometimes paddled, or "slatted," by the upperclassmen.* The slatting may have been an offshoot of initiation practices in the Alabama lettermen's club known as the "A Club." The brutality — not to say stupidity — of these initiations seems to have been unusual among SEC schools.

---

*By 1957, a number of recruits had secured a commitment from Whitworth that this type of harassment would be ended.

Some of the hazing associated with the initiation was perhaps not too extreme — shaved heads, carrying animals to class, military drill in the quadrangle. The new lettermen survived being coated with syrup, rolled in corn flakes and deposited in the middle of the Alabama backwoods to find a way home on their own. Fortunately, Gary O'Steen recalled, there were still people back then who would open their doors to strangers who needed to use the phone in the middle of the night.

But the slatting had gone past reason. Former lettermen from earlier years were invited, and booze flowed freely. Then the new lettermen reported to the gym, usually having resorted to drink to blot out what they knew was coming.

In the A Club room, a list was posted with each new letterman's name, and veterans signed up for those they wanted to swat.

"They've got a long table with a mattress on it," one player recalled, " . . . and you stand in front of it, reach down between your legs and hold on to your balls . . . and you pick out the people you want to hit you . . . your five . . . and you get five licks. They'd bust a paddle about on every lick . . . if they called it a bad lick, you'd have to take another one . . ." The slats were substantial — ordered every year for the purpose — 1 x 4 pine, with something like baseball handles cut into them.

Naturally, many athletes ended up with severe bruises on their backsides from the slatting sessions. Sammy Smith, who taunted his tormentors, ended up with blood running out of his shorts. Mothers who were shown the damage were horrified. Nevertheless, the slatting continued during Bryant's first two years at the University, and was moderated by intervention of the dean only in the initiations of 1960.

THE 1956 TEAM won two games and tied one, and lost to Auburn 34-7. After the season, in a straw poll among Birmingham football supporters, 295 of 352 replying found the Whitworth staff "not qualified." In a raucous Birmingham alumni meeting after the season many cries for Coach Whit's scalp were heard. Attendees called for a vote to recommend Whitworth's firing before the next season. After an initial count of a show of hands was disputed, the alumni president, Bob Davidson, invited supporters and detractors to assemble on opposite sides of the room. The motion of no confidence was narrowly defeated, but it was clear that, barring a sensational next season, Whitworth would be history when his contract expired in December 1957.

Off the record, Whitworth told Naylor Stone of the *Birmingham Post-Herald* that he knew the season would be his last. But he and his staff still had some hope that they could at least restore their reputations with a winning season in 1957. Trainer Jim Goostree, hired that summer, recalled that coaches were optimistic going into the season. "There were a number of athletes on campus, and we worked hard, they responded good in the summertime, put a lot of effort into preseason exercise programs and doing things that normally any athlete doesn't really enjoy doing," he recalled. "I supervised that and thought that we were making headway and certainly anticipated a better football season."

Those hopes were quickly dashed. In the opening game of 1957 at Tiger Stadium in Baton Rouge, prize LSU sophomore Billy Cannon was overpowering against a disorganized Alabama team. Cannon ran for 140 yards, 75 in a single burst in the fourth quarter, and scored two touchdowns.

In its next game, Alabama managed to tie Vanderbilt 6-6. But a trip to Ft. Worth to play Texas Christian resulted in another disastrous drubbing, 28-0 — and TCU actually lost four fumbles. Whitworth was so disgusted with the team's play that he and the other coaches spent only moments in the dressing room at halftime, perhaps hoping that some leadership would emerge among the players. But when Marshall Brown, a senior halfback who later was a student coach for Bryant, jumped up and began haranguing the team, other players told him to "sit down and shut up."

A 14-0 loss to Tennessee and a 25-12 defeat by Mississippi State at Homecoming ended all doubt. Fully aware of Whitworth's situation, the Alabama players speculated often about whom would be chosen to replace him. Few of the players wanted Paul Bryant.

Carl Valletto, the ex-Marine, remembers that most of the older players were hoping that Red Sanders, Bryant's old mentor from

Vanderbilt, then at UCLA, would get the call "because we had heard about the travesty at Junction down at Texas A&M, and being regimented like we were under Whitworth it was hard to imagine what was going to happen. We were looking for the best that we could get and at the time nobody . . . was hoping we got Bear Bryant. "I can assure you, no one was looking forward to him coming, no football players," Don Heath, a junior center from Anniston, said. Many thought Bryant was making too much money in Texas to come to Alabama.

Chuck Allen, a tackle and commerce major from Athens, recalls that many of the players were pulling for Ray Graves, Bobby Dodd's top assistant at Georgia Tech, "because we heard they played a lot of volleyball over there."

But Alabama alumni were united. Rumors of Bryant's return, and a clear, fervent wish for such an event, spread through the state. One factor decidedly in favor of a return by Bryant was a pending change in the University administration.

The University's reputation had been badly hurt, in early 1956, by its disastrous handling of the enrollment of the school's first Negro student, Autherine Lucy. University President Dr. O. C. Carmichael and the trustees had underestimated the potential for opposition to Lucy's enrollment. The campus erupted in riots. Lucy and a student radical were expelled. The *Montgomery Advertiser* reported that more than thirty top educators left the University. At the end of the year, Carmichael resigned. To replace him, trustees turned to a bright young Kentuckian, Frank Rose, the president of little Transylvania College in Lexington, Kentucky. Rose had leadership qualities absent in Carmichael, and he was enough of a politician to keep on good terms with both the segregationists and the moderates on the board.

Oddly enough, it was Bryant who was first asked for a recommendation about Rose, not the other way around, according to E. Culpepper Clark, who wrote about the hiring in his book *The Schoolhouse Door*. A member of the board of trustees, Ernest Williams, had heard Rose speak at a national convention of the Kappa Alpha fraternity, and was impressed. Rose had been named one of the top ten outstanding young men in America by the Jaycees, on a list that included Robert F. Kennedy.

Another trustee, John A. Caddell, had also heard good things about Rose. Caddell, who knew Bryant, called him to ask him about Rose. Bryant gave Rose a warm recommendation. On September 5, 1957, the board announced that Rose would be the new president effective as of January 1, and arranged to cure his only apparent defect, the lack of an earned doctorate, by awarding him an honorary one the next year.

Though still not officially in office, Rose did not dally in showing the alumni that he understood the importance of football at Alabama. Whitworth was told that he would not be retained, and was allowed to make the announcement himself, which he did on October 21 to the Monday Morning Quarterback Club in Birmingham.

Soon afterward, two athletes from Biloxi, Mississippi, Richard Strum and Norbie Ronsonet, ran into Whitworth in front of the First National Bank Building in downtown Tuscaloosa. Whitworth, in tears, went up to the boys and put his arms around their shoulders.

"I'd have given anything in the world to see you guys succeed as football players," he said. "I apologize."

Alabama was about to get a new coach who was not likely to apologize for anything.

CHAPTER TWO

'Only More Determined'

P aul Bryant was 44 years old in 1958, in the prime of his life and in full possession of his remarkable abilities. Though not yet famous, he had established himself as a man who could turn a losing football program into a winning one with dispatch.

He was a big man, and his physical presence contributed to the powerful impression he made. He was still strong enough to grab a 220-pound tackle by the shoulder pads and jerk him to his feet with apparently little effort.

People would always turn to look at him when he entered a room, and fall silent when he began to speak in his deep, rumbling bass. In public and with the media, he would affect the persona of a laconic, somewhat humorous, good ol' Arkansas boy. Furman Bisher, the sports editor of the *Atlanta Journal,* and other writers not from Alabama found this pose hard to take, and sometimes wrote caustically about Bryant's tendency to mouth platitudes. But when Bryant exclaimed "Merciful Heavens," or talked about "What their mommas and daddies taught them" on his weekly television show, Alabama faithful were enraptured.

In private, he could turn sharp and sarcastic and few who felt the lash of his tongue ever forgot it. A reporter who asked a dumb question, an alumnus with what he regarded as a silly request, underlings who presumed that he was a regular guy with whom you could crack jokes on an equal footing, would get at least an icy glare and often a rebuke.

Bryant talked a lot about going first class, and he wore fine silk or tweed jackets and Countess Mara ties when he knew he would be on display. Sometimes he did not care what kind of sartorial impression he made, and then he wore baggy khakis and white shirts. His hats, in the late '50s, tended to be nondescript brown fedoras. It would be years before he adopted the jaunty checkered number he made famous. He smoked unfiltered Chesterfields or whatever cigarettes someone else had. He drank, and sometimes to excess, but not in front of his players. He liked the ladies.

He went to church on Sunday, referred to The Lord and to prayer frequently, and late in life was probably genuinely religious. In 1958, he clearly believed that God helps those who help themselves.

He had a violent temper, and could be profane, intolerant, rude and overbearing. He made much of a prohibition against profanity on the practice field, and would fine himself $5 when he slipped. But like most of the men in coaching and around him, he used gutter language on many occasions when it suited him. "Turd" was a favorite noun.

He seldom said no to a former player, and most of them have stories about how he helped them or even comforted them in times of trouble.* But to the players who first encountered him in 1958, he was simply the most demanding and uncomfortable man they had ever seen. Other coaches had driven them to hard, physical training. But no one in their experience had stated so plainly what he would demand of them and then demonstrated so forcefully that he meant every word.

James Beall, a manager and administrative assistant to Bryant who is now a successful banker, filled in for Bryant's secretary on occasion, and sometimes ran errands for him in the coach's first year at Alabama. Once Beall put through a call from Bobby Dodd, but when Bryant picked up he found an operator still on the line. He chewed Beall out, saying, "Don't ever put me on the phone again unless the person who is calling

---

*Bryant's long time radio producer Bert Bank said that it was not unusual for Bryant to direct him to send some of the money he earned from his radio broadcasts to former players who needed help.

me is on the other end of the line, I don't give a damn if it's the president of the United States, you make sure you get him on that line before you put me on the line."

Beall has another story about Bryant that indicates the coach's disdain for failure of any kind.

Beall's name was pronounced "Bell," but, though corrected from time to time, Bryant persisted in using his own pronunciation. "We were out there practicing," Beall said. ". . . about 40, 50 yards up the way there was a manhole. Coach Bryant came over and said, 'Beel, go stand on that manhole and don't let anybody step on it, because if they do they'll break their leg, so you stand on it so they can see where it is.' So I was up there standing on it . . . [Marlin] Dyess breaks through the line and he's heading straight for me, and I'm thinking, well they are going to blow the whistle, so they blow the whistle, but nobody stopped. And I'm thinking . . . I can stay here and get killed, or I can move and somebody'll break their leg and Coach Bryant will kill me.' So in a split second I decided it was better for them to kill me than Coach Bryant, and they hit me . . . Coach Bryant came up and told Coach Bailey, 'He has got to be the dumbest son of a bitch that ever lived. He can't even get out of the way of a goddam play.' I've got cuts on the side of my face . . . and that was his only comment; there wasn't any 'good job.' . . . He just didn't take any prisoners."

The players who observed him in his first year at Alabama feared him, not only because he had the power to make their lives miserable with a brutal practice session, but also because he demanded from them what few others had — total dedication and intensity in every minute of practice and every minute of a game.

Ken Roberts, who played center for Bryant over two seasons, assessed Bryant as a supreme egotist who somehow felt justified in his behavior even when it was wrong. "I know he knew he could do things wrong. But to him it did not really matter. If I did it wrong, it's okay, I'm Paul Bryant. It'll be all right, y'all will just have to . . . ignore it."

Roberts recalled riding to Anniston with Bryant and some of the other Anniston boys when the head coach was going to make a speech to a booster club there. Bryant told the boys a story about receiving a letter from Jack Dunn, a local booster and former classmate, telling him what good boys and great players the young men were.

Bryant had written Dunn back saying something like, "I don't give a damn what you think, I want to see how they do on the field."

Roberts recalled: "And then he looked at us . . . it was like he did not understand . . . he said, 'and I don't think Jack's ever forgiven me for that.' He could have said, 'Jack I appreciate your input, and let me see how they look on the field.' But he didn't do it that way . . . he said, 'I don't give a damn what you think.' He didn't understand why Jack would get offended at that."

The outlines of Bryant's youth and early years have been often told. Youngest boy in a family of 12 siblings (three died in infancy), he was raised in Arkansas in hardscrabble circumstances that today we would think of as abject poverty. His father, from a family of farmers, was in ill health, unable to work steadily when Bryant was a boy. "I was a mama's boy," he said in his autobiography, *Bear*.*

He was a unruly, even wild, youth, large for his age and fond of fighting. He earned his nickname by wrestling a sideshow bear when he was 14. When he was 13, the Bryant family moved to Fordyce, a football hotbed in south central Arkansas, and there he first took up the game that became his life. It was a perfect match. Football had everything that Paul Bryant liked — strength, violence, cunning and intense competition.

Bryant loved to win. If you beat him at anything, even pitching pennies, he'd "stay there until he beat you, and beat you worse than you beat him," says Bert Bank, his longtime radio producer. Winning football games, from the first day he had a shoemaker nail cleats to his street shoes, became what he lived for.

Hank Crisp, who had connections in Arkansas, brought Bryant to

---

*Years later, after his mother passed away, Bryant was filming a commercial for South Central Bell, in which he was directed to say, "Call your momma." He ad libbed, "I wish I could call mine." It astonished the ad executives, and it made a great commercial.

Alabama in the rumble seat of his Ford coupe in 1931. "He was just like any other kid, only maybe more determined," said Merrill (Hootchman) Collins, an elderly "retainer" who was at Alabama even then. Poorly prepared for college, Bryant spent a year taking remedial subjects at Tuscaloosa High School. But by the time he graduated in 1935, he had become president of the student body and gotten engaged to "the prettiest girl on campus," Mary Harmon Black. The two were married that June.

Bryant frequently downplayed his abilities as a player, but observers

Paul and Mary Harmon Bryant.

such as Red Drew, who coached Alabama's ends at the time, said he was outstanding, with defense a strong point. The legendary sportswriter Grantland Rice told Benny Marshall that Bryant would have made All-American in 1935 if he had not broken his leg against Mississippi State. There's no doubt that he was dedicated — he played against Tennessee with the bone cracked.

Bryant's first coaching job was under his mentor, Frank Thomas, at Alabama, and then he moved to Vanderbilt for four years under Red Sanders. He would have been head coach at Arkansas at age 28 had not the attack at Pearl Harbor and World War II intervened.

Bryant immediately joined the Navy, and he had an affection for the Naval uniform for the rest of his life. Richard Strum, the halfback from Biloxi who retired as a Navy commander, was often asked by Bryant to wear his uniform when he visited practices. Bryant did go overseas, but most of his naval career was in a fitness program. At the war's end he was coaching a football team at North Carolina preflight at Chapel Hill.

Bryant had made the acquaintance of the owner of the Washington Redskins, George Preston Marshall, and when he was released from the Navy it was with Marshall's help that he was offered the head coaching job at the University of Maryland. He brought 17 of his Navy players to the campus and the team won six out of nine games.

Curly Byrd, the Maryland president, said at a year-end banquet that Bryant could coach the Terrapins for his lifetime, but Byrd, a former coach himself, did something Bryant couldn't tolerate. He reinstated a player Bryant had dismissed for a rules violation, and fired one of his assistant coaches. Bryant quit.

Among highly successful people, there often is a turning point that indicates strength of character, an early determination to become the master of one's life. Perhaps this was such a moment for Bryant. Thirty-one years old with a wife and two children, he was confident, or arrogant, enough to stand on principle. He was not out of work for long. Almost immediately, he got and accepted a telegraphed offer for the head coaching job at the University of Kentucky.

Bryant coached at Kentucky for eight years, winning 60 games, losing 23 and tying 5, and developing All-Americans in Bob Gain, Vito (Babe) Parilli, Doug Moseley, Steve Meilinger, and Ray Correll. He tried to leave Kentucky for Arkansas in 1952, and was persuaded against it. But when legendary basketball coach Adolph Rupp was rehired even after a point-shaving scandal, he knew he would never be Number 1 in the Bluegrass State. It was February 1954, and the only decent head coaching job still open was at Texas A&M. He accepted over the phone, negotiating a favorable financial deal later.

His first year at Texas A&M saw the legendary bloodletting at the small town of Junction. Unwilling to subject his first practices to the eyes of alumni, opponents and everyone in the media except his friend and later biographer Mickey Herskowitz of the *Houston Post*, Bryant loaded the Aggie players on buses and took them to an old army base owned by the college. For ten days, the players were subjected to the full Bryant treatment — two-a-day practices, no quarter given. Over half quit, including all five of the team's centers. That fall, A&M won only one game, against Georgia, 6-0.

Bryant's 1955 team turned around to 7-2-1, and in 1956 the Aggies went undefeated and won the Southwestern Conference championship. The team's 34-21 win over Texas that year filled supporters with exhilaration and gratitude. A group of alumni bought Bryant's house from him, giving him a $10,000 capital gain, and of course let him continue to live there. He was given a percentage of the gate at Aggie home games during the 1957 season.

Bryant's 1957 A&M team, though thinner at some positions than in the previous year, won its first eight games, and was rated number one in the country. But then it began to dawn on Aggie faithful that Bryant's alma mater might be calling. In fact, Alabama and Bryant were talking seriously. After Alabama's fifth loss, 7-0 to Tulane in Mobile on November 9, though still not officially in office, Frank Rose took a small delegation to Houston, supposedly in secret, to meet with Bryant. Fred Sington Sr., president of the Alabama Alumni Association and Ernest Williams, who headed the athletic committee of the board, went along. Bryant's Aggies had just won their eighth game, beating SMU, 19-6.

In the meeting, which lasted most of the day, Bryant expressed concern about the status of Crisp, the man who had signed him to an athletic scholarship. Eventually, Crisp came to Texas to confirm to Bryant that he was happy to step aside as athletic director. Bryant asked for complete freedom in choosing his staff, and a long-term contract. Both were agreed to. Bryant's salary was set at $17,500 (Rose earned $20,000), and he was promised a house for himself and his family.

At the end of the day, the deal was sealed with handshakes. The official announcement was to be delayed until the end of the season. But word of the meeting had been leaked, and reporters were clamoring outside the door when the session was over. The news media in Texas and in Alabama would not let go of the story, which made things extremely unpleasant for Bryant. He was still under contract to Texas A&M, and he knew that rumors of his departure would adversely affect his Aggies. It happened almost immediately.

The Houston newspapers printed this headline on November 16: "Bear goes to Bama." The next day, Texas A&M lost its first game of the year, 7-6, to Rice.

Rose did not help matters much the following week when he said in a speech to the Alabama State Chamber of Commerce that the University would hire a coach with "a remarkable record in his profession."

"This is a problem we must solve for once and for all," Rose continued. "We expect to get a man who is a good recruiter, who can recruit well in the South, and who knows the South, a nationally recognized man."

To a lot of folks, that sounded just like Bear Bryant. Still worried about his game with Texas, Bryant wrote and publicized a letter to Rose withdrawing his name from consideration and disingenuously recommending Jim Tatum of Maryland for the Alabama job. But when asked by Mickey Herskowitz to say once and for all that he wasn't interested, Bryant said, "I wouldn't want to say that because I might do it."

In the traditional Thanksgiving Day showdown, the Aggies lost to Texas, 9-7. After the game, Bryant made the statement that would be remembered ever after as "Momma called."

"This is one reason, and one reason only, why I would consider going to Alabama. That's the fact that some think that they need somebody," he said. "Some think I could help them. It's my school and if I was convinced that I could help it, then I'd certainly consider going. Remember how it was when you were a kid out playing and heard your mother calling you? If it was for chores or something, you wouldn't be very anxious to answer. But if you thought she needed you, you'd get going in a hurry. That's the way I feel about this. That would be the only reason in the world I'd consider the possibility."

Herskowitz, in his book *The Legend of Bear Bryant,* recalled this event in Bryant's hotel room after the game.

" . . . I was standing at his elbow, when he took a phone call from an old Alabama classmate," Herskowitz wrote. "I could not hear the exact words, but there was no problem guessing the question: 'Look, Paul, I won't tell anybody if you ask me not to, but everybody is going crazy over here wanting to know if it's true. Are you coming back?'"

"This was an old friend Bryant had known nearly 30 years. He said, 'It's sonsabitches like you who cost me the national championship,' and he slammed down the receiver."

In its final game of the year, Alabama lost ignominiously to Auburn, 40-0, on a day so cold that spectators built a fire in the bleachers at the north end of Legion Field. The tearful Whitworth bid his players good-bye, accepting all blame. A few days later, on December 3, 1957, the front pages of most Alabama newspapers carried the news: Paul Bryant had signed a ten-year contract to be head coach and athletic director at Alabama.

CHAPTER THREE

Man on a Mission

F rom his very first meeting with the Alabama players, on December 9, 1957, Bryant began to indoctrinate them with his beliefs, philosophy, and theory of winning. He made it clear that he was going to do things his way, and that his way demanded their total commitment. He did not much care if a given individual did not wish to give such a commitment, or was unable to. Bryant knew that there would be enough who did, and that he eventually he would win with them.

Bryant met often with his players, and because he so often emphasized common themes, it's impossible to say exactly what he said at that initial meeting. It is often confused with another on January 10, 1958. But if the details and timing are fuzzy, the messages aren't.

Most say that he barely mentioned football in the December 9 meeting.

Crisp introduced him and then left the room. Bryant said that he had accepted the job because his school needed him, and he couldn't say no. He said he hadn't come for money: "I could buy and sell any one of you. I came here to make Alabama a winner again."

He said that what had gone before would be forgotten, that this was to be a new start.

"He looked like a man on a mission," Don Parsons, a sophomore guard from Houston told Naylor Stone of the *Birmingham Post-Herald* that day, "and before he reached the front of the room, you could sense

Paul W. Bryant Museum

Bryant with the members of the team in December 1957, the fateful first meeting. Front row (L-R): Red Stickney, Charles Spano, Billy Rains, Danny Wilbanks. Behind Stickney: Bill Hannah. Middle between Stickney and Spano: Marlin Dyess. Middle between Spano and Rains: Mack Wise. Middle between Rains and Wilbanks: Jerre Brannen. Right corner behind Wilbanks: Dick Strum, Bobby Skelton (against wall).

that everyone was beginning to feel new hope."

"Everything from here on out is going to be first class," Bryant told the squad, "which includes living quarters, food, equipment, modes of travel.

"'And my staff and I are going to see that you play first class football.'"

He talked about taking pride in yourself, in your family and your school. "How many of you have written your mothers this week," he asked. "How many made up your beds this morning? How many went to church on Sunday? How many said your prayers last night?"

He said that he would expect a 110 percent effort from everyone, and that those who were not prepared to make that kind of commitment would do just as well to go ahead and leave. "I don't know any of you and I don't want to know anybody . . . I'll know who I want to know by the end of spring training.

"If you're not committed to winning ball games, to making your grades, go ahead and get your stuff and move out of the dorm, because it's going to show. Pull out so we can concentrate on the players who want to play," he said. "You can have all the God-given ability in the world, but if you don't hustle, you won't play. We're going to start somebody else in your place."

Bryant took no questions. Closing after 23 minutes, he said, "I'll see you people in a few weeks, and believe me, we're going to get down to business."

Immediately after the meeting on December 10, Bryant flew back to College Station to prepare his Aggie team for its last game under him, against Tennessee in the Gator Bowl. Texas A&M alumni were furious with him for leaving, and as Bryant wrote, "It didn't take a genius to see nobody had any heart for the game." He challenged the players to demonstrate their personal pride, and A&M lost a close game, 3-0.

The game was played on a Saturday night. On Wednesday morning, January 1, 1958, Bryant was in his office in Tuscaloosa at 5:30 a.m.

Bryant spent much of January filling out his staff, moving his family, and studying films on all the players. He also took time for several personal appearances at which he tried to explain his approach to football to the anxious and supportive Alabama faithful. One specific occasion was the Bessemer University Club's third — and last — banquet honoring the freshmen players. If not completely rude about it, Bryant was at least skeptical of the rationale for the banquet. "We hadn't won a game," Morris Childers, a player on that team said, "and Bryant . . . was rather insulting. . . . I do remember that he jokingly said that he had never seen anyone celebrate a team that hadn't won a game." According to Childers, Bryant's attitude was, "Why are you having this banquet, this is a bunch of kids that hasn't done anything." Only 15 of the 31 freshmen attending remained in the program a year later.

Bryant had been burned when Texas A&M had been put on probation for recruiting violations resulting from the involvement of overeager alumni. So he took this occasion and others to impress on the Alabama alumni that he intended to keep the recruiting process clean and urging them to stay out of it. "I have heard some bad stories," he said. "If anything is wrong, come and tell me.

"If you are giving anybody any money, for anything, I want you to stop right now. I've done it, and I found out if you pay 'em, they'll quit on you," Bryant told the alumni.

That was a big change. It had been entirely common, in earlier regimes, for Coach Hank Crisp to peel off a few bills for players from time to time, to pay for dental work, or to provide clothing. One source says that after Bryant was hired, Crisp paid off a large standing bill at Tuscaloosa's finest men's store, Black, Friedman and Winston. A Birmingham alumnus, in Sammy Smith's first year, picked him up at the dorm and took him to a clothing store where he bought the young player a new suit of clothes and the most expensive shoes the youngster had ever seen.

So Bryant's remarks must have startled some of the alumni, and they certainly caused some discomfort among the Alabama freshmen. "The previous fall, I knew guys were going down to a filling station and getting money, I don't know if it was $5 or $10 . . . payola, food money, whatever," Bobby Boylston, a former quarterback from Atlanta, remembers. "I never got any . . . but I go to the banquet and a nice man introduced himself to me and said, 'Bobby, here's $5. And when you get back to Tuscaloosa I want you to buy yourself a nice dinner.' Well, I took the $5. I was glad to get it. It was lot of money then. And I'm sitting there with that $5 in my pocket, now I don't know whether to give it back to the guy . . . or what. Anyway, I kept the $5 and went back and bought myself a dinner." But Boylston never got any more money, and Bryant's approach did control the abuses; Alabama was never placed on probation while he was head coach.

Recruiting for 1958 had been an immediate concern, of course. As soon as he announced his move, Bryant had huddled with Crisp to assess potential prospects. To work with Crisp, he hired Jerry Claiborne, a former Kentucky player, 28 years old, as assistant head coach. Claiborne had coached under Bryant at Kentucky and Texas A&M, and had then accepted a job as head defensive coach at Missouri under Frank Broyles. Soft-spoken, highly intelligent, and fully infused with the Bryant approach, Claiborne moved immediately to Tuscaloosa, spending a few nights in the dorm and then sleeping in a guest room in the home of Alabama publicist Finus Gaston.

Working closely with Crisp, Claiborne hit the recruiting trail and arranged for Bryant to talk by telephone to blue chip players considering Alabama. The results turned out to be outstanding — among those signed were Billy Neighbors, Pat Trammell, Jimmy Sharpe, Billy Richardson, Tommy Brooker, John O'Linger, and Bill Rice. The group was the nucleus of Bryant's first national championship team.

The remainder of the staff Bryant hired fully met his requirement that it be made up of "dedicated men who must believe in the head coach and his plan." Carney Laslie, a senior at Alabama when Bryant was a freshmen, was named assistant athletic director. Laslie had coached with Bryant in the military, at Maryland, Kentucky and in College Station. Laslie knew football and was a tight-fisted administrator. Players had been accustomed to helping themselves to socks from the athletic department's stores. Laslie made sure they turned in a dirty pair every time they got a clean one. Any player carried away enough to give a chin-strap to a girlfriend or a young fan would find his laundry money docked by $1.50. Laslie's miserly ways suited Bryant, who never received a high salary and who was known for paying his assistants poorly.

Phil Cutchin, named offensive coach, had played quarterback at Kentucky, served as an infantryman in World War II, and then coached with Bryant in Lexington and at Texas A&M. Cutchin, for one, says he was not intimidated by Bryant — "He wasn't hard to get to know, and he was a super guy to work for . . . you just can't imagine how good he was to work for," Cutchin said.

Sam Bailey, another college quarterback, had never played under Bryant, but had coached for him at Texas A&M for two years. Bailey was very calm, quiet compared to the younger assistants, a highly effective administrator. Bailey moved into Friedman Hall with his wife Mildred, and soon his steady hand had a moderating influence on behavior in the dorm. (On a Sunday soon after their arrival, Mrs. Bailey came in to the chow hall — now to be called the dining room — for dinner. The athletes had seldom seen women there, and Mrs. Bailey's beauty and style made a powerful impression.)

The Baileys' son, Darryl, known as "Beetle," became a favorite of the players. Darryl and Bryant's son, Paul Jr., (called "Cub") were frequent spectators at football practice.

The firebrands on the staff were all former Bryant players. Pat James, the line coach, had played for Bryant at Kentucky and was a standout in the 13-7 Sugar Bowl win over Oklahoma that ended Bud Wilkinson's 32-game win streak. James's fierce attitude frightened some of the players and was admired extravagantly by those who found it easy to give James the constant physical effort he demanded in practice.

Bobby Drake Keith, only 23, and Gene (Bebes) Stallings just 22, the youngest coaches on the staff, were veterans of the Junction experience. Each was delighted to be offered a full-time job with Bryant. Keith had trained to become a petroleum engineer, but job prospects were slim in the winter of '58 and he had been considering going to work for Bum Phillips as an assistant coach in high school. Then he got a call from Bryant. Elmer Smith, originally chosen for the Alabama staff, had decided to return to Texas A&M, and Keith was offered the job.

Stallings had been a student assistant at A&M in the fall of 1957, and was graduating in January 1958. Unlike Keith, he wanted to be a coach, and when Bryant offered him a full-time job at $4,500 a year he thought he was getting "the very best job in the world."

Another former Aggie, Dee Powell, was signed on as a student assistant until the summer, after which he would leave to fulfill his military obligation. The fact that Powell was a short-timer led some Alabama players to believe that he had been designated as the staff hatchet man, and at least one player would find Powell's personal attention, later in the spring, almost too much to bear. Bobby Luna, a hero in Alabama's 61-6 Orange Bowl win over Syracuse in 1953, was also hired as an assistant coach.

Hayden Riley, a combination football and basketball coach from Florence, was hired as an assistant in both sports. Bryant's old end coach, Red Drew, was called upon for scouting duty. Marshall Brown, Tommy Lewis, and John Snoderly, all former Alabama players, were chosen as student assistants. (Another coach, former Memphis State player Bob Ford, joined the team in the fall.)

The Alabama trainer was Jim Goostree, a Tennessean who had been hired by Hank Crisp on the recommendation of Moose Johnson, who was from Goostree's home town. When Bryant arrived, he had made it clear that none of the coaches from Whitworth's staff would be retained, but Goostree's situation was uncertain. After working in limbo for a while, Goostree finally caught Bryant in the hall.

"Well Coach, don't we need to visit?" Goostree asked, and Bryant said, "Oh yeah, I've been wanting to talk to you, come on down to my office."

"The minute we walked in," Goostree recalled, "he wheeled around and sat down on the corner of this conference table, and looked me right in the eye, sitting down, he towered over me somewhat. He said, 'I know more about you than you know about me, and if you want to . . . if you like me, and I like you, after spring practice, you've got a job at Alabama as long as you want one.'"

"Well, I've got 50 percent of that whipped already," Goostree blurted. "I had better get out of here and go to work on the other half." (Bryant retained only two other staff members from the Whitworth era — publicist Finus C. Gaston and athletic business manager B. W. Whittington. Bryant did find jobs for several other coaches with Alabama connections.)

It was a highly effective, deeply professional and disciplined staff,* imbued with Bryant's approach to football, and still in most cases somewhat in awe of their leader. Bryant at this point in his career was the decision-maker on all matters of consequence, and it was obvious to the players that the coaches, even Claiborne and Laslie, feared Bryant's temper and remained constantly aware of his whereabouts during practice sessions. When the little chain at the top of the steps to Bryant's makeshift wooden tower rattled, all eyes would cut toward the center of the field to see where the top man was headed. He seldom descended to bring congratulations.

---

* Bank told Bryant one day that the assistant coaches were so good that even he could have won with them. "No you couldn't," Bryant told him.

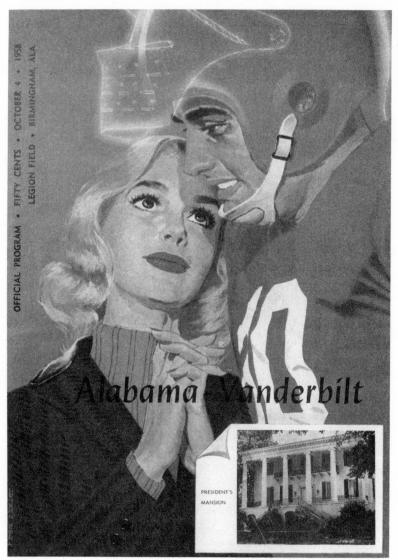

OFFICIAL PROGRAM • FIFTY CENTS • OCTOBER 4 • 1958
LEGION FIELD • BIRMINGHAM, ALA.

Alabama-Vanderbilt

PRESIDENT'S MANSION

CHAPTER FOUR

Mythic Connections

The fifties are thought to have been a boring decade, and in truth it was a time so different than what we have become accustomed to that it is hard to remember how things really were. The civil rights movement was beginning to take hold, and a few beatnik followers of Jack Kerouac were sometimes seen, but the great majority of citizens seemed content. The USA was the best country in the world, and the South was the greatest region.

In 1958, we were closer by eight years to the end of World War II than we are, in 1996, to the last days of the Vietnam conflict. A war hero, Dwight Eisenhower, was president.

Elvis Presley had shaken the foundations of music, but in 1958 he was in the Army. The threat of Communism still seemed enormous.

Most people could get no more than three television channels, and to change from one channel to another, they had to get up and walk over to the set. The largest commercially available televisions were 21 inches diagonally. It would be years before color TV became affordable. Bank credit cards, McDonald's hamburgers, and interstate highways were in their infancy. Computers were huge, incomprehensible things that mutilated cards people were not allowed to fold or spindle.

Heroes were still heroes. No one thought of searching garbage for insights into the character of famous people. People did not yet know that Charles Van Doren had cheated, or that the U. S. was sending spy planes over the USSR. Fidel Castro seemed to many to be an idealistic young revolutionary preferable to the corrupt Cuban dictator Fulgencio Batista.

Football was simpler, too.

College teams played nine or ten games, and then the season ended. Fewer than 20 teams received bowl bids at the end of the 1958 season.

Only a few games were televised — generally just one a week for the entire country. No Alabama game was televised in 1957 or 1958, and Bryant's Sunday television show with film of the previous day's game was an innovation for the state. Stadiums were smaller. Alabama's total paid attendance for 1958 was fewer than 325,000, including 44,000 at the Alabama-Auburn game at Legion Field in Birmingham. The term "recreational vehicle" had not entered the nation's vocabulary, and only a few pioneers held tailgate parties from their station wagons.

Substitution rules were strict, and players played on both offense and defense. It was not unusual for an individual player to be involved in 80 to 90 plays in a single game. Alabama's largest traveling squad numbered few more than 40, and fewer than 30 generally appeared in a game. African-Americans did not play football for major colleges in the south.

Players were smaller. In its opening game against LSU in 1958, Alabama's starting line averaged only 196 pounds. The biggest player on the Alabama team officially weighed in at 215 pounds.

Rivalries were intense, but few players dreamed of getting rich playing football. There were no agents haunting the campus hoping for a chance to represent a future multimillionaire. Some players did go on to professional football — but the big money days wouldn't begin until 1965, courtesy of Joe Namath and Sonny Werblin. Arnold Palmer, the PGA's top money winner in 1958, won the enormous sum of $42,607, that year, and that included winning the Masters' Tournament.

But 1958 was a year in which sports, and especially televised sports, began to become less about sport and more about money. In baseball, the Dodgers and the Giants deserted New York for the west coast. Late in the year, the Baltimore Colts' dramatic overtime win over the New York Giants in the NFL playoffs captivated a nationwide television audience.

Between January and May 1958, one hundred or so hopeful athletes took a shot at a place on the Alabama roster. They were a remarkably homogeneous group — mostly from Alabama, mostly Christian Protestants. Their hair was universally cropped into flat-tops. They wore chinos, open-necked sport shirts, and penny loafers. By today's standards, by and large, they were almost incomprehensibly naive. It would not have occurred to any of them to mount a student protest, to proclaim atheism, or to question an elder. If they didn't always obey authority, they always felt guilty when they didn't.

They had grown up in a time during which football had a special place. The game was a powerful source of pride and self-esteem for individuals, families, towns, cities and the entire state. The mythic connections to the Lost Cause of the Confederacy were part of the reason.

As sports historian Andrew Doyle wrote in an article in *The International Journal of the History of Sport,* Southerners "regarded the rest of the nation with a complex mixture of assertive pride and defensive hostility, and intersectional football gave full rein to both of these sentiments." When Alabama beat Washington, 20-19, in the 1926 Rose Bowl game, Doyle says, its display of "masculine strength and virility . . . became proof that the martial prowess and chivalric grandeur of their mythologized ancestors [were] still alive in the modern world."

It was not simply that football gave the South a way to excel — it was a way to excel in the virtues that Southerners most valued. Few people from Alabama had been exposed to "the North" and fewer still had an understanding of the advantages a strong industrial base, top quality educational establishments and progressive attitudes afforded their rival region. So they didn't really believe that they were disadvantaged. All they knew about the North was that people there looked down upon them and thought of them as bigoted, pellagra-ridden and lazy. What better way to prove otherwise than to kick ass in a hard, physical game.

The passion to demonstrate validity as a region carried over into local programs. High school life in the cities and small towns of Alabama was centered around football. Every boy with athletic ability played football, and many families made substantial sacrifices to free their sons from chores to attend practice. Bands existed mostly to perform at football games, with majorettes and dance teams as the centerpiece for halftime shows. Competition for cheerleading positions was intense, and the chosen enjoyed the highest status.

On the brisk fall Friday evenings, pep rallies resounded through the halls. Students sang fight songs adapted for local consumption. Whether the team was winning or not, principals and coaches called for 'school spirit' and few resisted. Around dark, headlights strung out toward the neighboring towns, as the parents, siblings and classmates of the players motored into rival territory for the epic battles that were a significant element in town pride.

Sipping coffee bought from the band boosters before the game, maybe furtively tilting a bottle, the veterans of earlier teams mingled behind the grandstand, replaying old memories and handicapping the game. Then they filed into their seats and stood solemnly for both school songs, the opening invocation, and the National Anthem. Children too young to appreciate the immensity of the occasion gamboled on the pathways in front of the bleachers. Students seated themselves around the band, and when "Two bits, four bits, six bits and dollar," was called leapt to their feet and yelled themselves hoarse.

The next week, around the filling stations, Sunday school classes and honky-tonks, townsmen replayed the most recent contest and looked ahead with high anticipation to coming games. Coaches were lionized or bitterly criticized, depending on success. Boosters endlessly analyzed the prospects and talents of individual players.

A victory over a traditional foe, or especially by a small town school over a city rival, meant much. If Elba could beat Dothan, or Tallassee beat Sidney Lanier, why, that implied a superiority that was shared by all the citizens who supported the winners. Such events were celebrated with the deep satisfaction that comes with righteous victory. For a shining moment, the humiliation of earlier losses was avenged, sacrifices were made worthwhile. Conversely, a loss would cast depression among the boosters.

Football was a way to gain recognition and approbation, which was accorded even the average athletes on a winning team. The swiftest and the strongest — who often became quarterbacks, halfbacks, fullbacks or ends — earned a special status. Many were offered summer jobs and special deals on clothes and automobiles by local alumni, who sometimes were hoping to influence their choice of a college.

Seldom were more than a few of the best players on a high school team singled out by college coaches for scholarship consideration. When a high school athlete was actually offered a scholarship, he incurred a responsibility toward his family, town and school that was a heavy one for an 18-year-old to carry. Success became important beyond its personal meaning.

Alabama football was deep in the blood of many who had never set foot in a college classroom, and fathers groomed their sons with a single goal in mind. Sammy Smith's father took him to Alabama games from an early age. "I would sit there in the stands, either cold or wet or bored," Smith said, " . . . didn't know what was going on . . . and he'd say, 'I want you to look out there at those red shirts . . . you're going to be wearing one . . .'" Danny Wilbanks, another senior on the team, said his "whole family was Alabama, and they talked to me about Alabama all the years that I was growing up, and I'd listen to Alabama on the radio on Saturday afternoons, listen to hear them call Hootie's [Ingram] name and Corky Tharp and Bobby Marlow and all those names . . . I just knew that I wanted to go to Alabama . . ."

The fathers of such players basked in the success of their sons and in their position as football insider. "What do you hear from your boy?" was a frequent question, and it must have been delicious to offer to peers tidbits about the inner workings of the Alabama program.

It is a rueful fact, though, that it is much easier to excel in high school than in college. Some young men mature early, and then cease to develop. Some young men are a step slow, some are injury-prone. Some, gifted with exceptional talent, have never had to work for their accomplishments, and are unable to do so when asked. Few have the luck, the skill, the mental toughness and the durability to play college football.

The players who did get the golden chance to play in college knew that failure would be publicly noted and that their family would have to bear the attendant obloquy. When they returned home, disgraced, their presence would be noted sourly in the barbershops and local coffee roundtables where burghers assembled daily. "No guts," someone might comment, and from that date until death, there were many among the local boosters who thought first of the word "quitter" when they encountered a local boy who tried but failed to play at the college level. Many fathers, their pride and status a victim, could never find it in themselves to forgive their sons for quitting, whatever the motivation.

By far most of the players on the Alabama team in 1958 were the first in their families to attend college, and few could have hoped for a college degree without football. Playing for Alabama was a ticket out — if not to athletic glory, at least to the promise of a better future than one could ever hope to achieve in the coal mines, cotton mills and small farms in which their parents toiled.

What that meant was that the 100-odd players who in January 1958 were placed under the power of Paul Bryant were soon faced with a dilemma. Either "pay the price" — endure the brutal physical demands of the new coach's practices — or give up their scholarships and admit failure. Quitting meant they might not complete their college education. On a deeper level, it meant forfeiting the rituals of football combat from which, for much of their conscious lives, they had gained identity and status.

At that point, of course, none of them could have known then that their new coach was going to become a legend. Even the prospect of playing in an actual football game seemed immensely remote. Quitting or not quitting soon became the central preoccupation of a great many of the players. The objective became survival.

About 85 of the returning players were either veterans of the Whitworth years, redshirts, or rising freshmen, listed in a pre-spring training roster released by the University and published by the *Birmingham Post-Herald*.

Especially highly regarded, at least by the press, was Billy Rains, a second-team all-SEC guard from Moulton. Rains was married and he and his wife were expecting their first child in the summer. In his first two seasons, Rains had frequently been singled out by Coach Whitworth and the media as hard-working and dedicated. He also made the all-opponent team selected by that year's national champions, Auburn.

Sid Neighbors, a two-year letterman from Northport, was the team's biggest lineman at 228 pounds. His brother, Billy, later became an All-American at Alabama. Neighbors was "as broad as a fireplace," a teammate said, and was always fighting to keep his weight down. Still, he had started every game at tackle in 1956 and 1957.

Another returning tackle, Dave Sington, was the son of an All-American, Fred Sington Sr., who had played in the Alabama line alongside Ears Whitworth. The elder Sington was president of the Alabama Alumni Association and was one of the men who had gone to Houston to haggle with Bryant over his contract. Senior Pete Reaves, a tackle from Bessemer, was listed on the Alabama roster, but Reaves had decided to give up football to concentrate on baseball, where he was a star pitcher.

A number of seniors returned at the end position. One, Baxter Booth, a laconic farmers' son from Athens, had played 320 minutes in 1957 and considered himself a first-stringer. Another was Charlie Gray of Pell City — often called Charlie Tom — who had played more than any other end in 1957. Gray, whose father had been a star at Birmingham-Southern, had caught 60 passes thrown by Bobby Skelton in his senior year at Pell City High.

Seniors Willie Beck and Ralph Blalock had both lettered at end in two previous years, but neither stayed long after Bryant arrived. Dodd Holt, a varsity non-letterman from Jasper, also returned as a senior end. Jerre Brannen, another product of the great Anniston teams of 1955 and 1956, returned as a junior letterman. Brannen's quiet, religious nature belied a fierce competitive spirit.

In the backfield, two senior quarterbacks were returning.

Bobby Smith, serious and intense, was the son of a filling station owner and mechanic from Brewton. Smith had not been actively recruited and had been astonished when an Alabama coach approached him after his team from T. R. Miller had lost its game in the state basketball tournament in Tuscaloosa and asked him to try out as a football player. Smith had been ecstatic at being offered a scholarship, and he had paid off, having started most of Alabama's games in 1957.

Another senior, Bobby Jackson from Mobile, had also lettered in 1957, but had been hampered by a knee injury. The mercurial Jackson did not glory in contact work, and so was called, ironically, "Jarrin' Jack." His major assets were an elusive running style and ten-second speed in the 100-yard dash. Whitworth had tried to use him at halfback, but sportswriters in Mobile were critical of that move, and Whitworth may have blamed Jackson for that, and punished him. At any rate, Jackson's talents had not been fully used before Bryant's arrival.

A talented senior returned at fullback, Danny Wilbanks from Tallassee. Wilbanks had been a four-letter man at Tallassee High near Montgomery, and ran 35 yards for a touchdown when Tallassee beat Sidney Lanier, the big Montgomery high school, in 1954. That contest had practically depopulated Tallassee for the night. Auburn had courted Wilbanks extensively, and two of his teammates accepted scholarships there. But his family ties to Alabama football were decisive.

Wilbanks had played 115 minutes in 1957, and scored three touchdowns. Big and powerful at 197 pounds, he was counted upon to bring muscle to the offense around the goal line.

Many of the Alabama players were impressed by the talent of Benny Dempsey, the senior center from Brantley, the only child of a hardware store owner. Dempsey had been one of the most heavily recruited players in Alabama history. (It was an open secret among the Alabama players that Dempsey's cousin, James Beall, had been given a scholarship to help persuade Dempsey to sign.) At 6-1, 207, Dempsey had the physique of a Charles Atlas, plus speed and quickness. But he lacked fire. ("Goddam, Dempsey, that wouldn't have been a foul in basketball," Crisp whined at him one day at practice.) But Alabama had a lot invested in him, and he was the favorite of some influential alumni.

Another senior, Ken Roberts, had shared center duties with Dempsey for two years. Roberts was one of a number of outstanding Anniston athletes developed by the late Billy Bancroft. His father owned a restaurant in Jacksonville.

The dedication of the seniors was to be sorely tested. In group and individual meetings with them, Bryant made it clear that they and their needs were not a priority for him. "I don't care if every senior in this room gets up and walks out," he said in one meeting. "Because for you to play, you're going to have to be twice as good as a junior or sophomore, and I doubt very seriously that any of you are."

There were 23 juniors. Among them, competing with Dempsey and Roberts at center, was Jim Blevins, son of a gasoline distributor in Moulton. Blevins had been offered a scholarship when he finished high school in 1952, but instead joined the Army and ended up in Korea, returning to school in 1956 a married man. Another center prospect was Donnie Heath, one of the four Anniston players recruited by Moose Johnson from the championship 1956 team, whose father was a machinist who built looms for the ribbon mills in Anniston. Heath, who had a wacky sense of humor, was known as "Loco."

Premier among the returning junior guards was Don Cochran, who had played on state championship teams at Woodlawn of Birmingham. Built low to the ground, Cochran was called "Duckbutt" by his friends. Sammy Smith — immersed by his father in the grandeur of Alabama football from his childhood and named after Slingin' Sammy Baugh — also returned. Bill Hannah, younger brother of Herb Hannah, had returned from the Marines in 1957 and played a year — at 240 pounds — under Whitworth. He and Valletto were the oldest men on the team at 24. Dave Sington's older brother Fred Jr., a junior in eligibility, was back on the squad after a two-year hitch in the Navy. Fred was surprisingly fast for a big man, and could outrun some running backs.

Valletto, the son of an immigrant steelworker from Pittsburgh — the man who had fought with Don Kinderknecht on behalf of Richard Strum — was back as a tackle/end.* Among others were Charlie Coleman,

---

*When Alabama used an unbalanced line, tackles became weak-side ends.

a beefy 230-pounder from Mobile, who was back at Alabama after a year at East Mississippi Junior College; and Joe Campbell, a barber's son from Chattanooga, who was hearing a call to the ministry. Chuck Allen, a running mate of Booth's from Athens, could play either end or tackle.

There was talent among the junior running backs — notably Marlin Dyess from Elba, not yet known as "Scooter," and Bill Knight, who played at Shades Valley. Both were track athletes who could run the 100-yard dash in under 10 seconds. Another halfback, Red Stickney, a high school All-American from Key West, Florida, gained over 2,000 yards in his senior year, but was finding college competition tougher. Mack Wise, a former teammate of Dyess, had been held out a year to recover from an severely torn muscle.

Dyess was small even by the standards of the day — less than 150 pounds. In his first meeting with Dyess, Bryant was amused. Rubbing his hands through Dyess's crew cut, he asked, "What the hell are you, the water boy?" But Dyess became a great favorite of Bryant's, and he was often kidded by his teammates about the soft treatment he got in practice.

Another halfback, Dick Strum from Biloxi (one of the players Whitworth had been so apologetic to) was trying to recover from a knee injury he got in the game against Mississippi State in 1957. On that day, his knee was so severely dislocated that the bone protruded through the flesh, and when trainer Jim Goostree saw it, he just turned his head and threw a towel over it. The knee had improved with therapy, and was being heavily taped. Strum was hoping it would be all right.

Bobby Skelton, also a junior, who had been a high school passing sensation from Pell City, was expected to challenge Jackson and Smith for the starting quarterback job. Another junior, Gary O'Steen from Anniston, was sometimes listed as a quarterback, sometimes as a halfback, and was the single back that most Tide players hated to tackle in practice. The 1958 season was already underway before the Alabama staff finally decided where to place him permanently. There were two other quarterback candidates — Laurien (Gooby) Stapp, from Montgomery, a lefthander and an outstanding punter, and James (Jap) Patton, a sophomore from Tuscumbia (his older brother Houston had played quarterback at Ole Miss; a younger brother, George, became an All-American at Georgia).

There evidently had been no shortage of athletes available to Whitworth and his staff. The early 1958 roster listed 16 players who had been redshirted—held out of play so they would retain their eligibility for an additional year. In that group were an intense pre-med student from Huntsville, Milton (Butch) Frank, son of a former football coach; Buck Burns, a center from Tuscaloosa, whose father was a municipal judge; and Duff Morrison, a halfback from Memphis. Morrison, Burns, Red Stickney, and Gary O'Steen had first met in a game for high school All-Americans, played in Memphis. End Jerry Spruiell, another former teammate of Bobby Skelton's who had only played one year of high school football, had also been held out a year and was listed as a sophomore. Guard Johnny Gann from Sylacauga had been held out because of injuries.

The sophomore group included four players from the coal mining town of West Blocton, near Tuscaloosa. The wheelhorses were Walter Sansing and Tommy White, who both played tailback in the Notre Dame box under the highly capable Morris Higginbotham. Along with them came tackle Roy Holsomback, a rangy, rawboned backwoodsman, and guard David Hicks, who had played blocking back in the single wing and who could almost stay up with White and Sansing despite his size. Another sophomore guard was Don Parsons, a Birmingham native whose family had moved to Houston before his high school years. Parsons's ambition had always been to play for the Crimson Tide, and he sent his high school films to an uncle in Birmingham. The uncle showed the films to Fred Sington, Sr., and he had intervened to get Parsons a scholarship.

Gary Phillips, another sophomore guard, had been recruited by Bud Wilkinson at Oklahoma. But he had been told by an alumnus that it was a sure thing — that Bear Bryant was coming back — and since he wanted to practice medicine in Alabama, he decided that the University was the place to be. Jack Rutledge from Birmingham had been a fullback

in high school, and averaged 9.1 yards a carry at Woodlawn. But his
speed was not great, and his upper body strength made him an obvious
selection for the interior line. Rutledge was already balding a little, and
he looked enough like John Patterson, who was then campaigning for
governor of Alabama, to be called "Governor."

Among several ends moving up from the freshmen team were Gary
O'Steen's younger brother, Henry, bigger and more physical than his
brother; Bobby Boylston, a former quarterback from Atlanta; Bud
Moore, whose family had moved from the country to Birmingham's
West End when he and his brother were teenagers; and Morris Childers
from Fairfield, who had really wanted to go to Auburn, but had not
gotten an offer from the Tigers.

Along with Sansing and White, there were several touted backfield
prospects. Charles Rieves, as big as Wilbanks, was a talented fullback
from Rolling Fork, Mississippi. Ferdy Cruce from Florence was "a
natural talent, probably the second or third of fourth best ball player we
had on the team . . . speed deluxe," Gooby Stapp said. Buddy Wesley, a
halfback who had played with his roommate Sammy Smith at Talladega,
would demonstrate his greatest abilities on defense. Wesley was nicknamed "Tarbaby" because he was as silent as the effigy Br'er Rabbit had
constructed.

Several sophomores had been recruited out of Tennessee — two
cousins of Harry Gilmer, Joe, an end, and Jerry, a quarterback from
Kingsport; Eugene Harris, known as Clarabelle (for the character on
TV's "Howdy-Doody Show") because of his red-hair and freckled face,
a center/guard from Cleveland; halfback Glen Jones from Clinton; Sam
Locastro and Walter Reitano, linemen from Memphis.

Another twenty-odd other players, at least*, took a shot at making
the Alabama squad. These were a mixed bag of junior college transfers,

---

* Dave Sington said there were many more. "We had three players per
locker," he said. "They brought 'em in from the Army, the Air Force, they had
one old boy from the Seals, I don't know where got them all. Lots of them only
stayed about a week."

military returnees, and miscellaneous prospects who received an invitation from someone to come and try out for the Crimson Tide.

Included in this group were Wayne Sims, a guard from Columbiana, who had been recruited by Mississippi State as a quarterback and then farmed out to Holmes Junior College for two years. Told by Mississippi State that he was too small to play in the SEC, Sims had agreed to play for Murray State in Kentucky as a junior and had already shipped his things north. But then an acquaintance of Sims, Ehney Camp, a former Tide player who was with Liberty National Life Insurance Company, suggested Sims go to see Bryant about a scholarship at Alabama.

Sims decided to give it a shot. When he was admitted to Bryant's office, the coach looked at him and said, "Son, you like to play football?"

Sims said, "Yessir."

Bryant asked, "You want to play at Alabama?"

Sims said, "Yessir."

"You get back down here to start the second semester," Bryant said. "I got to have somebody because I can't win with who they left me."

End John Paul Poole from Florence was another non-roster player who, discouraged by the program under Whitworth, had agreed to be drafted and served 21 months in the Navy. Back in school, Poole went to see Bryant, who said, "If you can help us, we'll help you."

Another end, Norbie Ronsonet, a former teammate of Richard Strum in Biloxi, had flunked out the previous year, and enrolled at Perkinston Junior College in Mississippi. An Alabama alumnus from Biloxi assured Ronsonet that everything was fixed for his return to Alabama, but when he got there, Bryant was out of town and Jerry Claiborne professed no knowledge of the deal, causing "the Cajun" some discomfiture. Things eventually worked out, but oddly neither Poole nor Ronsonet was listed in the Alabama media guide issued in the summer of 1958.

Bryant, in his autobiography, characterized the athletes he inherited in 1958 as "fat and sloppy." The players' initial impression of the new coach was that he was not a man to trifle with.

For one thing, Bryant displayed little indulgence for the careless attitude that characterized the team's approach to classes, meetings, and life in general. That came across in his meeting with the squad on January 10, 1958.

Notified to assemble for a meeting at 1:15, most of the players arrived in plenty of time. When Bryant, after consulting his watch, began the meeting, he started by calling out a name: "Gilmer? Where's Gilmer."

Jerry Gilmer, the quarterback prospect from Tennessee, did not respond.

"Is Jerry Gilmer in this room?" Bryant called again. Somebody said, "Coach, I don't believe he's here."

Bryant turned to Carney Laslie. "Dammit, Carney," he said, "go upstairs and pack his things. He's off scholarship."

Some suspected that the whole deal was a setup — that Jerry Gilmer had decided not to return at all, and that Bryant was taking advantage of that. Whatever the case, no one came late to meetings after that. (Gilmer returned in the fall, was redshirted because of injuries, and never played.)

Following that little episode, the room was silent as a stone. Bryant then began for the first time to talk in detail to the players about his plans and expectations. "I have come to Alabama for one reason," he said. "To build a winning football team. We are going to do two things. We are going to learn to play football and we are going to get up and go to class like our mommas and poppas expect us to. And we are going to win.

"Ten years from now you're going to be married with a family, your wife will be sick, your kids are sick, you are sick, but you will get your butt up and go to work. Because we are going to do that for you. We are going to teach you how to do things you don't feel like doing."

Some of Bryant's remarks were very welcome to players who lacked the glamorous reputations or the political connections of others. "We're going to look for 11 players who want to win," he said. "I don't care who you are, where you are from, whether you played last year. I don't care if your folks have money or don't have money. We're going to look for people who want to win and be a part of this team, and of the tradition that Alabama football has had over the years."

Many in the group of players were anticipating tough rules like the ones Whitworth had tried earlier to implement — curfews and strict prohibitions on drinking and smoking, but Bryant surprised them. "As far as training rules are concerned," he said, "I don't have any training rules. If you are man enough to come out on the field and give me what I expect of you . . . and go out and stay out all night and mess around, go ahead and do it.

"There's only one thing I expect . . . When you are out in public you represent this football team and you represent the state of Alabama, and you are to act accordingly. If you don't you will have to answer to me." On other occasions, Bryant would say, "if you want to smoke and drink, come by my house and do it so you won't embarrass the University."

Bryant met with the squad virtually every day during the spring of 1958. At these meetings, he repeatedly stressed the same themes — go first class, take pride in yourself, give 100 percent at all times, make your Mommas and daddies proud. And he met one-on-one with every player.

The individual meetings were a chance for Bryant to make some judgment about a player's commitment and intensity. That was fine for Don Cochran, who knew he was one of the better players on the squad, and who hated to lose. His high school team at Woodlawn in Birmingham had been overpowering. All Cochran wanted to do was play for a winner.

Cochran had started every game as a sophomore. When it became known that Whitworth was leaving, he had been contacted by a number of schools. Several offered attractive packages. The University of Miami's Andy Gustafson promised he would find Cochran's wife a job in the Miami area if he would transfer. But Cochran, who had heard that Bryant was hard but fair, wanted to stay.

When he went to his interview with Coach Bryant, the head coach immediately challenged him. "Why did you get Coach Whitworth get run off?" he asked.

Cochran replied that he didn't think he had. "I was just one of many people and I did the best I could at whatever I was trying to do," he said. "But most of the time I didn't know what I was trying to do. I'm not making excuses."

Gathering his courage, Cochran continued, "Coach Bryant, I've heard terrible things from all these different sources about how bad things are going to be . . . but they also told me you were fair. And I'm just going to tell you right off, you're not going to run me off. I'm going to be here."

Fixed with an icy glaze, Cochran began to regret his boldness.

Then Bryant grinned, and said, "Well, we'll see."

Bryant asked Jim Blevins, who had just returned from a tour in Korea, if he had "picked up any bad habits in the Army."

"I'll take a drink now and then," Blevins said.

"Well, if you really feel like you need one, come out to the house, because that way you won't get into trouble," Bryant said.

When Dick Strum came in for his interview, Bryant asked him to sit down, and then pulled out an electric razor and gave himself a shave.

"How's your Momma?" he asked?

"She's fine," Strum said.

"Do you write her?" the Coach asked.

"Nossir," Strum replied, "I call her on the phone."

"Well, you know you don't have but one," Bryant said. "Write her."

Donnie Heath arrived a half-hour early to his interview just in case his watch was wrong. Once inside Bryant's office, Heath introduced himself.

"Yeah, you were number 52, played on last year's team," Bryant said, "I've seen some film and wasn't very impressed with what little I saw of you." Heath was told he'd get an opportunity.

Gary Phillips, the sophomore pre-med student from Dothan, was waiting outside Bryant's office when Ken Roberts's interview was finished. Phillips asked Roberts what Bryant had asked.

"He asked me if I had a car, and I said, 'Yessir,' and he asked me if I had a girl friend, and I said, 'Yessir,'" Roberts said. So when Phillips was asked by Bryant what was on his mind, he blurted: "Well, Coach . . . I don't have a car and I don't have a girl friend."

"Yeah," Bryant replied. "And you ain't too big either."

Phillips was deflated but perked up when Bryant added, "But one of the best linemen I ever had was Stubby Trimble, and he weighed 185 pounds and didn't have but one hand."

THE ALABAMA ROSTER BEFORE SPRING TRAINING, 1958

	Age	Hgt.	Wgt.	Class	Letters	Hometown*
Left Ends						
Charlie Gray	20	6-1	187	Sr.	56-57	Pell City
Baxter Booth	21	6-2	191	Sr.	56-57	Athens
Buddy Wood	20	6-4	192	Jr.	57	Guntersville
Don Coleman	20	6-1	190	Jr.	V	Birmingham
Joe Gilmer	21	6-2	185	Jr.	RS	Kingsport, Tenn.
Henry O'Steen	19	6-2	200	Soph.		Anniston
Bobby Boylston	19	6-3	195	Soph		Atlanta, Ga.
John Paul Poole	24	6-2	174	Sr.		Florence
Left Tackles						
Sid Neighbors	23	6-1	228	Sr.	56-57	Northport
Chuck Allen	20	6-3	219	Jr.	57	Athens
Joe Campbell	20	6-3	206	Jr.	V	Chattanooga
Bill Smith	23	6-2	214	Soph.	RS	Augusta, Ga.
Roy Holsomback	20	6-3	195	Soph.		West Blocton
Darrell Nettles		6-3	225	Soph.		Pine Hill
Harold Beaty	19	6-2	225	JC		Benton, Ark.
Left Guards						
Bill Hannah	24	6-0	221	Jr.	57	Indianapolis, Ind.
Jim Blevins	23	6-3	217	Jr.	57	Moulton
Bland Walker	19	6-0	202	Jr.	57	Eutaw
Jimmy Norred	21	6-2	220	Jr.	V	Talladega

* In Alabama unless otherwise indicated.

Milton Frank	20	5-10	187	Soph.	RS	Huntsville
Don Parsons	19	6-0	200	Soph.		Houston, Texas
Russell Stutts	18	5-11	185	Soph.		Birmingham
David Hicks	19	6-0	215	Soph.		West Blocton
Charles Coleman	21	6-0	225	Soph.	JC	Mobile

Centers

Benny Dempsey	21	6-1	207	Sr.	56-57	Brantley
Ken Roberts	21	6-0	201	Sr.	56-57	Anniston
Donnie Heath	19	6-0	198	Jr.	V	Anniston
Elliott Moseley	20	6-0	205	Soph.	RS	Selma
Buck Burns	19	6-0	210	Soph.	RS	Tuscaloosa
Jasper Best	20	6-0	195	Soph.		Gordo
Eugene Harris	19	6-0	195	Soph.		Cleveland, Tenn.
Jack Rutledge	19	5-11	195	Soph.		Birmingham

Right Guards

Billy Rains	21	5-11	205	Sr.	56-57	Moulton
Sammy Smith	20	6-1	202	Jr.	57	Talladega
Don Cochran	20	5-11	195	Jr.	57	Birmingham
Pete Reaves	21	6-0	199	Sr.	V	Bessemer
Charles Spano	22	5-11	210	Sr.	V	Navastoa, Texas.
Cecil Thornton	21	6-2	210	Sr.	V	Centre
Gary Phillips	19	5-11	195	Soph.		Dothan
Sam Locastro		6-2	190	Soph.		Memphis, Tenn.
Johnny Gann	20	5-11	208	Jr.	RS	Sylacauga
Wayne Sims	20	6-1	194	Jr.	JC	Columbiana

Right Tackles

Dave Sington	20	6-1	226	Sr.	56-57	Birmingham
Don Owens	21	6-1	212	Sr.	56-57	Memphis
Carl Valletto	24	6-2	214	Jr.	57	Oakmont, Pa.
Fred Sington	23	6-1	224	Jr.	RS	Birmingham
Sammy Barranco	20	6-1	205	Soph	RS	Lake Wales, Fla.

Charles Cornelius	20	6-0	206	Jr.	RS	Ashland
Dan Pitts	19	6-3	225	Soph.		Red Level
Walter Reitano		6-3	210	Soph.		Memphis
Bobby Johnson	19	6-3	210	Soph.		Centre

Right Ends

Willie Beck	20	6-2	192	Sr.	56-57	Northport
Ralph Blalock	21	6-2	196	Sr.	56-57	Cullman
Jerre Brannen	20	6-2	191	Jr.	57	Anniston
Dodd Holt	20	6-1	193	Sr.	V	Jasper
Jerry Spruiell	20	6-0	190	Soph.	RS	Pell City
Paul Wood	22	6-1	190	Soph.	RS	Thomaston, Ga.
Bud Moore	19	6-2	200	Soph.		Birmingham
Morris Childers	19	6-1	190	Soph.		Birmingham
Larry McCoy		6-0	190	Soph.		Tuscaloosa
Norbie Ronsonet	20	6-1	190	Soph.	RS	Biloxi, Miss.
Gary Elkins	19	5-11	180	MTF		Gadsden
Steve Anderson	19	6-3	205	MTF		Helena, Ark.

Quarterbacks

Bobby Smith	21	6-1	181	Sr.	56-57	Brewton
Bobby Jackson	22	6-1	187	Sr.	57	Mobile
Robert Skelton	20	5-11	171	Jr.	57	Pell City
Jimmy Woodward	23	5-10	172	Sr.	RS	Tuscaloosa
Jerry Gilmer		5-11	175	Soph.		Kingsport, Tenn.
Laurien Stapp	19	5-11	175	Soph.		Birmingham
James Patton	19	6-0	170	Soph.		Tuscumbia

Left Halfbacks

Gary O'Steen	20	5-11	174	Jr.	57	Anniston
Red Stickney	21	6-1	180	Jr.	57	Key West, Fla.
Dick Strum	21	5-10	172	Jr.	57	Biloxi, Miss.
Bobby Sirmon	21	6-0	190	Jr.	RS	Georgiana
Arland Carter	20	6-0	187	Soph.	RS	Fort Payne

Walter Sansing	19	6-0	190	Soph.		West Blocton
Duff Morrison	20	6-0	175	Soph.	RS	Memphis
James Hester		5-11	175	Soph.		West Point, Ga.
Allan Mauldin	19	6-0	175	Soph.		Childersburg
William Wesley	19	5-10	175	Soph.		Talladega

Right Halfbacks

Marlin Dyess	20	5-6	147	Jr.	57	Elba
Bill Knight	20	6-0	184	Jr.	57	Homewood
Mack Wise	20	5-10	177	Soph.	RS	Elba
Neal Pierce	21	5-9	160	Soph.	RS	Anniston
Ferdy Cruce	19	5-11	175	Soph.		Florence
James Loosier		5-11	185	Soph.		Memphis, Tenn.
Glen Jones	19	6-0	185	Soph.		Clinton, Tenn.
Tommy White	19	5-10	175	Soph.		West Blocton

Fullbacks

Danny Wilbanks	21	6-0	201	Sr.	57	Tallassee
Cecil Hurt	20	5-10	180	Jr.	V	Birmingham
Bill Parker	18	5-10	191	Jr.	V	Gadsden
Bob Bryant	20	5-11	190	Soph.	RS	Brewton
Charles Rieves	19	5-11	200	Soph.		Rolling Fork, Miss.
James Wood	19	6-0	190	Soph.		Thomaston, Ga.

Ages and Classes are for 1958 season
V—Varsity non-letterman
RS—Redshirt
MTF—Mid-term freshman
JC—Junior College Transfer

The following players appeared on depth charts but couldn't be found on an official roster: Hall, Trawick, Petty, Demore, Scott, Silver, Carpenter, James, May, Mills, Nixon.

CHAPTER FIVE

Controlled Violence

B y the time he arrived at Alabama, Bryant's teams had won 91
games and he had a robust and richly deserved reputation as a
psychologist and motivator. Getting superior performance from
moderately skilled athletes was perhaps the accomplishment he savored
most. But there was much more behind his coaching success than
motivation. Through the years he had worked out a comprehensive
approach that addressed every aspect of a winning program. They are
articulated in his book, *Building a Championship Football Team,* which
was written by Gene Stallings, and published in 1960.

The first requirement was complete control — the complete support of the college administration, sole responsibility for hiring his
athletic staff, and a long term contract. Bryant's book said that without
the long term contract, a coach "might have to revert to such a practice
as playing individuals of questionable character because of their immediate ability, rather than weeding them out and concentrating on solid
citizens."

He demanded of himself a definite plan for success, dedication, and
tough-mindedness that permitted "decisions that are unpleasant."

Drake Keith, who went on to considerable business success as
president of Arkansas Power and Light Company and so ought to know,
regards Bryant as one of the best planners he's ever seen, in business or
elsewhere. The planning extended to every aspect of the program —

administration, testing and selection of players, the teaching of fundamental football techniques, offensive and defensive techniques, scouting
and game preparation, game administration and halftime adjustments.

The sole objective was winning. And because football is a game of
violence, Bryant's plans began with figuring out ways to "out-mean and
physically whip our opponents." His emphasis on "butting heads" led to
charges that he taught brutality in football. Brutality is in the eye of the
beholder, but Bryant did not teach patty cake, and the degree to which
he had defined and codified the techniques of controlled violence was
exceptional.

There was no particular secret about it. In *Building a Championship
Football Team* he said this about the use of gang tackling to demoralize
opposing ball carriers: "Frankly we want the first man to the ball carrier
merely to hold him up, and not let him get away, so we can unload on
him. You can punish a ball carrier when one man has him "dangling,"
and the others gang tackle him hard."*

The book goes on to say that he didn't teach piling on, or intention-
ally trying to injure an opposing player. To the people being held up and
pounded, that must have been a subtle distinction. Bryant and his
coaches sought the physical intensity they knew they needed to win by
constantly emphasizing hard hitting and praising it when it occurred. In
practice, even after the whistle had blown to stop play, a hard lick would
get oohs and aahs from the coaches. "If somebody was walking back to
the huddle and I could get a good shot at him, I'd put him on the
ground," Gooby Stapp said. "And when you did that about four coaches
would be helping you up saying that's what we're looking for . . ." Jerre
Brannen was another player who gained attention this way. "You'd
throw [a block] at somebody," Jap Patton said, "a coach, whatever. What
would happen, we would have scrimmages . . . and somebody would
make the tackle . . . and the first thing you would do, you'd jump up in
a good football position . . . looking out for Brannen."

---

*The book is out of print and difficult to find. A later edition, revised by
Stallings, leaves this passage out.

Bryant describes in his book specific techniques for linemen to use on defense, and credits O. A. (Bum) Phillips, a member of his Texas A&M staff who went on to fame as a pro coach, for devising the numbering scheme. The book describes in detail how a defensive player is to attack his opponent. For example, here is the description for the "5 Technique": "The 5 technique man lines up on the outside eye of the offensive tackle . . . with the feet staggered (outside foot back in most cases). On the snap of the ball, he employs a forearm flip charge into the tackle. As he makes contact, his back foot is brought up even with his front foot."

Coaches drilled players on these techniques until they were mastered. Joe Campbell recalled being in a group of four being taught by Pat James how to correctly "pull" from a line position. "I think we spent the entire 20 minutes with one person pulling and another person snapping the ball . . . and one person holding the dummy . . . the one that was pulling liked to died . . . we were blocking the dummy and we didn't do it right, so we did it over and over again . . ." That sort of attention was simply unheard of under Whitworth's staff.

Bryant was ever vigilant, from his tower, in watching how techniques were taught. After his playing days, Don Cochran worked for Bryant as a graduate assistant. Once the head coach spotted Cochran teaching a particular technique less completely than he expected. "That's wrong," he roared from the tower, and descended to demonstrate so both Cochran and the player would understand not just the first steps of a move, but several more after them.

In meetings before and after practice, Bryant would thoroughly discuss plans and techniques with the assistant coaches and go over details until he was certain his way was understood. Once on the field, the teaching method was to describe the technique, demonstrate the technique, and then ask the player to perform it in one-on-one sessions. They would make you "do it and do it and do it" until they were sure you understood, Bobby Smith said. Then it would be perfected in three on three drills, and then in full scrimmages.

Smith, a starting quarterback the previous year, had things to learn, too. One of the very first times he threw a pass in practice, Smith was caught watching his receiver by quarterback coach Phil Cutchin.

"Who are you looking at?" he shouted. "You don't do that, you look at the halfback first, that's your first key. You look at the linebackers, and they'll tell you where to throw the ball . . . and then you will know where your receivers are."

"Nobody had ever told me that those linebackers are watching your eyes . . . those halfbacks," Smith said. "I might have been smart enough to figure that out . . . but Coach Bryant's first staff were great teachers and they knew football and they were organized to teach what they wanted taught." Smith said.

Bryant placed a lot of emphasis on quickness, which began with the correct stance. "If they came along and kicked your hand and you fell forward, your stance was wrong," Don Cochran said. "And if they shoved you and you fell backward your stance was wrong. You had to be in position to move left, right and forward and backward with the same momentum . . . techniques was the main thing we worked on . . . Quickness, always. Everything we do is quickness."

"We would come off that ball so fast," Charlie Gray recalls. "The first thing to make contact would be the forehead of your helmet . . . just like that, pop, before he could respond. And once you made contact, you learned to feel pressure. If you sensed that he wanted to go one direction, that's the way you'd take him."

No detail was too small for the attention of the Bryant staff. Even before spring practice began, while "voluntary" conditioning drills were underway, the skill players spent extra time in the dorm after supper.

"The centers and the quarterbacks had to go downstairs in the dorm every night after supper," Bobby Skelton said. "Sam Bailey was coaching the centers. All the centers would line up with the ball, down in position, and he would get down on the floor and make sure that everybody's hands were under there the same way . . . you had to put it under there and put the same amount of pressure and everybody had to have the same tone or pitch in their voice. We'd stand there and just go down the line, just 'hip' . . . so everybody would sound the same." Later, Bryant had the managers dunk the balls in buckets of water so center and quarterback would know how the ball would feel if it rained.

The analytical Butch Frank was deeply impressed by Bryant's attention to detail. "Here they were teaching 20-year-old players who had been playing football since they were 8 or 10, how to put your hands down in a stance . . . how to put your toes. How to make your first step, how to make your second step. The minutest detail for every lineman of every technique, it just fascinated me. . . . Nothing was done without a reason."

A particular favorite of Coach Bebes Stallings was the "9 Technique" — in which the defensive player's initial move was to "deliver a hand or forearm shiver to the head of the offensive end." Pat James taught the same basic thing to guards in the "2 Technique."

The objective was to stun the opponent and free yourself up to find the ball carrier or to play the quarterback option. To James's mind, the result of a properly executed "2 Technique" was a bloody nose.

The biggest change many remember is the extent to which Bryant emphasized quickness and the use of the head in blocking and tackling. Under Whitworth (and in most programs), tackles were made with the shoulder, on the opposite player's number. The Bryant staff taught Alabama players to stick their foreheads into the opposing players around the belt buckle.

The technique wasn't dangerous because the players constantly exercised to build up their necks and because the emphasis was on hitting with the front of the face, not with the top of the helmet. "It wasn't necessarily in tackling that you were trying to butt them down," Jack Rutledge said. "He was not using the head as a spear, to hurt . . . he was using the head as a point of aiming, a point of position . . . His whole emphasis was, you've got to keep your eyes open . . . all the coaches . . . had to get around behind . . . so [they could] see [the player's] eyes . . ."*

*In 1965, the NCAA rules committee ruled that no player could "deliberately and maliciously use the helmet or head to unnecessarily butt or ram an opponent."

The second major area of emphasis was conditioning. Bryant expected his players to be able to play an entire game and still emerge fresh. The emphasis on stamina was relentless.

Bryant wanted "somebody who after an hour of playing football would say, 'I'm warmed up now, let's go,'" Bill Knight recalled. "He always said, 'you all keep me in the ball game . . . and that big old boy that's been working on your ass for three quarters is going to be stepping on his tongue, his guts are going to be hanging over his belt, and he's going to throw up and you've got him.'"

Never was a player allowed to sit or lie down on the practice field; never did a player walk from one practice session to another; and never could a player take the luxury of a quick rest at the end of a scrimmage play. This approach was especially tough on the bigger players, and some were unable to adjust to it. But it did pay off. In the 1958 season, Alabama went three games in the middle of the season without calling a single time out. Late in the game, when opponents began to flag, the Alabama players would get a lift by realizing they were still fresh. "You'd just sit there and laugh at them," Gary O'Steen said. "Really, you just felt so good, you were dancing around over there, these old boys sucking wind, we'd say, 'Oh boy, we've got you now.' That was one of the best feelings in the world."

There was much more to Bryant's approach to motivation than the inspirational speech in the locker room. Clearly, he used his intimidating presence and manner to literally frighten players to perform. The fear he generated was not so much of physical punishment or of being 'run off' — though that was there, too. The fear was based on the suspicion that Bryant knew better than they themselves the limits of their endurance. "You didn't have the fear of being punished so much, you had the fear of not living up to his expectations," Charlie Gray said. "You were afraid that you would be caught that one time that might lose the team the football game . . . The things that he did made you make a commitment. If you weren't going to make a commitment to play football his way, then he wanted you gone. And once you made that commitment, then you were afraid. You were afraid of failure."

The coach used both positive and negative techniques to achieve a high level of commitment. He talked constantly in his meetings about taking pride in personal appearance, grades, family, school and state. When he saw or heard something that led him to believe this kind of pride wasn't being displayed, the player involved would hear about it, and more than often not would end up running extra laps after what had already been an exhausting practice. Or Bryant would "break their plate" — take away their eating privileges and laundry money, a considerable penalty for the impoverished athletes.

On the positive side, the "Red" and "White" teams were allowed through the chow line before others, and they got better food. Players on the traveling squad each got four game tickets, which were usually sold at scalpers' prices, providing a welcome supplement to income.

Bryant and his coaches were not averse to using physical means — striking, kicking or butting a player — to make a point. In those days, players expected some "putting on of hands," and Bryant's staff was as tough as any in this regard.

The most frighteningly physical of the coaches was Pat James. It was not unusual for him to go one-on-one, totally without pads, with a player. James, his baseball cap turned around backward, would get so fired up during such drills that he would foam at the mouth, his face within inches of the face of the player being chastised. "You call that a block, that wouldn't stop a girl, Tennessee's going to break your ass in two," James might yell.

James gloried in the rough-and-tumble world of the lineman, and maintained the belief, often expressed, that bloody noses and busted lips made for better ball players. Once, Butch Frank recalls, eight players were lined up against each other in a half-line blocking drill. James challenged the offensive linemen to use a technique he had shown them to come up under the defensive man's chin and deal him a sharp blow.

"I want to see four bloody noses," the coach yelled, and his wish was granted. Then he put the defensive players on offense, called for the same thing, and was rewarded with four more.

Another time, James and Don Cochran were side-by-side running in from a practice that evidently hadn't been tough enough for James's taste. James flung his arm backward and caught the trotting Cochran across the mouth with the back of his hand, bloodying his nose and lip. "You ain't bleeding anywhere. You're going to have to get mean, Cochran," he cried. Cochran, who would have gone through a wall for Bryant, did not even get upset. "If you were a winner, Coach James was the greatest guy in the world," he says. Others were not so sure.

In one scrimmage, James, ostensibly teaching a technique, popped the huge tackle Charlie Coleman in the face. Coleman said, "Oh yeah, I think I know what you mean," and hit James with a forearm that knocked him to the ground about six yards away. James got up and said, "Hotalmighty, if we had 11 that mean we'd beat anybody."

The other coaches were more restrained. Bebes Stallings, who had an iron grip, would grasp a player behind the arm above the elbow and propel him to a desired place or into the right stance. But Stallings was always in control of himself and more apt to show patience than some of the other coaches.

Bryant himself, on occasion, would become so involved in a drill or technique lesson that he would go briefly head-to-head with a player. Bud Moore and Benny Dempsey both remember the head man descending the tower in a hurry and heading toward their practice group, early in the spring.

"He came off that tower, and I thought he was coming after me," Dempsey said. "He blew the whistle . . . he's running, he had on those big old boots . . . and had on a big old coat, big and floppy . . . everybody just froze in their tracks . . . ."

Moore was afraid he was in for it, too, but Bryant sailed past him and grabbed the big ex-marine, Carl Valletto, by the face mask. Suffused with anger, or doing a good job of making the players believe he was angry, Bryant twisted the helmet until Valletto fell to the ground. The exact words are lost, but the message was clear. "Valletto was considered the toughest man on the team," said Bobby Boylston. "He made an example of Valletto right away . . . and that got a lot of people's attention."*

At other times, Bryant would use his baseball cap to swat a player across the face to make a point. Wayne Sims has a favorite story about one such incident during a drill in which he was pitted against freshman Billy Neighbors in a "board drill":

"Billy weighed about 300 pounds at that point, and he was short," Sims says. "I would fire out on him and Billy would just flip me. Coach Bryant would get on me and drag me back and I'd fire out again and he'd flip me off. Coach Bryant said, 'Get over there and get on your knee.' And in a minute he called me back up there and he said, 'Boy take that hat (helmet) off,' and he took that baseball cap and he popped me about twice across the nose . . . I was hunting a gate, I would've left, but I was afraid Coach James would have caught me before I got there. He said, 'Now do you think you can block him?' So I got down and fired out and Neighbors was so scared he was running backwards faster than I could go . . . I couldn't even keep up with him. Coach Bryant said, 'See what you can do when you want to?'"**

It may have been on the same day that, dissatisfied with Gary Phillips's technique, Bryant kicked him in the rear when he assumed his stance and then slapped him with his cap.

"That was the closest I came to losing my scholarship," Phillips says, "because I turned around to hit him. And he saw I did, and he said, 'Gary, I have to treat you like a you-know-what to get you to do it right.' And I said, 'Coach, that's the way you outlined it in the meeting.' And he got back down and . . . showed us what he wanted us to do."

Bryant's radio producer, Bert Bank, visiting practice one day, had been disturbed by the treatment Bryant dealt one player who had not performed to his satisfaction. "You were pretty tough on him," Bank commented to the coach. "You watch him Saturday," Bryant responded.

---

*About this time, Bryant "broke Valletto's plate." "I know I had to feed him, he wasn't allowed in the chow hall . . . I would put bottles in my pocket and I fed him for about a week," Strum recalled.

**Duff Morrison once expressed to Bryant some concern about blocking a much taller player. "He ain't but 11 inches tall when he's lying on the ground," the coach said.

Along with the physical pressure and the self-induced emotional pressure of trying to live up the expectations of coaches, parents and home towns, players had to master a mental challenge too. They were, after all, in college, and attending classes. Beyond that, they had to learn the Bryant approach to football, which was more detailed than any they had encountered before.

Bryant would bring SEC officials into meetings to go over football rules, interpretations and enforcement. Players were given play books to read and memorize, and were expected to know not only their own responsibilities but those of other players. During the season, they were given tests on the defensive and offensive plans for upcoming games. Poor grades resulted in extra running.

Bryant's staff paid great attention to statistics to analyze opposition teams and players. The game plan for Vanderbilt listed all of the plays that the Commodores had run against Missouri and the yardage gained on each snap. A chart prepared for the game with Memphis State — hardly a feared opponent — listed every passing and running play against three opponents and predicted the plays Tide defenders could expect in different situations.

The use of game films to grade player performance was as old as the camera, but Bryant and his staff took emphasis on grading to another level. Bryant was one of the first coaches to film and grade scrimmages and even half-scrimmages to assess players.

In his book about football techniques, Bryant stated flatly that grading the game film determined "who to play and who not to play" in critical situations. On the Sunday following the game, the assistant coaches would spend hours running the game film and grading every player who played. Late Sunday afternoon, after a brief practice session to work out soreness, the coaches would review the film with the players and cover the grades in a squad meeting. Bryant personally determined who would move up or down as a result of the grades. The new depth chart was posted before practice on Monday.

Grades were based on a simple formula. An assistant coach graded every player that played a given position. If a player completed his assignment, he was given a "+". If he failed to complete his assignment, or was "whipped" on the play, he was given a "-". If the player was on the field but wasn't involved in the play, he was given a "u", for "ungradeable."

Then the total pluses and minuses were added and divided into the number of pluses. So if a player was involved in 40 plays and had 20 pluses, his grade would be 50. If a player completed an initial assignment, but did not get up make another block or pursue, it was possible to get both a "+" and a "-" on the same play.

Coaches also scored every player on "RBIs" and "errors," terms lifted from baseball. An RBI meant an outstanding play, such as an interception, causing or recovering a fumble, or a particularly effective block. Fumbles, blowing an assignment badly, or letting a receiver get loose behind you were errors.*

Grading was strict, and those who played dreaded the session in which the grades were covered. "There wasn't any such thing as a half-way . . . you either got a minus or a plus," Rains said, "If you didn't block your man and keep blocking him and staying with him, if your knees hit the ground, then you just got a minus."

"We'd go over the films with our position coaches," Rains recalls. "Hours and hours and hours of just nothing in the world basically but criticism. . . . On the good plays, they'd never give you an 'attaboy' . . . because Coach Bryant . . . strived for perfection more than anyone I've ever seen . . . he thought you could whip Godalmighty. That was his mentality. He thought if you gave it enough effort, if that effort was good enough, that you could whip Him. He coached that way for the whole time."

In his book, Bryant says that to play winning football, a player should grade at 61 percent. But big plays offset low grades in Bryant's mind. He wrote, "We would rather have a boy make three or four RBI's, even though his grade is only 50–55 percent . . . than have a boy get 65–68 percent and never make any big plays."

---

* The grade sheet for the Georgia Tech game can be found at the end of Chapter 19.

Errors were not tolerated for long. "A player who makes two or three errors a game simply cannot play for us," Bryant wrote. He proved the seriousness of this statement during the 1958 season, and particularly after games against Tennessee and Mississippi State.

Bryant never criticized a player on his television show, or to a reporter beyond saying, "The ends need some work." But in the squad meetings with players he did not mind singling out poor performance in an individual or a group. Buddy Wesley feels that players sometimes became more concerned about their individual grades than they were about actually winning the game. An error, such as a 15-yard penalty or a fumble, earned special attention at practice. Wesley, for example, was flagged for a late hit in the LSU game. In a scrimmage the following Monday, he carried the ball on ten or more running plays in a row. "I'm going to teach you [not] to get a penalty down there where it hurts," Bryant said. That day, Wesley was carried off the field by the managers. That was the kind of lesson you didn't forget.

Finally, many remark upon an element of guile and calculation in Bryant. He was always looking for an edge, a way to take an advantage. He "had a little slyness about him . . . a lot of gamesmanship in him," Charlie Gray said, "Coach Bryant liked to pull tricks . . . liked to show off . . . he liked to outfox the other guy across the field . . . and he tried to figure out how to do that . . . and so everything that Coach Bryant did, whether it was in just . . . idle conversation . . . or the trenches . . . he was always trying to outcoach the other fellow, in one fashion or another . . . ."

Calculation, Phil Cutchin said, "was his long point. He could read a group pretty well. If he felt they were self-satisfied, he'd do every thing he could to send them out on the field second half with a different attitude . . . ." Even Bryant's anger seemed to be a tactic. "He had a tremendous ability to recognize the emotional aspect of the players and of the team, and he knew and thought about what that emotional aspect was as he went into that game," Drake Keith said. "He would get upset . . . but he didn't get upset unless he thought it would do good to get upset."

CHAPTER SIX

Bump, Bump, Bump

Methods and planning aside, an immediate factor in Bryant's plans for building a winning team was the selection of the players on whom the success of the first season would depend. From the first days that his staff interacted with the Alabama squad, it was clear that the new coach applied vastly different criteria to player selection than had Whitworth. The pressures this placed on the young men on the Alabama squad were to be a source of compelling drama during 1958.

The means by which the coaches began player assessments was a "voluntary" conditioning program that began immediately after Bryant met with the squad on January 10. The sessions were voluntary, but everyone knew that players who did not volunteer would find themselves looking for food and lodging elsewhere and lose their scholarships.

The conditioning took place in a third floor gymnasium that had been used, back in the 1930s, as a temporary dorm for players. Some of the players had not even known the space existed before the arrival of the new coaching staff. Immediately it became a dreaded place, an early testing ground for what Bryant liked to call "winning attitude."

The room measures about 75 x 100 feet, and while it was big enough for Detroit Tiger pitcher Frank Lary to loosen his arm up before spring training, it was too small to assemble the entire squad. So players went in shifts of 25 or 35, with guards and centers, or tackles and ends, together.

Once the players had filed in, wearing sweat clothes, a manager closed and chained the door. No one came in or went out until the "class" was ended.

What immediately impressed the players was the non-stop character of these one-hour sessions, and the organizational sophistication behind them. "Suddenly, from this boring undisciplined rabble, [we went] to an extremely regimented situation where everyone was equal," said Morris Childers. "One thing that clicked in my mind was that the fear factor of the upperclassmen . . . suddenly that was over. Everybody was brought to the same level."

Not a moment was wasted, and there were no breaks. The fiery assistant coaches — Pat James, Gene Stallings, and Dee Powell especially — were constantly at the elbows and ears of the athletes, pushing, cajoling, correcting, challenging.

In addition to providing insight into character, the upstairs drills were designed to heighten physical condition, improve quickness, and to build endurance. One drill became a trademark of the team that later excited Alabama fans. To replace the leisurely, rhythmic side-straddle hops of previous years, Carney Laslie taught the players quickness and motion on sound — hands to helmet, hands to side, hands to knees, hands to feet. The drill demanded concentration, put a premium on quickness and exposed players with a lack of either. On at least one occasion, early in the year, Laslie, dissatisfied by the effort one player displayed in these drills, sent him packing. "He was supposed to be [up around his head] and he hit his pads," Dave Sington said, "and Coach Laslie sent him in. The boy said, 'What are you talking about?' And Coach said, 'You're off, get your stuff out of the dorm.'"

Another exhausting drill that demanded quickness and stamina was the "grass drill," which called for the players to drop to the floor and get up as quickly as possible, time after time. In another, players were told to lock shoulders and drive against each other, this without pads, and they did blocking drills against the sleds that were backed up against the gym wall. The players did endless push-ups, and some recall doing situps and leg lifts in the hundreds, until their backsides bled. They were expected to swing from rung to rung on a horizontal ladder with their elbows bent and their arms supporting their entire weight. This drill was hell for big men like Dan Pitts.

Evidently Bryant had some concern about the legality of these sessions under NCAA and SEC rules, and one step he evidently took as a smokescreen resulted in a humorous incident recalled by Dave Sington. It began when Birmingham papers carried the following news in early February:

James To Coach Tide Mat Team
"University, Feb 4 — University of Alabama is broadening its sphere of intercollegiate sports, it was indicated today by an announcement of additional assignments for members of the football coach staff by director of athletics Paul Bryant.

Pat James will be the coach of Alabama's first wrestling team, Bryant said. James is the defensive coach of the football team."

The story went on to say that Jerry Claiborne was assigned as assistant track coach and Gene Stallings as golf coach. "While it is too late for Alabama to put out a varsity wrestling team this season," the story said, "James is expected to lay the groundwork for one next year."

There was wrestling, but it does not appear that Alabama had any intent of fielding a team. The clear intent was to use wrestling to test football players' strength, endurance and will to win, and that came as a shock to one of Sington's friends from Baylor Prep.

Sington ran into the friend on the way to the third floor. "I said, 'What are you doing here?' And he said, 'Aw, I'm going out for wrestling.' They got upstairs and they put that big iron chain on the door. He didn't know what to think. He had his wrestling togs, his wrestling shoes, tights, the whole works. I guess he thought he was going to wrestle. When you started those managers put that chain on the door, and I said, 'Well, you're here for an hour, anyway.'"

The boy did not return after the first session. Wrestling under James was not like wrestling anywhere else. "You wrestled for your life," Jack

University of Alabama Sports Information

Coach Pat James

Rutledge said. After one of these sessions, Tommy White usually found himself unable to do anything but crawl away from the mat.

"We had three sessions, agility, on the mats, and weights," Jap Patton said. "And if you got weights first or last, you were a dead man." As the sessions continued, some of the exhausted players — too weak to even stand — would crawl to a small trap door that opened out onto the building's roof, and there would vomit up the meals that had been served earlier in the cafeteria. Eventually, the managers thoughtfully provided buckets to catch whatever was thrown up.

On the first day of these drills, Chuck Allen, the junior tackle from Athens, waited his turn on the steps outside the locked door. When a manager unchained the door, all was quiet for a moment. Then the ends and centers began to stumble out, covered with sweat, many of them bleeding and smelling of vomit. Allen spotted his buddy Baxter Booth.

"My God, what happened?" Allen exclaimed.

"Run. Don't do it," Booth blurted. "It's the worst thing you've ever seen."

It was exhausting work, and the coaches found it so as well. Dee Powell remembers how drained he was at the end of these grueling days. But the coaches knew the objective.

"It was fairly simple to find out who had ability. That was easy enough," Powell said. "But it took a lot more to find out who was going to stick in, who was tough enough to win when it was hard. We challenged them . . . we checked them and checked them again. We weren't going to have a team that couldn't take it."

Some players fell victim to injuries. Although the coaches constantly screamed to players to "stay down, stay on the mat" during the wrestling matches, it was hard to display the required aggressiveness without seeking leverage. Travis Best, a sophomore lineman, separated his shoulder. End Larry McCoy, the sophomore from Tuscaloosa, injured his knee in a match with Bobby Skelton. Donnie Parker, a sophomore fullback from Gadsden, broke his collarbone in a similar way while wrestling Jap Patton. Neither McCoy nor Parker ever played after that. Jerry Spruiell was more fortunate. He and Don Coleman made the mistake of standing upright in a bout and then fell. Spruiell took the impact for both on his extended left arm. The elbow popped out of joint briefly, but Goostree resorted to whirlpool and ultrasonic treatments and Spruiell continued to practice. He also carried a twenty-pound barbell for a couple of weeks to try to straighten the arm.

While some fell by the wayside, others like Butch Frank found the drills a forum in which they could display the kind of aggressiveness that impressed the coaches and earned them a chance to play. Frank had talked with his father, a former coach, about how he meant to approach practices under the new coach.

"I came to the conclusion that there was only one chance I had, which was 200 percent," Frank remembers. "I went home and got in terrific shape. A lot of guys did not understand what this was going to be. Because I was in shape, I was able to go through all the drills, [and] I was able to wrestle with the large linemen. I pinned a couple of large lineman. It got his attention."

Frank, who was known for his dedication throughout his career, also impressed teammates with his approach to school work. He would even take books on road trips. It was not unusual for him to say to a roommate, probably playing Rook or poker in one of the dorm rooms, "Wake me up in 30 minutes so I can study," and quickly drop off to sleep. "Except he didn't trust me, and would set his alarm, too," Jap Patton remembers.

Those who stayed eventually built themselves into the best condition of their lives. And some thrived on the intensity. Don Cochran, the guard from Birmingham, said he voluntarily went through two hours of the drills, instead of one. Roy Holsomback remembers that Don Parsons did the same. Most of the players found this kind of dedication beyond them, and some tried without success to use classroom requirements or labs to provide an excuse for missing a session.

Bobby Smith and Jim Pitts tried another approach. Smith, who lived in Brewton, and Pitts, from Red Level, would occasionally hitchhike home together. One Friday, the two finished classes early and decided to head home. That meant they'd need to rearrange the time of their third floor workout, scheduled for late that afternoon. They asked Pat James if he would let them work out early.

"That was the biggest mistake we ever made in our lives," Pitts said. "We felt like we would not have to work very hard, but Coach James took us upstairs and he almost killed both us. We wrestled until we couldn't get up off the mat. Finally Bobby and I waited until the next day to hitchhike home . . . we were too tired to try to go."

As the third floor drills continued, the players came to feel that Paul Bryant and his coaches did not care whether any one of them, as individuals, succeeded. "It was survival, that's all it was," said Chuck Allen. "It was the mental thing . . . reaching down so hard and so deep into what you had . . . they didn't really care, and it was pretty obvious at that point . . . 'we're going to do it our way, and I don't care, you either get on the wagon our get out.' They were totally committed to that way, that way was the correct way, and [they didn't have] any doubts at all." It was around this time that a much-remembered phenomenon began — the late-night bump-bump-bump of trunks being dragged down the dorm stairwells by players who had had enough.

Those who stuck with it, though, were shedding their losing attitudes and beginning to believe in themselves. Jerry Rich, a freshman from Gadsden who had only arrived on campus in January because of a shoulder injury, was one who began to feel a sense of accomplishment from simply enduring. "You mentally changed, you felt like you . . . could handle anything that showed up," Rich said. "You had gone through so much hell."

As the conditioning drills continued through February and March, the players began to long for a change, any kind of a change, to break the demanding cycle. But Bryant, involved with administrative details, kept putting spring training off to the point where the players were praying something different. When spring drills actually began on March 19, though, they were no relief. Conditioning had just been a prelude. The real challenges were just beginning.

CHAPTER SEVEN

Junction East

I f there is a parallel in Alabama football history to the Junction experience at Texas A&M, it took place in March and April 1958, the team's first spring practice under Paul Bryant.

Junction had several factors absent at Alabama: the heat, which was more intense in the Texas summer than in the Alabama spring; the remoteness from civilization; the rustic facilities, including a practice field that was full of "goatheads," a kind of cockleburr; and the fact that practices took place twice a day. At Alabama, the practices went on for a longer period, and the basic idea was the same. "We used the same drills and the same practices at Alabama as we did at Texas A&M," said Phil Cutchin. Years later, Bud Moore asked Bryant if Junction had been that much tougher than the first spring at Alabama. "No it wasn't," Bryant told Moore. "'I meant for it to be that tough at A&M, and I also meant for it to be that tough at Alabama, because I wanted you boys to take pride in that red jersey, because I had worn it.'"

One difference about the Alabama experience was the amount of press coverage. Sportswriters in Alabama were much less critical than the big-city media in Texas. During preseason, most papers did not send reporters to Tuscaloosa every day to cover practice, which meant that Bryant kept negative stories about tough practices and quitting players to a minimum. The state of Alabama football being what it was, Bryant could do no wrong.

The Alabama players had already been impressed, during the conditioning drills, with the Bryant staff's intensity and with the detailed organizational plans it brought to every aspect of the program. When spring drills began, all were struck with the vast difference between Bryant's practices and the relaxed approach of the Whitworth era.

To begin with, there was a daily schedule, drafted by Bryant himself, mimeographed and posted for all to read. When he drew his equipment, each man was given a jersey that indicated not only his relative status at the time, but also what he would be doing for every minute of practice.

The practice field was a short walk from the dressing rooms in the athletic building. After the athletes passed between two women's dormitories, they could see the makeshift wooden tower, 15 to 20 feet high, near the center of the practice area. The field itself was chalked off into sections, each designated by letter or number. Part of the field was fenced off, and canvas curtains could be raised to provide privacy.

Practices were divided into five, six or seven 15 or 20 minute segments. In the practice of March 29, for example, the "5th 20" had Coaches Cutchin, Keith, Bailey, and Snoderly working with one group on offensive pass routes; Laslie, Stallings, Luna, and Brown with another group on pass defense; James and Powell with guards, a center and a quarterback on blocking in the middle; and Claiborne and Lewis with the other guards and tackles on the blocking sled.

At the end of each period, the managers, Bert Jones or Gary White, blew a whistle and called out the assignments. Players and coaches were expected to sprint to the next station and the next drill. "It was the first time I had ever gone through a practice that there wasn't a little slack time, somewhere," said senior Billy Rains. Players slow to jump up from a tangle learned better. "Redbird, nobody makes money on their ass except a prostitute," Bryant once told Red Stickney. "He picked me up like a fly and just held me in his face . . . my feet were off the ground and he shook me . . . threw me backwards and I did a flip and came up running," Stickney said.

Adding to the rigor of the practices was the virtual taboo — not unique to Alabama — against drinking water during practice.

"Abstinence [from water] was a form of discipline," acknowledged trainer Jim Goostree. "The theory back then was that if you drank water it was a show of weakness," Russell Stutts said. One concern was controlling cramps, and the players were given potassium and salt tablets, which only increased their need for liquid. Duff Morrison "took 13 salt tablets and two potassium . . . this big — things they give pregnant women — because my legs and calves would cramp so much." One day he lost 16 pounds off his 179-pound frame. Jasper Best, who had played at 205 in high school, was down to 182 and after practice might weigh as little as 162.

"They thought as long as we were losing weight we weren't in shape," Best said. Players would become so dry they would sometimes resort to desperate means. "We'd use sweaty towels or anything else you could get your mouth on, you'd be so cotton-mouthed," Marlin Dyess said. At breaks, they might be given frozen orange segments or chips of ice to suck. But there was never enough. The coaches attempted to extend the prohibition beyond the practice field, exhorting players to avoid liquids until dinnertime. This was impossible to enforce. Once in the showers, the players drank themselves soggy from the streaming shower heads.

The depth chart that Bryant posted for the first day of spring practice listed 95 names. It was radically different than one Whitworth might have posted had he still been the coach.

Willie Beck and Ralph Blalock, both senior ends, and Jimmy Woodward, the senior redshirt quarterback, were gone, as were about a dozen others who had found the early conditioning more than they were willing to bear. The remainder of Whitworth's returning starters, with the exception of Charlie Gray, found themselves listed below players with less experience.

David Sington, Ken Roberts, Bobby Smith, and Danny Wilbanks were all Crimson "B" teamers, essentially second string. Billy Rains and Benny Dempsey were White "A" — third string at this point. Baxter Booth, Sid Neighbors, and Chuck Allen were each listed fourth at their positions.

The demotions were not welcome. "I guess that was one of the most sickening feelings I ever had in my athletic career," said Rains. "I just couldn't believe it was happening."

By the third practice on Saturday March 22, ten more players had eft, and several more were near the ends of their ropes. These included Booth and Allen, the longtime teammates from Athens.

The way Booth remembers it, Allen suggested that the two hang it up. Allen says, "Baxter and I convinced each other . . . that we didn't have to take this shit anymore." In any event, after practice on Saturday the two went home to tell their parents that they planned to quit.

Booth knew the decision wasn't going to be popular with his father, so when his parents asked him what he was doing at home Saturday night, he stalled for time. "Aw, I just came home to see y'all," he said. The next morning at breakfast, he tried to drop the word casually. "I think I'm going to give up football," he said.

"You're going to do what?" Booth's father said.

"I've just had enough down there," Booth replied.

"I'll tell you what you're going to do, you get your ass right back down there," Booth's father said. Booth did.

Allen, too, had reconsidered. He remembered a statement Bryant had made about the players who were leaving.

"You know, you can quit anytime you want to," the coach said, "but the first time you quit is hard. If you are going to quit, I want you to quit on me now, because I don't want you to quit in a game. You know, the next time will be easier. And the next time will be even easier."

"I just didn't want to go back to Athens . . . everybody else had always quit," Allen said. "I wasn't that great a player. I just didn't want to be thought of as a quitter."

Having decided to stay, Booth decided to fight for his position among the projected starters. Bryant had said that any player who felt he wasn't getting a fair shot could challenge any other player, and if he won in a fair contest, would get the other player's jersey.

Booth went to see his end coach, Gene Stallings. "Coach, y'all ain't giving me a chance," he said. Stallings said, "Let's go see Coach Bryant."

Bryant was sitting behind his big desk. "What do you want?" he asked.

"Well, Coach, I just don't think y'all were giving me a chance."

"Where do you think you ought to be playing?" Bryant inquired. By now, Booth knew the answer to this one.

"First team, the red team," he said. "That's what I was last year."

Asked who he wanted to challenge, Booth choose Jerre Brannen, who was rated the first string right end. Tuesday afternoon before practice, the entire squad gathered around to watch.

"He tackled me three times, I tackled him three times," Brannen said. "He blocked me three times and I blocked him three times." Then came a drill in which each tried to prevent the other from catching a ball lobbed to him over the other's shoulder. "You'd just kill each other," Brannen says.

When the coaches voted, they chose Booth, and the two swapped jerseys. Booth was feeling much better about his situation until he found out the next day that Brannen had challenged him back. "So we went through that shit again, and I won again . . . and then we go practice . . . crawl off the field, just worn out, beat up . . . and the next day he's challenged me again."

Booth may be a little off on the details — newspaper reports say the rematch was a few days later and that it was declared a draw. Anyway, Bryant called a halt at this point, giving both the players a red jersey. Having seen the toll it took and realizing that any jersey swap was temporary, the players stopped volunteering for such activities.

Others were wondering about their football futures, too. Red Stickney, the highly touted halfback from Key West, was one. Stickney's father was a shrimp fisherman who had been badly injured in an accident, and his parents were divorced. Stickney was perhaps the best example on the team of the sensational high school athlete who struggled to meet expectations at the college level. Bryant, recognizing that he had speedier halfbacks, moved Stickney to fullback, which also meant linebacker. Stickney had never played that position.

Coming in from his first practice after the switch, bloody, tired, a tooth loose, Stickney was approached by Bryant, who asked, "Redbird, how do you like that old fullback?"

Stickney said, "I don't know."

"Well, you'll learn to like it," Bryant responded.

But Stickney did not like it much better a week later, and late one night he called his mother. "Momma, I'm coming home," he said. "You know how much I love football. I just don't understand what's going on here."

Stickney's mother convinced him to stay at least until the morning, and he went on to practice in the afternoon. While he was getting dressed, Bryant came over, grabbed his jersey and said, "Hey, Momma's boy, I heard you are not having any fun. I heard you called your Momma last night wanting to go home. You want to go home and cry in Momma's lap? Give me that jersey. You don't deserve an Alabama jersey."

Stickney was stung. "No, I want my jersey," he said, and grabbed it back from the coach.

"Let me tell you something, Redbird," Bryant said. "You'd better smile."

The other players — and many witnessed the event — called Stickney "Smilin' Jack" for six weeks. He never learned how Bryant found out about the call to his mother.

Sophomore Gary Phillips, the pre-med student from Dothan, was another player who was finding the going rough. Signed on as a guard, Phillips had been praised by Bryant in the early spring. But later on, he was listed down in the depth charts and found himself working out at end.

"I had never played end, never been told in high school or anywhere how to play end, and they had two pulling guards and a blocking back playing on me and about killed me," he said. "So I got the impression, well, heck, they don't intend to play me, I'm too small. Why put up with this if they're not going to coach me on what to do. So I told a couple of friends, Mack Wise and maybe Roy Holsomback, that I had had enough, that I wasn't going to play, so I was going to quit."

Holsomback remembers going to the bus station with Phillips to make the call to his father, who owned a service station in Ft. Walton Beach, Florida. "So he goes over to the phone booth and he calls," Holsomback recalled, "about to cry, you know."

Phillips says he told his father, "Daddy, they don't plan to play me up here, and I believe I can just work my way through school, or go somewhere else, and I'm going to quit. And Daddy said, 'Well, I guess you can come home and pump gas, son. I thought you was tough.'"

As Holsomback recalls it, Phillips said, "Goddammit, I am," and slammed the receiver down so hard part of it broke away. "I never thought about quitting after that," Phillips said.

Perhaps it is not surprising that the players were feeling somewhat uncertain under the constant physical and mental pressure of the spring drills. In the early part of the spring, Bryant and his coaches were still assessing talent and testing each players dedication. They tried a number of different players at center, moving Blevins and Phillips to center and trying Rutledge and even the tiny Scooter Dyess at fullback.

Blevins, the tough ex-Marine, had caught Bryant's eye for his combative nature. He displayed it one day for everyone, including the parents of Red Gann.

Gann's parents had come up from Sylacauga to watch practice, the first time they had ever done so. Gann was matched up as a middle guard against Blevins at offensive center. Richard Strum saw the whole thing.

Blevins was a little punchy, he said, and "he'd look at you funny and shake his head . . . he would get down over the ball and the sweat would run down his nose . . . to this day I can see the sweat dripping off his nose . . . every time he'd get down over the ball, he'd shake his head and Johnny Gann would haul off and knock the hell out of him."

"I kept working on him with my elbow a little too much," said Gann. "I got in a few times, he kind of blew his cool . . . ."

Strum continued: "Jim said, 'Johnny, don't do that any more.' Johnny said, 'Well you moved.' The next time it happened, boy they came up swinging. Johnny stopped to take his helmet off, that was a mistake because Blevins didn't."

"He caught me with a right cross," Gann recalled. " . . . my four bottom front teeth came out . . . spitting teeth and blood everywhere . . . and they finally sent me to the doctor, I went to the doctor, they looked at me, and I went back out and finished practice." Gann's parents were horrified, but that was football under Bryant.

Bert Bank, Bryant's radio producer, was at the practice. "I said to Bryant, 'Why in hell didn't you stop that fight?' He said, 'None of your damn business.'"

There was continuing discussion among the coaches about who would play quarterback. The coaches had seen little of Jackson, whose knee was hurt. Until the middle of spring practice, they believed he would have to have surgery. Smith had the most experience, and he and Skelton were both skilled passers. But Bryant had never been a passing coach, even with Babe Parilli, and the blocking ranks were too thin to consider building an offense around throwing.

Sophomore James Patton (nicknamed Jap not because he had Asian features, but because his initials J. A. P. were once carved into a toy gun he had) looked strong defensively, and so did Smith. Gary O'Steen was showing outstanding skills as a runner, but he was anything but polished. Laurien (Gooby) Stapp was an outstanding punter, but he lacked experience.

The coaches also fretted about the centers, despite what looked like experience and depth with the seniors Dempsey and Roberts, the big redshirt Buck Burns, Blevins, and others. Donnie Heath was having an outstanding spring, impressing the coaches with his intensity. When he made a picture-perfect head-on tackle of Charlie Rieves, splitting his helmet, Bryant was ecstatic. He let Heath sit out the remainder of the drill and sent the manager for a brand new helmet.

But it was Dempsey who got the most attention. Perhaps on the basis of the films, the Alabama coaches suspected that Dempsey was not a winning player by their definition. Blessed with great ability, he could not or would not extend the effort the coaches demanded.

The dissatisfaction began to show one day when outdoor drills had been cancelled. The coaches took the centers inside and timed them on the quickness of their snaps. "A center had to be able to snap the ball back to the punter within seven-tenths of a second," Dempsey recalled. "The punter had to be able to get the ball in the air within a second and a half . . . and then the ball had to hang anywhere from three to four seconds, and a man that couldn't run 40 or 50 yards in six seconds couldn't play . . . by the time the ball went in the air and came down, the linemen ought to be under it."

Dempsey had been practicing on the Red team. But when he went to pick up his "basket" after the indoor session, it had a green jersey in it — fourth string.

Dempsey was shocked. He thought he had been given the wrong basket, and protested to the equipment manager. "I've got the wrong color jersey," he said. "No you don't," the manager said. He showed Dempsey a note that said, "See Coach Bryant."

"I walked in his office and he was looking down at his desk reading something and he didn't even look up," Dempsey said. "And he said, 'Have a seat over there, Dempsey.' I sat down, he looked up and he said, 'You were reported to me for loafing yesterday in the gym.'

"I said, 'Coach, I don't know who said that . . . I was doing the same thing the other centers were doing, snapping back as fast as I could snap, snapping to Bobby Jackson, and then on punts, the same way.'

"He said, 'Well, you were reported to me for loafing by one of the coaches. As far as I'm concerned, I would have given $10,000 for you as a freshman, I wouldn't give ten cents for you right now.' So I knew that I had had it."

CHAPTER EIGHT

'Bleed 'Em and Gut 'Em'

W hat happened to Dempsey and several others that spring and fall directly raises the question of the coaches' attitudes toward players who, because of character, laziness, or "un-willingness to pay the price," did not fit into Bryant's plans.

Bryant knew that his ultimate success depended on the quality of his players, and he had identified specific traits which he used to select those he recruited. He had had no say in the selection of players inherited from Whitworth. It is his attitude toward these athletes that is in question.

Many of the players, seeing the intense pressure placed on some of their peers, believed the intent was "run them off" — to make things so rough that the players would quit and give up their scholarships. In 1961, an unnamed SEC coach was quoted in *Sports Illustrated* as saying that it was obvious "that the practices were made so brutal that untalented players were forced to quit."

That statement misses the mark. It's true that the pressure had the effect of forcing some players to quit, but it wasn't only less talented ones who left. Some of the best athletes on the team were among those pruned out. As Bobby Luna saw it, "There were some football players down there that never should have even been there, and there were some good football players down there that had a lot of crap in their neck, thought they were gods, big time deals. They hadn't won any football games, they were just having a ball on the University's money."

Bobby Boylston, the former quarterback from Atlanta, saw it this way: "You were a tool for him to get to where he wanted to go. He stood right there and told you. 'I'm going to win, you can be here if you want to be. I don't care whose face I have to step in.' Coach Bryant really didn't care whether you quit. . . . when they got through, there was a mutual respect, he respected them and the guys respected Coach Bryant once they realized what he was doing . . . but Coach Bryant didn't care if you quit, I don't think he had one second thought no matter who quit. He was a tough sucker. He didn't care what happened."

In 1958, grant-in-aid scholarships were given for four years, and once signed supposedly became something of an entitlement: Play by the rules, come to practice, make your grades, and you can stay until your eligibility is used up. Notwithstanding, there is plenty of testimony that in his first year Bryant sent some players packing and that the players so treated went quietly. In *Bear,* Bryant himself says that "I had one boy saying he was going to quit, and I had to nip that in the bud so I went to his locker and took all his things and threw them into the street."

Bryant cut some players from the practice field. It almost happened to Bud Moore, the end from West End in Birmingham. Moore was a tough player who loved contact. "I hated to see Bud Moore come across the line," Morrison said. "That sumbitch was tough." One day at lunch Moore had eaten too many of the savory turnip greens served up in the dining hall, and during practice he became nauseated. He came in for some close attention by the head coach, as James Beall recalled: "Coach Bryant got down off his tower, and said, 'I'm going to show you how it's done.' And [Bryant] went one on one with [Moore] and didn't have any pads on him. Telling Bud to hit him, hit him . . . Bud was sick . . . he said, 'Coach, I got sick at lunch today . . . because of turnip greens,' so . . . Bryant was, 'I don't give a damn, you hit me, hit me' and he actually just drove him into the ground . . ."

Once Moore began to vomit, he couldn't stop, even when Bryant called a break for all the players to gather around. The continued spewing irritated Bryant. "Well, if you can't handle it any better than that, you are through," he said, and sent Moore to the showers.

Moore did as he was told. Shaken and feeling terrible, he was found in the showers by Stallings. "Come with me," he said. Moore wrapped a towel around his waist and followed his end coach to Bryant's office.

"Just say, 'Yessir' or 'Nossir,'" Stallings advised Moore.

"So I knocked on the door," Moore said. "He opened the door, big old rascal standing there, still in his coaching clothes, and he says, 'Boy, what do you want?' and I said, 'Well, Coach Stallings said you wanted to see me.' And he said, 'Yeah, these coaches tell me I'm making a mistake by running you off. I don't know about it myself, but you've got a uniform if you want it.' And I said 'Yessir.' And he slammed the door."

Volatile as he was, Bryant approached nothing without a plan, and many players comment on his ability to read individuals and understand what made them play better. His coaches insist that the intent was not to force players out, but to get the most out of them and see if they were willing to "pay the price" of being in a winning program. "You can't help the team if you quit," said Phil Cutchin.

"Sometimes we were disappointed to see that the kid didn't stick," said Drake Keith. "In most cases I'd say that was true . . . you hate to lose 'em because we didn't have a whole lot to work with, but if they were not going to be there when we . . . really needed them, it was better all the way around for everybody to know it at that time . . ."

Coach Bryant "hated to see kids quit," said Keith, " . . . but once they did . . . he felt like, if you quit now you're going to quit in a game. I don't think he really enjoyed seeing it . . . he'd rather see a kid fight, and hang in there, not give up."

Stallings agrees. "He probably hated it, too, he just didn't let his emotions show . . . he had a job to do and you know he wasn't trying to win friends, he was trying to win games . . . if a guy left, that was his choice . . . ."

The players themselves are divided. Jim Blevins said, "Coach Bryant didn't run anybody off . . . those of us that stayed eliminated those others . . . that's the way I look at it. It's a personal thing, but you know . . . had I not . . . done what was necessary and felt the way I did about it, somebody would have eliminated me . . . ."

Bryant seldom relented toward a player who quit: "Football players don't quit," he said. But several of the players believe those placed under severe pressure might have rehabilitated themselves. "It was a test," said Butch Frank. "I think he was testing all of us, every minute. That was one of his modes for finding out the few who could, despite not having much talent, stay in there and win."

In *Bear,* Bryant said, "My plan was to bleed 'em and gut 'em because I didn't want any well-wishers hanging around."

It's clear that in the endless meetings before and after practice, the coaches thoroughly discussed the tactics they used to test and motivate individual players. There were three main approaches: kick butt; pet; or ignore. Marlin Dyess and Butch Frank, for example, needed only an occasional kind word to keep them motivated. But for Benny Dempsey, the tactic was clearly "kick butt."

Dee Powell, headed for the military in the summer, was evidently designated the butt-kicker. The young veteran of the Junction bloodletting became Dempsey's constant companion during practice.

Charlie Tom Gray was Dempsey's roommate. "Benny . . . never did play up to his potential, Coach Bryant knew that," he said. "Coach Bryant had studied films for three years on all the boys . . . he knew the ones that had talent . . . he was going to make football players out of them or he was going to run them off."

"I'll be honest with you," said Wayne Sims. "[Dempsey] was probably mistreated. He was one they set out to make an example of because he was so much bigger, a hell of an athlete. I don't know if I could have stayed if I had been [Benny]."

"I'd look down at the guards and centers practice and they'd have Dempsey by the ass, throwing him into the blocking dummy," said Bill Knight. The coaches taunted Dempsey, too, daring him to quit, telling him he wasn't tough enough. "Everyday after practice," Dempsey said, "I was the only one that had to stay . . . and they ran me ten yard stop and starts . . . get down in the stance and run ten yards. And ten . . . ten . . . ten . . . and when you got to where you couldn't run any longer, they'd pick you up by the back of your shoulder pads and throw you as far as they could throw you . . . anyway, they did that to me, I don't know how many days . . . ." But Dempsey, whatever his other failings, would not quit.

"He would come in, and he would be so tired," said Gray. "But after supper, he was rarin' to go."

Holding on as best he could, Dempsey was helped by one person who was a friend to all of the Alabama players, Merrill (Hootch) Collins. "Hootchman . . . would come out on that field and help me get in . . . he knew I was still out there," Dempsey said.

Hootch, or frequently Hootchman, Collins was 70 years old in 1958, a spindly, ribald caricature of the old southern retainer. Wearing an Alabama cap, usually seated in a cane bottom chair in the breezeway that led from the athletic building into the building just north on University Boulevard, Hootch had been around the Alabama athletic department long enough to refer to Paul Bryant as "boy."

Hootch was born in 1888, the son of a former slave, he said. He told Richard Strum that his first nickname was "Shag," because he helped shag baseballs at Alabama baseball practices. He first went to work for the University in about 1900, as a janitor in the supply store which was located then in Woods Hall.

The athletic department, he once told an interviewer, had a half-interest in the supply store then. That led to Hootch's connection to athletics, and when the football team took trips in those early years, Hootch would go along to take care of whatever 'valuables' the players put aside during the game. He seems to have retained these duties continuously through the regimes of Wallace Wade, Frank Thomas, Red Drew, and Whitworth. By the time Bryant arrived, Hootch's sole function was to make coffee for the coaches.

Trainer Jim Goostree always maintained that his formal job interview at Alabama was with both Crisp and Hootchman, in the breezeway outside the athletic building. Later that summer, Goostree remembers the following encounter with Hootchman:

"I was in a pair of shorts working in the training room trying to clean it up," Goostree said, "and [there was] a great big window fan in there.

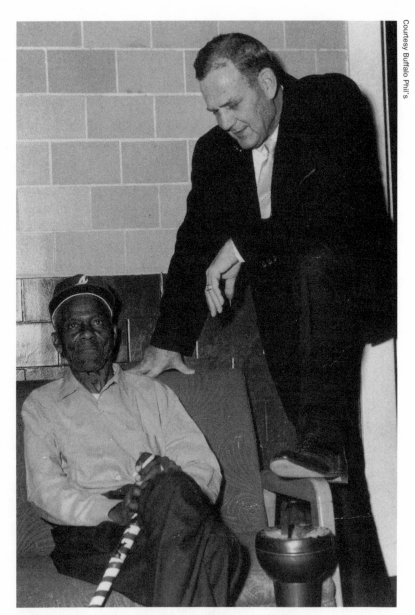

Coach Bryant with Merrill (Hootchman) Collins.

I turned it on and it sucked all the red clay dust out of that parking lot right into the building. And . . . so I couldn't work with it on, that marble floor was right over the boiler, and it was real hot in there, and I was trying to clean up, and . . . Hootch was sitting out back in that breezeway, and I just needed help bad . . . I decided I'd go out and ask him to help me. So I went out there, and I said, 'Sir, what do you do around here,' and he was sitting in an old cane bottom chair with a pillow in it, and he said, 'I is retired. In the summer time around here, everybody is retired.'"

So while Hootch's formal duties had ended by the time Bryant arrived, he would still ride with the managers, in the equipment van, to all of the football team's games. If for some reason he couldn't go, and in later years when he was too frail, he kept up with his boys on an ancient Philco radio that he kept near his cot. For years, he lived in the cramped boiler room in the basement of the building adjacent to the athletic department.

Hootch knew the players, all of them, and remembered their names for years afterward. Many developed a fondness for him, bringing him warm meals from the dining hall, giving him 50 cents out of their laundry money every two weeks, and occasionally buying him a bottle of whiskey. Hootch attended all A Club initiations, and was accorded the honor of the "last slat" for all of the new members.

James Booth, who played basketball at Alabama from 1960 to 1964, said that Bryant took an interest in Hootch's health. One morning, Booth was visiting with Hootch when Bryant arrived at the athletic building. Bryant assigned Booth the duty of bringing Hootch a warm meal every day. Bryant had also ordered business manager B. W. Whittington to take Hootch to the Social Security Administration to make sure he got his "pennies."

Hootch died in 1968. Not long before his death, Richard Strum was passing through Tuscaloosa and looked the old man up. Bryant had moved him into some old "Negro" housing not far from where the Bryant museum is today. "I had him a fifth of Jack Daniels," Strum said, " . . . and I knocked on that door . . . it was pitch black . . . he said,

'Come on in.' I couldn't see anything, didn't know what he looked like but I gave him that bottle and shook his hand . . . and that was the last I ever saw of Hootchman . . . ."

The University took spring holidays in early April 1958, and Bryant sent his players home, using the break to move to the next phase of his rebuilding plan — beginning to settle on the players who would actually get playing time, and teaching them the offensive and defensive plans they would use when the season began. When the players returned, Bryant announced, the practices would be closed to visitors and the press.

The first two practices after the return were long and arduous, and they were followed by what the newspapers called a "punishing series of wind sprints" that left the players gasping. Bryant was contemptuous of the team's conditioning, even at this point. "I don't guess there's a half dozen kids who have ever been in shape in their lives," he said. Comments like this from the head man were a signal to all that there was more pain to come. Bryant and the coaches used sprints, like the wrestling before them, to challenge and test not only the condition but also the commitment of their athletes. It was around this time, the third week of spring practice, that Bryant singled out halfback Ferdy Cruce for special attention.

Cruce had been moved to the Red team around the end of March. There is no doubt that he was tremendously talented, but Bryant expected his players to demonstrate the will to win at all times in everything they did.

Actually, Bryant's rancor was not specifically directed at Cruce to begin with. He was upset with the performance of the Red team, which had failed to score in several attempts around the goal line. Said Dave Sington: "He told us if we score, we'd go in. Anyway, Bert Jones [the manager, who was officiating for the scrimmage] said we were offsides or something, so we didn't make it. Coach Bryant said, 'I'm going to clear the stadium and I'm going to run y'all until you die.'"

Jap Patton, who was watching from the sideline, recalled what happened next.

"They did a 50-yard sprint . . . and Cruce finished right along with everybody else . . . Bryant took off running and ran down there and grabbed Ferdy in the nose guard and was [shaking him] I think he might have hit him, he looked like, if you recall, how when . . . Sugar Ray Robinson beat Carmen Basilio, how his face looked . . . that's the way Ferdy looked, he had got hit in the face. And Coach Bryant asked him if that was as fast as he could run. And he said, 'No sir.' And the next sprint he beat them 20 yards."

The constant pressure on Cruce and others made an impression. Running one day after practice, Richard Strum recalls, "All of a sudden I started to vomit . . . but I kept running . . . and barfing over my shoulder . . . and I could hear the coaches, 'There's a man that wants to play, there's a man that wants to play.'"

As the practices continued, injuries, major and minor, began to deplete the availability of players for practice. The depth chart posted for April 11 showed 18 players injured — among them fullbacks Red Stickney and Danny Wilbanks, guards Don Parsons and Butch Frank, and tackles Don Coleman and Sid Neighbors.

Having himself played with a broken leg, Bryant was impatient with injuries, and Goostree was expected to keep the list of non-combatants small. "Unless there was bone showing through, you didn't get out of practice," said Ken Roberts. Charlie Tom Gray remembers lying in bed hoping that he would be lucky enough to break his leg. Chuck Allen could be heard apologizing to his body every day for what he was getting ready to put it through.

Said Gary Phillips: "The first time I broke my nose, it swelled really wide and was blue and sore, just the wind would hurt, and I was sitting there, I was hoping that I wasn't going to have to practice . . . I guess Goostree had told Coach Bryant that I had broke my nose . . . anyway, he came down the steps and stopped and said, 'Well, Little Buddy, how's your nose?' It was all swelled up, I said, 'It's pretty sore coach.' I was wanting him to say, 'Well, you just run today,' or something. He just said, 'Well, you're just handicapped.'" Phillips practiced in pads.

The constant pressure to play through pain made it difficult for marginal players like Dodd Holt, the senior end from Jasper. Consistently placed near the bottom of the depth chart, Holt suffered from a sore shoulder and a sore knee, and he began to feel like cannon fodder. "They wanted bodies . . . they didn't care if they were walking or whatever," Holt said. Placed at the end position against pulling guards and blocking backs, in the evening Holt would "go to [the] dormitory with involuntary tears and muscle tremors for about four hours," unable to sleep. By the end of the spring, in trouble on his grades and beaten down physically, Holt called it quits.

Sammy Smith remembers one scrimmage when an injured hip was really bothering him.

"A bruised hip is really painful," Smith said, " . . . and I was the last man getting back to the huddle for about three consecutive plays. Everything was speed, speed, quick, move. I was dragging, I was dragging my leg. And the whistle blew . . . from the tower, and everybody froze, because somebody's going to get it . . . a coach or a player, somebody."

Bryant came over to Smith and grabbed his face mask: 'What's the matter with you?" he growled.

"Coach, I'm hurt," Smith said.

"Hurt, goddam, I'll teach you what hurt is," Bryant said. "He started shaking me," Smith said, " . . . and I stiffened my neck . . . I was already totally exhausted . . . . I stiffened my neck for a while, he kept shaking it and hollering . . . in my face, and finally my neck just got weak, and I kinda, I believe, that I was put down on my knees. And he was shaking me, I thought my neck was going to break and he was saying, 'Football players always are hurt, you've got to play with the hurt. I'll teach you what hurt is.' He was hollering and screaming . . . and then he let go of me and I ran to the huddle and I never felt that hip again. He said you could play through the pain. All football players have to do that, real football players."

It seems likely, as Don Parsons says, that Bryant's contemptuous attitude toward injuries meant that some players never had a chance to heal. Parsons, himself plagued throughout his career with a neck injury, said of Bryant: "He wouldn't let them get well. I mean if you had an injury . . . and you could walk, or run, or trot, or whatever, you damn sure better be out there . . . and there were quite a few kids that . . . could've maybe possibly . . . been okay . . . in the long run." Goostree, who on occasion would overrule Bryant on a player's fitness for game or practice, was under constant pressure to make players available.

Allen remembers this story about how Bryant dealt with injuries.

"Coach Laslie used to handle the wounded type guys," he said, "and they were all out in sweats, and one day Coach Bryant looked over there and he saw more guys in sweats than there were in pads . . . and he went over and talked to Laslie and they started running and they ran damn wind sprints the whole practice while we were over there scrimmaging, doing whatever drills . . . the next day, all them sonofabitches was back in pads."

Sid Neighbors, the two-year letterman at tackle, was one of the walking wounded, having taken a blow to the head. Sitting out in the breezeway with Hootchman and some of the other players one afternoon, Neighbors was enjoying his status.

Many players remember this story. As Bud Moore recalls it, "We had a bunch of pea gravel around there in the parking lot, and Sidney had this gravel and he's trying to ring it off everybody's headgear . . . talking and carrying on, and everybody else in pads, waiting and dreading like the devil to go out to practice.

"Coach Bryant walks out," said Moore, "and he walks over and puts his hand on Sidney's shoulder and he said, 'Sidney, how are you feeling?' And Sid said, 'Oh, Coach Bryant, my head's still hurting me bad, I hear ringing in my ears, sounds like a telephone ringing.'

"'Bryant said, 'Well, Sidney, next time it rings, you answer it, because it's me telling you to get your fat ass out to practice.'"

CHAPTER NINE

'Poor Coaching'

B y the eleventh day of spring practice, Bryant and his staff had begun to identify the players who would carry the burden when the season started the following September. Before that practice on April 11, 1958, the four-deep showed two red teams and 14 additional players with an "(x)" by their name that meant "also have red jersey." These 36 players got to go first in the chow line and who got to eat steak when others were served a chopped concoction known as "dinosaur burgers."

At quarterback, Bobby Jackson and Bobby Skelton were listed one-two on the red team. Jackson was not much of a passer — Skelton kidded him "that every time he threw the other team put on the punt return" — but even though he was hampered by a knee brace, he had quick feet and great speed. The knee was so much improved that Goostree, the team doctors, and the coaches had decided against an operation. Gary O'Steen also had earned a red jersey, but was ranked third. The coaches were still unsure how best to use the talented junior from Anniston.

If there was no Billy Cannon in the backfield, there were several backfield players of roughly equal ability, enough to provide considerable depth. Mack Wise and Marlin Dyess, the former teammates from Elba, were one-two at right halfback. Behind them, Ferdy Cruce and Bill Knight were both listed as wearing red jerseys as well.

Four players had earned red shirts at left halfback — Duff Morrison, the sophomore from Memphis; Richard Strum from Biloxi; Buddy Wesley from Talladega; and Allan Mauldin, a sophomore from Childersburg. Wesley's promotion had been dramatic.

"We had one of those night scrimmages out at the stadium and I had a hell of a night," he recalled. In the middle of practice, [Coach Bryant] comes out there and takes my blue jersey off and puts on a red jersey . . . and after that, I was either first or second string the rest of the time . . . . I was cracking some people." Not long thereafter, Bryant made Wesley a fullback so he could play linebacker.

Walter Sansing, the former tailback from West Blocton, was listed first at fullback. Behind him in order were James Wood, a sophomore from Thomaston, Georgia; Cecil Hurt from Woodlawn in Birmingham; Charlie Rieves from Rolling Fork, Mississippi; and Jack Rutledge, Hurt's former teammate from Birmingham. Rutledge was soon moved back to guard.

The first four at left end were the steelworker's son, Carl Valletto; the veteran Charlie Tom Gray, Skelton's old target from Pell City; Henry O'Steen, Gary's younger brother from Anniston; and Buddy Wood, junior letterman from Guntersville. On the right side, Jerre Brannen and Bobby Boylston were listed one-two. Baxter Booth's aggressiveness had earned him a red jersey, and Bud Moore, resurrected by Stallings, had one also.

Two returning players, the veteran Bill Hannah and Dave Sington, had the first team tackle positions. Behind them with first team privileges were Sammy Smith from Talladega; Dave's brother Fred Jr.; and big Dan Pitts from Red Level, survivor of the one-on-one practice with James.

Only four guards were listed with red jerseys on this day. On the left side were the Woodlawn zealot, Don Cochran, and behind him, Billy Rains. The aggressive Jim Blevins from Moulton and Gary Phillips, the pre-med sophomore from Dothan, were one-two on the right side.

At center, Buck Burns, the big redshirt sophomore from Tuscaloosa, had moved in front of the veteran Ken Roberts. Wayne Sims, the junior college transfer from Sylacauga, was listed third. Benny Dempsey, seemingly written off by the coaches, was fourth string, but still ahead of Elliott Moseley and Jasper Best.

A number of others who might have been listed were hobbling. Donnie Heath was the most seriously injured. "I was going down under a punt," he recalled. "The minute you heard the kicker's foot hit the ball you were supposed to look up and find the ball. Anyway I got blasted from the side . . . and I knew at that time . . . I had never been injured before, in high school or college . . . and I had a feeling my football career was over, because I never had a feeling like that in my life. It felt like my knee was torn half in two . . . ."

Neighbors's head was still ringing. Butch Frank's feet were bothering him. Chuck Allen, Danny Wilbanks, Red Stickney, and Tommy White were all on Goostree's list, along with a dozen others.

On Friday night, April 12, Bryant called for a scrimmage at Denny Stadium, and the results muddled the quarterback situation. Gary O'Steen had a terrific night, throwing a 65-yard pass to Dyess for a touchdown, and then running the option for 75 yards and another score. Jackson was injured slightly, and Bryant promptly promoted O'Steen to the first string.

A few days later, the team lost John Paul Poole, the returning Navy man. A more serious student following his Navy tour, Poole was having trouble meeting the competing demands of football and the engineering curriculum. Poole went into see Bryant.

"I told him that I wasn't sure that I was going to be able to . . . because of the rigors of electrical engineering . . . that I wasn't going to be able to play football and get my class work done," Poole said. "And it was very critical that I do that, because I was coming up on my senior year and graduation was very important to me. He understood. We had a real good, cordial talk, and then I left . . ."

The next day Bryant was visited by Naylor Stone of the *Birmingham Post-Herald,* and the coach told Stone that while he hated to lose Poole, "Quitting was the thing to do . . . we want our youngsters to get an education." Bryant's handling of Poole, then and later, showed clearly how much he respected players who were not afraid to talk to him about their problems. Those who quit without doing so would find it very hard to earn his respect again.

Another scrimmage a week later failed to impress the head coach. "With the exception of Wayne Sims, Milton Frank, Duff Morrison, Mack Wise, Jim Patton and two or three others," he told reporters, "it didn't look like either team cared about winning. We hope to find some more in the movies, but if we don't we'll just play with those I mentioned. I don't know anything about coaching people who don't care about winning."

The next day, the captains for the annual A-Day game, Baxter Booth and Charlie Tom Gray, divided the squad into Red and White teams, and they practiced separately after that. The game itself, won by the White team, 13-0, played in wet conditions at Denny Stadium April 26, showed that the Alabama players had learned to be more aggressive, but at a meeting the next day with reporters, Bryant declared himself to be "terribly disappointed."

Indeed there was little to be encouraged about. The quarterbacking in particular was woeful.

On the Red team, Bobby Smith was hobbled and played only sparingly. That left the Red quarterback job to Gary O'Steen, and he was rough around the edges. The Anniston junior led the game in rushing with 34 yards, but fumbled twice, and both led to White touchdowns. O'Steen's former Anniston teammate Jerre Brannen recovered both fumbles, and ran one into the end zone.

Jackson was not 100 percent, either. He had injured his Achilles tendon the week before the game, and was still wearing a knee brace. He lost two fumbles and gained only 13 yards in 8 tries. His backup, Jap Patton, was more successful, completing four of nine passes.

Several running backs played well. Ferdy Cruce caught three of Patton's passes for 51 yards, ran 10 times for 38 yards, and despite losing a fumble was clearly the game's standout offensive performer. Dick Strum gained 34 yards for the Reds, and Marlin Dyess got 26 for the Whites. But Buddy Wesley and Mack Wise each lost a fumble.

The top two fullback prospects played well. Charlie Rieves gained 27 yards at fullback for the Whites and Danny Wilbanks got 15 in three carries for the Reds. Evidently learning to like fullback, Red Stickney blocked and tackled with distinction.

Punting, handled by Brannen, O'Steen, and Gooby Stapp, was good but not flashy. Aware of the presence of scouts, Bryant did not allow either team to attempt a quick-kick. Fred Sington missed two field goal attempts and one extra point.

Line play was rugged, already characteristic of the aggressive Bryant style. Brannen, Butch Frank, Don Cochran, Baxter Booth, and Wayne Sims were singled out by writers. Donnie Heath, his knee wrapped and bandaged, played most of the game and recovered a fumble.

Benny Dempsey's father came up from Brantley for the game, only to find that his son's name had been left out of the program. " My Daddy didn't even know what my number was," he said. Dempsey played the entire game at tackle, not center. After the game, his nemesis, Coach Powell, put his arm around Dempsey's neck and congratulated him on playing a good game.

"I wish you'd tell Coach Bryant that," Dempsey said.

In his press conference the next day, Bryant was blunt. In his column in the *Montgomery Advertiser,* Max Moseley quoted him:

"There were some bright parts of the game, but that continuous fumbling ruined the whole show. We just could not handle the ball at all. It was not all of the quarterback's fault, the centers had a poor night too."

"What was the reason for the center-to-quarterback troubles?" Naylor Stone of the *Post-Herald* asked.

"Poor coaching," Bryant replied.

"We can't say that, can we?" Stone asked, surprised.

"Why not," Bryant shot back. "You asked for quotes didn't you?"

"I can't say exactly that our spring training was a complete success," Bryant continued. "At least we found out something about the boys we have. We found out the boys who have the talent, the boys who have the desire, and lastly the boys who want to play."

Writers differ on what the head coach said about what would happen next. Moseley heard, "We'll name our best squad and that may be 11, 15, 19 or 22 men that we think are our best. Then we'll name another group that we'll term our squad to work with and it'll consist of the boys who have shown the desire and who haven't quite reached the point where they are good enough. The third group will be the boys who have not shown any desire or talent."

Zipp Newman of the *Birmingham News* wrote it more bluntly:

"[Bryant] said the squad would be broken into three groups, 'those we will play, those we will try to play, and those who will not be invited back to play.'" Nobody in the press commented on the fact that, technically and perhaps morally, Bryant lacked the authority to force players to leave.

A few days later, the publicity department issued a release naming 24 players to a "100 percent club" for "100 percent effort on the practice field . . ." The list evidently was meant as both a carrot and a stick — and it is notable in hindsight for those it included, and for those it didn't.

At quarterback, Bryant included Smith, Skelton and Patton, but not Bobby Jackson. That may have been because Jackson — talented enough to play professional football — was not known for relishing contact.

Among other backfield players, included Morrison, Allan Mauldin, Dyess, Wise, Tommy White, and Stickney. Notably absent were the star of the spring game, Cruce; the most talented fullbacks, Wilbanks and Rieves; Gary O'Steen, and Wesley.

Wayne Sims and Heath were on the list at center. Senior Ken Roberts was not included, and neither, obviously, was Benny Dempsey.

At tackle, Bryant singled out Jim Blevins, Bill Hannah and Dave Sington, leaving Chuck Allen and Valletto off the list.

Cochran, Sammy Smith, Butch Frank, and Jack Rutledge were the guards on the list. That left out Billy Rains, an all-SEC performer the previous year.

There were five 100-percenters at end: Charlie Tom Gray, Baxter Booth, Jerre Brannen, Bobby Boylston, Henry O'Steen, and Buddy Wood. But the same release said that Wood was being moved to center and Boylston would be moved to tackle.

Right around the end of spring practice, a key player returned to the Alabama roster — tackle Pete Reaves.

Reaves had played on championship teams at Bessemer High School, and had enjoyed some success under Whitworth in his sophomore year. It was his extra point that provided the margin for Whitworth's first win at Alabama, 13-12, over Mississippi State, in 1956. But he had played sparingly in 1957 and his outlook on football had soured by the end of the season. An outstanding pitcher on the Alabama baseball team, he was excused from spring training.

Alabama baseball coach Happy Campbell knew Reaves was a tough competitor, and he told Bryant he ought to consider him. Then Bryant either saw or heard about in incident at a baseball game that spring.

Alabama was playing Auburn, and Reaves was pitching. "I never did like Auburn, okay?" said Reaves.

"I think there was a guy on second," he said. " . . . a boy hit the ball to the outfield, left field as I recall, so I naturally go behind home plate to back up the catcher. Well, the ball got by the catcher and I reached down to get it, and when I raised up, the guy tried to run over me. So I just gave him a little flip over my shoulder and he landed on his butt.

"I just was casually walking out to the mound . . . didn't think anything about it, and I heard someone say, 'Watch behind you,' so when I turned around he jumped at me and I just cold cocked him and that was it."

A few days later, Bryant sent for Reaves. They agreed that Reaves would give football another try that fall.

If the other Tide players were expecting a break after the end of spring practice, the coaches soon disabused them of that hope. The coaches began a "voluntary" program of "track class" — sprints and other drills — that was kept up until classes ended. Some of the players who had missed spring practice because of injury, such as Sid Neighbors, were given more attention. Dave Sington said that " . . . The guys that had been hurt, that finally got well for about a week or so, they took them downstairs in that . . . where the old coaches' office was, they had that one big room down there . . . they put them in full gear and took them down there every day . . . for about 10 days for their spring training." If that was technically illegal, it was tough to regulate.

Even the end of school did not end Bryant's expectations of the Alabama players. Before leaving for the summer, each of the players met with a coach. They were given a workout schedule for the summer that they were expected to follow. The schedules were extensive, often with different routines for every day of the week, and players were expected to practice their specialties as well. "I went to Anniston stadium . . . I don't know how many balls I punted that summer," said Jerre Brannen.

Billy Rains, who had played at 205 or 210 pounds under Whitworth, was told by the coaches he would need to be at 192, the same weight he carried as a junior in high school, when he returned in the fall. Back home in Moulton, Rains went to the Moulton high school field to run and rode a bicycle every day. He was also playing baseball that summer, catching for a semi-pro team. One day he overdid it.

"It was a triple-header," he said. "I had caught two games that day and we drove to T. M. Rogers and were playing that night . . . and a ball just popped out of my mitt and I went to pick it up." Suddenly, Rains felt his back go out. Unable to stand or sit straight, he rode back home to Moulton flat on his back in the bed of a pick-up truck.

Benny Dempsey didn't have a workout schedule. Already on academic probation in the spring because of a "D" in zoology, Dempsey had flunked out of school. He went home convinced his college career was over.

Dempsey's father, though, still hoped that his only son would play football under Bryant. "My Daddy got in his car one Sunday, right after I got home that summer," Dempsey said, "and drove to Tuscaloosa and went to Coach Bryant's house and talked to him a long time. To see if he could help me get back in school. And I told my Daddy before he went up there, I said, 'Coach Bryant's not going to do that Daddy, he'd have to do it for everybody else that got in the same situation, plus . . . me being a senior he's not going to do that.' And he wouldn't."

It is an indication of Dempsey's abilities that he was almost immediately offered a professional football contract with the New York

Giants. Realizing that his chances of ever playing again at Alabama were remote, he took the $1,500 bonus and headed for New York. His pro career, however, was short-lived. The Giants, who later that year went to the NFL finals, had Ray Witecha at center, an All-Pro for eight years, and depth behind him. Traded to Boston after the exhibition season, Dempsey hung up his cleats and headed home.

At least three players had something on their minds other than football for that summer. Fred Sington, Jack Rutledge, and Chuck Allen were planning to get married.

Bryant — and most coaches those days — were not enthusiastic about married players. Maybe it had something to do with a belief that unrelieved sexual tensions added to performance. But the main reason was probably that marriage required commitment, and Bryant did not want his players committed to anything but school, momma, and football. Since there were already a number of married players on the squad — among them standouts Jim Blevins, Don Cochran, and Bill Hannah — there was not much direct action he could take. Ferdy Cruce, Billy Rains, and Bobby Skelton were also married, as were Pete Reaves and Don Parsons.

Parsons, the Houston sophomore, had married his high school sweetheart when both were freshmen. The two had planned to wait until after college — Parsons at Alabama and his girl, Bonnie, at Texas Christian. But when Parsons went to Ft. Worth to see the TCU-Alabama game in 1957, he didn't like the way the TCU boys were behaving around his girl. When Bonnie came to Tuscaloosa for homecoming, the two crossed the border to Mississippi and tied the knot. Parsons had heard Bryant, at one meeting or another, say something to the effect that "all you Romeo SOBs, we're going to try to run your butts off" but he figured he could stick.

Rutledge went into see Bryant after spring practice, and was encouraged when the coach told him how well he thought he had done, and how he much he was counting on him at guard in the fall. Then Rutledge said, "Coach, you know [I plan] to get married."

Bryant "sat back in his chair and took [a drag on] that cigarette,"

Rutledge recalled, "and he said, 'You just forget every damn thing I told you. I don't think a married man can play on my team.'"

Chuck Allen had a similar experience. "I went in and he had that great big giant desk, and cigarettes and money all over it . . . everything else . . . Chesterfields . . . I told him, 'Coach, I'm getting married this summer.' He said, 'You're not asking me,' and I said, 'Nossir, I'm getting married this summer,' and he said, 'Well, you're off scholarship if you get married. If you want to, you can come back in the fall and if you make the first three teams, you get your scholarship back.'"

Fred Sington was nervous about even mentioning his plans to Bryant, but as his marriage date approached, his fiancee pressed him to clear his plans with the coach. Screwing up his courage, Sington went into Bryant's office and asked permission.

"Fred, I don't like my players to be married," Bryant said. "But in your case it may help."

With the help of Coach Laslie, many of the players had secured summer jobs. But Bryant and his staff, not satisfied after the spring game that the centers, ends and quarterbacks had worked together enough, cut some of the jobs short.

Around the end of July, Bobby Jackson was working with an outdoor crew drilling core samples for the Army Corps of Engineers at Redstone Arsenal in Hunstville. In the distance, a solitary pay phone began to ring. A passerby stopped to answer it, and then yelled out, "Is Bobby Jackson there?"

Jackson was sure someone had died, but when he picked up the phone, he was connected to Coach Bryant, who said, "Bobby can you get up here to Tuscaloosa?"

"Sure, I can quit. When do you want me?"

"How about tomorrow," Bryant said "I've got a job for you."

Jackson caught a bus that afternoon. Jap Patton, working on a pipeline in Michigan, also got a call, and flew back to Tuscaloosa. Soon a number of ends, centers, and quarterbacks were working out daily, earning their keep by picking up trash and helping to get Denny Stadium ready for the annual high school all-star game. A number of other players had also returned early in order to work themselves into shape.

It was too early for an official practices to begin, and Bryant hewed to the letter of the rules. Coaches were not allowed on the field with the players, but off the field they could and did set out practice schedules. Jackson, Bobby Smith, Bobby Skelton, Gary O'Steen, and Patton spent hours taking direct snaps from Jim Blevins, Ken Roberts, and the other centers. The centers also worked on linebacking skills, and the quarterbacks in the safety position, which they generally played on defense.

The players who returned early found evidence that Bryant had meant what he said about improving conditions in the dorm. New doors had replaced all those lost to the marauding apes of the previous regime. New, extra-long beds had been placed in every room. The greatest change of all was air conditioning in Friedman Hall. Bryant had prevailed on some local alumni to foot the bill. Nothing could have been more welcome to the players preparing for the opening of fall practice.

Courtesy Carl Valletto

Posing with Coach Bryant in the workout room on the third floor of the athletic building. Front row (L-R): Fred Sington (72); Carl Valletto (77); Don Cochran (62); Jim Blevins (54); Bill Hannah (66); Chuck Allen (74); Wayne Sims (33). Back row (L-R): Marlin Dyess (41); Red Stickney (30); Gary O'Steen (4?)

CHAPTER TEN

Last of the 'Riffraff'

It was hot — hot and muggy, as only river towns can get — in Tuscaloosa on Sunday, August 30, 1958, the day Alabama football players reported for the beginning of fall football practice. Moving into Friedman Hall, the players were pleased to find the improvements in the dorm, the oversized beds and the chill of the air conditioning. They would need the cool air, and badly, though many did not stay long enough to enjoy it.

In a letter to all of the players dated July 15, Bryant had provided broad hints as to the kind of practices the players could expect once they arrived in Tuscaloosa.

"Now is the time to begin getting in good physical condition," Bryant wrote. "You must report in good shape because our plans call for real hard work the first two weeks of practice. After that, we hope to simply sharpen up and rest up for each game.* Anyone failing to report in good physical condition would throw our plans out of kilter, so if you cannot report in good shape, please don't report at all.

"We are cognizant of the fact that some of you have weight problems," the letter continued. "We realize also how difficult it is for some to lose weight. On the other hand we know that you cannot play without getting your weight down, so in fairness to you and the team, we are

---

*This hope was never realized.

requesting some to be down to a certain weight before reporting here."

Then came this sentence: "If you are in this category, and fail to make the weight, we will assume that winning means little to you and there will be no place for you here."

The required weight was set in a postscript, and Bryant had hand-written a personal note on many of the letters. Buddy Wesley's note read, "Come in in racehorse condition."

In consultation with trainer Jim Goostree, Bryant had set the reporting weights low. For one thing, he wanted players in top condition and at their quickest. A secondary purpose was to see on the first day of practice just who among the players had been willing to make the sacrifices to report at the weight he demanded.

When Fred Sington and his brother Dave received the letter around the first of August, the postscript said they should each report at 218 pounds. When the brothers stepped on the bathroom scales, Fred weighed 244 and Dave 241. The two immediately began a training regimen that they never forgot. Rising at 5 a.m., they would eat a light breakfast and then join the Shades Valley High School team for its conditioning drills. Often, they would then go for further workouts at the downtown YMCA, eat a light lunch ("half a head of lettuce with some dressing") and then join the Shades Valley team again in the evening.

The elder Sington and his wife Joyce moved down to Tuscaloosa the last week in August, and on Sunday morning, Fred did some jogging and went by for a weight check. Goostree watched over his shoulder as the scales registered 218½. After taking a shower, Sington ran into Goostree again.

"I told Coach Bryant what your weight was," Goostree said.

"What did he say, Goose?" Sington asked.

"He said you'd better get that half-pound off or you ain't getting a uniform," Goostree replied.

Sington went back to his locker, put on sweat clothes and a rubber sweat suit, and worked out for another 45 minutes. Stepping on the scales, he weighed 212½, and when he reported in officially that afternoon, he weighed 211. Dave was at 213. They were the two heaviest men on the team.

Many others had worked hard, too. Pete Reaves challenged a hilly, ten-mile dirt road, and by the time practice began could run it easily. Ken Roberts, directed to come in at 192, worked out every day, skipped breakfast and ate a lot of Jello.

Butch Frank had worked hard, too, under a special incentive. In a letter to Butch that summer, Bryant had sent a fat package of offensive plays and a handwritten note that said: "Butch, I want you to be our fullback this fall." That was a surprising development. Frank knew he was not as big or as fast as Danny Wilbanks, Walter Sansing, or Charlie Rieves and he had never, ever, carried a football in an organized game. But he took Bryant at his word. Working as a camp counselor in Tennessee, he began to rise every morning at 5:30 to run the horse trails, frontwards and backwards. In the evenings, he chopped wood and worked with weights. He was determined to return in shape.

A number of players, however, showed less dedication. Sid Neighbors, the senior tackle, missed his target of 218 pounds by a dozen. Frustrated because his brother Billy, a freshman, was acceptable at 248 pounds, Sid quit. Before his death in 1991, Sid Neighbors told Thomas C. Ford, that in time he understood. "You have to have some goats, and I happened to be one of the goats. I regret I ever quit." But at the time, Sid was bitter and defiant. A few days after practice began, when the players were treated to a short cruise on a boat owned by the Gulf States Paper Company, Neighbors flaunted his new freedom by buzzing the boat while towing two attractive young ladies on water skis. Bryant did not see the humor.

At least three others reported overweight. One was Dan Pitts, the bulky tackle from Red Level. Pitts, who had played at over 240 pounds in high school, was told to come in at 195. He made a valiant effort and got just below 200. After he weighed in, he went with another group of athletes over to a nearby medical facility to have his pre-season physical examination. A manager, perhaps Gary White, came by and told him and several others that Coach Bryant wanted to see them.

"We went over there to his office, and he met us out in the hallway and explained to us how he had sent us [in] that letter the weight we were supposed to report at and that this group of young men didn't report at that weight, and when we got down to that weight, to come back and see him and he would consider letting us come back," Pitts says.

Pitts and the others started to walk away, in a quandary. Pitts, whose father had died in a farming accident, knew that he could never explain to his brothers back home that he was off the team. Just then, he heard Bryant call his name. He hurried back down the hall.

"Dan," Bryant said, "you go ahead and draw your uniform." Elated at the unusual circumstance of Coach Bryant softening his position, Pitts felt like the luckiest man on earth.

David Hicks, one of the foursome from West Blocton, which went 38-2 in three years under Morris Higginbotham, was given no reprieve and he left the squad, despite the opinion of his townsman and room-mate, Roy Holsomback. Holsomback had seen Hicks play as a blocking back in high school, and "he could stay up with Tommy (White) and Walter (Sansing) on the 100-yard dash. They would beat him but only by a couple of feet," he said. "I never did really understand it," Hicks said. "But he . . . he told us we didn't have a scholarship no more . . . I didn't think he could do it, but they did . . . I kinda felt bad about it . . . I could have made his team if they'd have given me a chance . . . ." Hicks went home to West Blocton, thought about playing at Chattanooga, and then got a job.

Holsomback's own experience that fall was strange, and his story reveals so much about the times, the players, and the pressures of the day that it deserves a full retelling.

Holsomback's father, a coal miner, had been laid off when the mines in West Blocton had shut down, and he scratched out a living by working on road crews. The family supplemented its food with government commodities — including beans "that even the dogs wouldn't eat," Holsomback said.

Strong but not very big or very quick, Holsomback was probably number four in ability among the West Blocton group. He had been thrilled when Alabama showed an interest in him. It was on a recruiting trip with his teammates that Holsomback had his first taste of a genuine beefsteak. "I looked at the menu and 6, 7, 8 dollars, and . . . [I just said] 'wow.' They brought a salad, and I never had eaten a salad. I cut off a piece of that meat and bit into it and I could not believe . . . I just sat there and sucked that juice . . ."

Holsomback had at first been injured and then sick during the spring, and he had received little attention from the coaches. He was the only player, he believes, who did not play a snap in the spring game. But he had made it through, and had completed a year of college, and he was determined to stick with it.

When he got back, however, he and some other players were told by Coach Sam Bailey that they were not going to live in the athletic dorm, but in some old wooden barracks left over from the war years, near the Black Warrior River.

Bailey — by all accounts a fair and empathetic man — was straight with the boys. "I think this is just a way of running you off, boys," he said. "Don't dare tell anybody I said this, but they are trying to get you off the team . . ."

Holsomback recalls: "So I go over there, there was a big hole in the floor . . . I went in there, threw my luggage up on the bed. I got my little radio and had to hook it up to the springs for an aerial . . . and Eugene Harris, I don't know who, some pretty good ballplayers, said, 'Holsomback, we're quitting. Are you going to quit?'"

"I said, 'Hell, no. The last meal I had at home was commodity beans, my momma and daddy are on welfare now, this is the only place I can get something to eat. I've gotta stay.'" A few hours later, a horn blew and a manager took Holsomback back to the dorm. Before long, he had worked his way up briefly to the White team, and he stuck for the next three years.

Two of the overweight players decided that they would make another effort to get their weight down to acceptable limits. The two were Buck Burns, the redshirt sophomore from Tuscaloosa, and Danny Wilbanks, the senior fullback from Tallassee.

Wilbanks had played 115 minutes in 1957, and scored three touchdowns. He missed most of the spring drills because of an injury, but was listed as the likely second-team fullback in the Alabama press guide. Directed to come in at 200 pounds, Wilbanks showed up weighing 205 on August 31. Summoned, as Pitts was, to see Bryant, he reported to the head coach.

"Wilbanks, what about this weight?' Bryant asked.

Wilbanks replied, "Coach, I'm reporting in the best shape I've ever been in."

"I didn't ask you if you were in shape, I said what about this weight," the coach replied.

"Well, Coach, I was weighing 212 when I got the letter, telling me to come back at 200," Wilbanks said. "I lost 7 pounds, and I'm in good shape that's just all I could get off in two weeks."

Bryant was cold. "Well, when you lose the rest of it, come back and see me."

Burns might have expected some leeway given the prominence of his father, the judge, a former classmate of Bryant's, and an honorary member of the A Club. But he got the same demand from Bryant, one that was reported in the local media: "They can come and talk to me after they get rid of the weight," Bryant told reporters. "They're not going to come out to practice like that. The price some of these kids paid to be ready, you know they want to play football."

Burns and Wilbanks went to the equipment manager and drew rubber sweat suits. The two stopped by Burns's home to pick up a key to the family cottage on the Black Warrior River. For food they took only some raw eggs, and on Monday morning, they began to work off their extra weight.

That same morning, Labor Day, September 1, 1958, some 66 hopeful Alabama players began a regimen of two-a-day practices that matched or surpassed the intensity of the previous spring. It was the beginning of a survival march through 16 days of steamy mornings and afternoons that blurred into what seemed like endless blocking, tackling, and running, running, running.

Conditions were brutal. It was much hotter than in the spring, and the strain of two practices every day — with the continuing prohibition of drinking liquids during practice — quickly pushed the players near exhaustion. Duff Morrison recalls himself and roommate Wayne Sims, both troubled with shin splints, "crying, supposedly grown men, 19, 20 years old, laying there crying because we had to go back" in the afternoon.

Thirty years later, after reviewing climatological records, a group of scientists in Alabama determined that "there were no environmental combinations at any time periods" in the months of August, and September in central Alabama "that would be considered safe for out-door practice in full uniform." "If practice is conducted outdoors in Alabama during August and September," they concluded, "copious amounts of water should be consumed prior to practice; frequent water breaks should be scheduled throughout practice . . ." But no one knew that then.

Things were getting serious now, dead serious. The opening game, against LSU, was scheduled for September 27. Bryant's young and enthusiastic coaches maintained a rigorous schedule during this period. They started the day at 6 a.m. with a staff a meeting, and wrapped it up with another session at 8 p.m. At these meetings, as in the spring, Bryant would go over plans for the practices, and the coaches would discuss the strengths and weaknesses of the Tide players. Bobby Luna, who didn't see his infant son awake for three months, figured out that he was making about 11 cents an hour. But the long hours built oneness in the staff. The wives of the young married coaches, too, grew close, later traveling together to the games and commiserating about their husbands' sched-ules. Football wives, in those days, were something like military wives and, by and large, they loved football, too.

The players were awakened at 6:15, ate the required breakfast at 6:45, and gathered for a team meeting at 7:25. Straight from the meeting, players went to the dressing room to put on their shorts, shoulders and helmets for the 9 a.m. workout. Practice lasted no more than two hours, but it was two hours of constant motion. Whistles would blow every fifteen to twenty minutes, sending the players charging to the next station on the round. Even without full pads, the heat of the late summer days was oppressive.

After morning practice ended, and after the players showered, they convened at 11:15 for a meeting with the coaches. Lunch was at 12:30, followed by a short siesta in the blissfully air-conditioned dorm. By 3 or 3:30 p.m., the players trickled back into the dressing room to don their full football gear for the afternoon practice. Dinner was at 7, and then there was another meeting with the coaches at 7:30.

The married players found little opportunity, and presumably had little energy, for conjugal pleasures. "Married, that's a misnomer," said the newlywed Fred Sington. "I would leave our apartment at 5 o'clock in the morning and come home at 10 o'clock at night. And I . . . don't know how we stayed married . . . I came home at 10:30 at night I was so tired that I just didn't want anything to do with anybody . . ." Later, during the regular season, Sington awoke one night to find his wife Joyce across the room in tears. Dreaming about practice, Sington had slugged her with a forearm.

On the very first day of two-a-day practices, Bryant and the coaches tested the returning players to their utmost. About an hour after the afternoon drills began, a huge thundercloud loomed over the practice field. Watching the sky, Bryant called the players together. A number of the young men cheered, anticipating an early end to practice.

But instead of sending the team in, Bryant said, "I'm going to let you take your shoulder pads off, we're going to do a little running to see what kind of shape y'all are in."

The coaches broke the players into small groups and began calling for "up and downs," of varying length. The players started off in their normal stance, shifted to full-speed running, and after the required yardage — 10, 20, 30 or 40 yards — dropped into their stance again as the whistles blew. Then it was the same process, again and again.

"A horse couldn't run that much," Jap Patton recalled.

"I believe everybody I can remember that day was down crawling on their knees, except maybe Marlin Dyess," Walter Sansing said. "They weren't only crawling, there was a lot of throwing up. I thought really that day that I was going to die, and I was in good shape. I came back in good shape . . . but not for that. That was . . . I saw coaches grab players by the seat of their britches and throw 'em because they were throwing up . . . they'd just make 'em go a little bit more . . . I'll always remember that . . . you'd be on your all fours trying to finish and your buddy over there would be throwing up, and the coaches would be yelling, 'you're not going to quit, you can't quit, you'll quit in the fourth quarter if you quit here.'"

Patton says that, "Butch Frank was even crying, and Butch was always a . . . cheerleader type. . . . it was terrible, it really was terrible."

Finally, exhausted, the players were given leave to go to the dressing room, but only if they managed to run off the field and through the gate. Patton, at that point the first string quarterback, wasn't sure he could make it, and stopped to say something to Coach Bryant, hoping to catch his breath. Bryant didn't go for it. "Get on off the field, you've got to run off the field," Bryant said.

"We ran 31 50-yard wind sprints," said Duff Morrison. "When we ran the 30th one, down to Coach Stallings, he let us get a knee . . . it reminds me of when I was a little kid, going round and round in a circle, I couldn't see the ball 10 feet away from me . . . he says, all right, if you can make it through the gate, you can go in . . . there were eleven of us . . . eight of us made it through the gate, three of us didn't make it . . . they got the fish eye and just rolled back and passed slap out." One of these was Dan Pitts, already weak from losing so much weight, who went to the hospital with what the newspapers called a "sun-stroke."*

It never did rain.

---

*A similar incident later effectively ended Pitts's career. "I can remember Dr. Tatum . . . the nurses putting the ice around me and saying, 'This is the same guy we had so much problems with before,'" Pitts said. "And I can remember old Dr. Tatum . . . I couldn't speak . . . couldn't move . . . but I could hear him say, 'If we can keep him alive until in the morning, he'll make it.' That's something that just sticks in my mind. Then after that, I had a long talk with Coach Bryant and Goostree advised me not to play."

It was clearer than ever that the coaches meant to eliminate some of the players. At noon and evening meetings, according to Gary O'Steen, Bryant would say, "Well, I've been watching the films and . . . there's going to be three of four of you that won't be here tomorrow. You know who you are."

" . . . Everybody knew he was talking right at you," said O'Steen. "And you'd go out there and bust it, almost die, and say, I made another one, and sure enough there'd be somebody gone, and there'd be a few less people in the meeting, and he'd say, 'Well, I told you. There's still three or four more of you, today's probably going to be the day.' And that's how they'd leave it. And you'd say what are we going to run into next? What are we going to run into out there today?"

Many did quit. Manager James Beall, in charge of returning books and ROTC uniforms for the players who quit, was making so many trips for that purpose that he began to defer them until the back seat was full. Beall's roommate, Don Owens, a senior, was one who called it quits.

A few days after fall practice began, the Associated Press quoted Bryant as follows: "The riffraff are fast eliminating themselves and we had two real good scrimmages."

In his book, *Bear,* Bryant contended that when he said "riffraff" he wasn't referring to players, but to hangers-on around the football program. That explanation just doesn't fit the circumstances. There were no "riffraff" followers at the practices that fall. "Riffraff" was indisputably Bryant's word for players not willing to meet his expectations.

With Wilbanks's status shaky, Bryant's reason for moving Butch Frank to fullback began to be more understandable. Soon the head coach was also putting tremendous pressure on the another fullback prospect, Charlie Rieves.

As Bobby Boylston remembers it, Bryant came off the tower and confronted Rieves. "I want to check your guts," he said.

"And so he did stop and goes, and Coach Bryant was right behind him, blowing the whistle," Boylston said. "It was very seldom he did that. Finally, Charlie said, 'I can't go no more.' And Coach Bryant said, 'That's what I thought.' So he took the red jersey off Charlie and put a yellow shirt on him right there. Charlie quit either that day or a few days later."

The heat and the constant pressure caused many, perhaps most, to consider quitting at least briefly. On the afternoon of the first day, even Bobby Jackson was ready to walk out.

During practice, the gates to the practice field were locked, and the managers were under orders not to open them without the approval of Coach Bryant. One day Hugo Friedman — a distinguished Alabama alumnus and supporter for whom Friedman Hall was named — arrived too late to get in, and rattled the gate in vain. Bert Jones one day opened the gate to let University President Frank Rose onto the field, and Bryant chastised him even for that.

"It was so hot I couldn't hardly breathe, couldn't talk," Jackson said. "I'd walk over to [the managers] and I'd say, 'Would you unlock the gate for me?' And they'd say, 'The only way you are getting out of here is to jump it. We don't unlock that gate until we're told to by Coach Bryant.'" So Jackson stuck it out. But not everyone could.

The most dramatic defection took place on the second day of practice. The way it happened became a legend among the players on the 1958 team. There are many versions among team members, and the story has no doubt gained color through retelling year after year, but most agree on the following main points.

One group of players was running skeleton drills, sort of half-scrimmages, with just one side of an offensive line running against a linebacker, defensive end, tackle and guard. Most say that Carney Laslie was in charge of the drill.

In the huddle between plays, the offensive center, Eugene Harris, the sophomore from Cleveland, Tennessee, who had responsibility for blocking the nose guard, play after play, was ready to quit. Reluctant to do so on his own, Harris tried to persuade Russell Stutts and Fred Sington to leave with him.

"Let's quit, Bulldog," Harris begged Stutts repeatedly.

Sington, who also was near exhaustion, replied stoically, "We can go one more play."

Finally, Harris abandoned ship on his own. As a play began, he brushed past the nose guard and took off toward the fence.

Laslie yelled, "Come back here, boy," but Harris did not slow down. He hit the chain link fence about four feet off the ground, and vaulted over the top.

Bryant may or may not have said, at that point, "Manager, if any other of these turds want to quit, open the gate for them."

Harris fled toward the dressing room, shedding equipment on the way. Apocrypha says that he was wearing only a jock strap by the time he reached his locker. At any rate, no one saw him again after that.

Laslie inserted another player in Harris's place and continued the drill.

Bill Knight, a serious student, and one of the team's fastest backs, realized in the first day of practice that he didn't have the stamina to play Bryant-style football. Instead of leaving, as many did, by slipping off from the dorm after lights out, Knight went to see Bryant to tell him of his decision.

Bryant was disappointed. "You were one of the players we were counting on," he said. But he did not try to persuade Knight to change his mind. "I've had a lot of good football players who could not play for me," he told Knight.

Talking with Bryant directly was important to Knight's self-esteem, and Bryant's handling of his request showed class. "I left his office feeling like a winner, not a loser," Knight recalls.

Another defector in the early two-a-days was quarterback Bobby Skelton. But Skelton's reasons for leaving were personal, not physical. The son of a professional baseball player, Skelton had married just out of high school, and had a new baby. "I was having some family problems," he said. Skelton talked it over with his close friend, Bill Hannah, who urged him to stick. But the next day, he went home.

Skelton's old teammate from Pell City, Charlie Tom Gray, was standing by a blocking dummy the next day when Coach Bryant approached. "Gray, where is Skelton?" he asked. "I said, 'Coach, I don't know were Skelton is.' He said, 'Well, he's not here. What do you think has happened?' I said, 'Coach, the only thing I can think is . . . that Bobby's always fussing and feuding with his wife . . . and I wouldn't be surprised if he didn't . . . just hitchhike home to take care of whatever domestic problem he thought he had . . .'"

By Tuesday afternoon, down on the Warrior River, Wilbanks was sure that he had met Bryant's weight requirement, and he and Burns came back and weighed in. Wilbanks had lost 13 pounds in two days, and Burns, too, had trimmed down greatly. Burns's high school sweetheart, Jo Del Laney, the daughter of Whitworth assistant coach Malcolm Laney, had never seen him so thin. "I could see his rib cage," she remembers.

The two were told to report for the Wednesday morning practice.

But Wilbanks found that merely losing the weight had not persuaded the coaches that he had the dedication to winning they demanded. He got extra attention in practice, running at times with all three backfields. And then, when the other players went into shower, he and Burns were kept on the field and supervised in extra running.

"I can remember running until I fell on the ground and Coach Cutchin and Coach Bailey picking me up . . . one by each arm, and we'd run a little bit more," he says. "And then I just could get off of that field, you had to get off the field, you could not fall on that field . . . you'd get outside the gate, you could crawl to the locker room if you wanted to, but you had to get outside that gate . . . so, I can remember finally getting in there and getting my clothes off . . . my uniform off . . . . I'd get in the shower and I'd get me a folding chair and I'd sit down in that shower with cold water just running . . . drinking it . . . I'd be so full of water when I got back to the dorm, I couldn't eat . . . so I'd finally wind up not eating lunch . . . and it would be time to go back to practice again . . . 2:30, specialty teams had to get out early . . . so I practiced Wednesday morning, Wednesday afternoon, Thursday morning, Thursday afternoon . . . Friday morning I could hardly put one foot in front of the other . . . . I'm down to like 188 pounds . . .

"I just made up my mind after practice . . . I'm still running extra, still running in all these backfields," Wilbanks continued. "I just made up my mind, 'these folks don't want me, they're trying to get rid of me.' I had a sister living in Cottondale at that time . . . I called her up when I got back to the dorm . . . 'I'm coming out there to stay with you, I'm quitting, I'm giving up football.'"

On the next day, Burns, too, had called it quits. Bobby Boylston was Burns's roommate. Between practices on Saturday afternoon, Boylston asked Burns if he wanted to go grab a sandwich before the afternoon drills. Burns said no, and when Boylston returned his roommate had moved out, leaving a note: "Boylston," the note said, "I can't take it no more."

For Burns, his family and his girl friend, Jo Del Laney, it was a bitter end to their expectations of a great football career at Alabama. The entire family bled crimson and white, and until his death in 1993, Burns regretted giving in to the pressure. "He made a quick decision in his life that he later regretted," his widow, Jo Del, said. "That's all I can really say . . . he knew he had the ability, and what he could have done, but Buck made a difference in a lot of other people's lives in other ways, so you know it's just something that you put behind you and go on . . ."

The fact that players as talented as Burns and Wilbanks would be considered expendable by Bryant made a strong impression on the remaining players. Henry O'Steen had played against Burns in high school and thought he was the best football player and toughest guy he'd ever seen. O'Steen thought, "My God, this man's serious, if he can run a player like Buck Burns off."

By the end of the first week of September, 20 players had left the team. Sammy Smith, the 100-percenter from Talladega, was one who called it quits.

Smith had a childhood sweetheart who was in school at Florence State. The two wanted to get married, but Smith had been intimidated by Bryant's statements about that. "He said, I'm not going to get anybody get a divorce that is married, but you guys better not marry," Smith recalled. "'I don't want you to get married, it's a distraction . . . you are here to play football." I saw what happened to the rule breakers. I mean he killed them after practice." Smith said. So on the second day of practice, when Smith's roommate, Buddy Wesley, headed over to dress out, Smith said, "Go on over, I'll be over in a little while," Wesley had a feeling that Sammy was leaving. Sure enough, he packed that afternoon and went home to Talladega. A few days later, the home air chilly, he enrolled at Florence State and got married.

Two other 100 percenters also left — Allan Mauldin from Childersburg, and Buddy Wood, the junior tackle from Guntersville, who signed a professional baseball contract. Don Coleman, the big tackle who had knocked Pat James flying, had also departed. Others leaving were Glen Jones, Bobby Johnson, Cecil Hurt, Sammy Barranco, and Bill Smith. Larry McCoy, hurt in the wrestling match with Skelton during conditioning, never recovered enough to play. Johnny Gann, who had lost his lower teeth in the fight with Blevins, had a more serious injury and was advised by his doctor to give up football.

But one additional player had been added: John Paul Poole, satisfied now that he could handle his classes, went to see Bryant and asked if he could try again to make the team. "He was not real happy about it," Poole said, but Bryant needed ends and said okay. Poole, moving against the current, put his things back into the dorm.

CHAPTER ELEVEN

'Couldn't Beat Vassar'

T he carnage was over by the 17th and 18th practices of the fall, around the tenth of September 1958. With the squad at a manageable 46 or so players, Bryant and his staff began the serious work preparing for the first game of the year against LSU.

Under Bryant's constant tutelage, admonition and encouragement during the daily meetings, the attitude of the remaining players began to lift. There was regret for the friends that had left the team, but also growing confidence that the worst was over. As Bobby Smith said, "We began to think we could win, that was the thing . . . you were taught football . . . all you had to do was take those techniques he gave you and you tried to the best of your ability and you began to see that it paid off."

There was no time to brood about the players who had departed. As far as Don Cochran was concerned, "I was not glad to see them go but at that point whatever Coach Bryant did was right." But for others there was pain and even some anger that lingered for years. "It bothered me a lot," Buddy Wesley said. "I didn't think he should have done some of the things, running some of those boys off . . . I know they were good athletes. [But] I can't second guess him. That was his way of doing things, and I guess he found out that that was the way for him." "I didn't have time to sympathize," Charlie Gray said. "I was looking out for my own well-being."

Bryant was certainly showing no remorse. Bert Bank has told friends a story about going for coffee with the coach at a Tuscaloosa hotel that fall and encountering one of the players who left. The player was clearly Danny Wilbanks, who having lost his scholarship, was working as a bellman.

As they passed, Wilbanks said, "Hello, Coach. Hello, Mr. Bank." Bank smiled and returned the greeting, but Bryant didn't even glance toward Wilbanks or break his stride.

Bank was disturbed and suggested to Bryant he might have been more polite. Bryant just glared and said, "He's a quitter. Hell, I wouldn't let him carry my suitcase in here. If I was supposed to be on the fifth floor, he'd be liable to leave it on the second."*

Bobby Skelton had returned to campus a few days after he left, seeking reinstatement. Bryant would not allow him back on the squad. "I'll tell you what you do," he told Skelton, "you come back in January and pay your way, and then we'll see how you do, and we'll talk about it after the spring." So Skelton got a job and stayed home in Pell City.

His loss wasn't causing great concern at quarterback. The seniors, Bobby Jackson and Bobby Smith, had almost as much talent and more experience. Furthermore, Gary O'Steen had shown a lot of promise running the option from the quarterback spot.

The best news was that Jackson's knee, almost put under the knife in the previous winter, was looking stronger and stronger, and he was displaying increased mobility. When practice began, the coaches told him to try playing without the knee brace he had worn all during the spring. "Bobby," Bryant said, " . . . if you get hurt, we'll operate on you and you'll have another year. Throw it away and let's see what happens." The knee was never a major problem after that.

In an early fall practice, Bryant had been pumped up by watching Jackson play halfback, and was still toying with playing him there as the

---

*After the 1958 season, Judge Burns told Wilbanks he had talked to Bryant and told him he had made a mistake on his son Buck and Wilbanks. According to the judge, Bryant admitted as much, saying "Yeah Judge, I sure did, I made a mistake with Wilbanks, it cost me three ball games, too."

game with LSU neared. But a full-scale scrimmage against the freshmen at Denny Stadium August 18 tilted the scales toward keeping the Mobile senior at quarterback. For one thing, Jackson had an outstanding day, running for 89 yards, scoring twice, and throwing a touchdown pass to Jerry Spruiell. And Bobby Smith was hurt in that scrimmage, severely twisting his ankle. That left Jackson and O'Steen one-two, with Jap Patton third among the quarterbacks.

When Smith returned to practice, limping on the bad ankle, he found a yellow jersey in his basket. To him and most of the others, yellow had a bad connotation — implying something about courage. "I'm not wearing that yellow shirt," Smith told the equipment manager. "I know what that shirt's for. My ankle's sprained, I can't hardly walk . . . and I'm not wearing it."

"Well, Coach said . . ." the manager began.

"Well, I ain't wearing it, give me one of those white or gray things, it doesn't have to be red, but I'm not wearing that yellow shirt," Smith said. The manager eventually relented.

Don Cochran, a player the team could ill afford to lose, had also been hurt in the scrimmage, and more seriously than Smith. Running down to cover a punt, Cochran collided with Bud Moore. "I went down, and tried to catch myself," he recalled. The fall dislocated Cochran's elbow. A bone from the lower part of his arm came out of the socket and was forced, beneath the skin, several inches up into the upper arm. "They got me on the sidelines and I guess I was screaming and carrying on . . . they couldn't put it back in so I went to the hospital, and they put me to sleep and got my arm back in there and they had one of these old metal casts on it . . . by that time it was about [as big as a leg]." The loss of Cochran at this point would have been devastating. Another guard, Joe Campbell, after working out all summer and gaining a spot on the second team, had been ruled ineligible because he had been out of school a semester.

The varsity buried the freshmen, 45-0, but Bryant was not satisfied. "Could you have beaten LSU today?" Benny Marshall asked him. "I don't think we could have beat Vassar the way we hit," he said. The scrimmage did boost the stock of Wayne Sims, the junior-college transfer from Sylacauga. "Sims . . . is head and shoulders above everybody else," Bryant said. Sims, from then on a Bryant favorite, solidified his starting position at left guard.

As the first game approached, the coaches also wrestled with substitution patterns that would allow them to have the right players in the game at the time. This was an incredibly intricate challenge, given the restrictive substitution rules in effect at the time.

Two Southern coaches, Wallace Wade and General Robert Neyland, had led the move away from unlimited substitution — "chicken-shit football" Neyland called it — in 1953. Players were allowed to enter a game once in each quarter. That meant, simply, that if you came out, you stayed out until the next quarter began.

The 1958 rule had been somewhat liberalized, but it was nothing like today's free substitution. It read: "A player is eligible to re-enter the game once in each period."

"Re-enter once in each period" — the practical effect was that players like Mack Wise or Marlin Dyess, outstanding offensively but not so great on defense, were placed at a disadvantage in Bryant's game plans.

When it had the option that year, the Tide usually kicked off. This meant that defensive standouts like Duff Morrison would start. If Dyess or Wise replaced Morrison, then Morrison could return, but only once in a quarter. If the ball changed hands often — and this was one reason Bryant hated fumbles — it was easy to end up with the wrong players on the field and no way to replace them. And there was really no way to have specialty players — punters or field goal kickers — because you couldn't be sure you could get them into the game. That meant that there had to be a number of qualified punters and place kickers among the regulars.

It was not even a simple matter to determine who was eligible to go into the game at any given time. The coaches devised a system — poker chips of various colors worn around the neck — to help keep up with it. That helped avoid penalties but didn't alleviate the frustration.

Aware that he lacked skill in many positions, Bryant was building his offense around the quarterback, especially Jackson. "We lined up in every set known to man and then let Jackson keep it," he says in *Bear*. The playbook was short — the offensive summary against LSU shows only seven running plays, half of them utilizing the quarterback keeper.

The other offensive weapon was the quick-kick. Coached personally by Bryant and Phil Cutchin, it came like lightning out of a two-back set. The right halfback (preferably Gary O'Steen, but all the halfbacks learned to do it) would cheat a little back and toward the middle. Taking a direct snap, the kicker would wheel to the right and hit the ball sideways off his instep. If the ball was struck just right — and O'Steen was a master — it would sail over the heads of the defensive secondary, spin end-over-end and roll forever.

Alabama coaches did have clear preferences about which players they would prefer to have in the game in given situations. The week before the LSU game, they designated Butch Frank, Chuck Allen, Billy Rains, and Red Stickney primarily for defensive situations. Marlin Dyess could play either halfback on offense, but would usually come out on defense if Morrison or O'Steen were available to replace him. Morrison "couldn't run, he wasn't big, he wasn't strong, he wasn't quick, but God he had stamina," Bill Knight remembered.

LSU opened its season on September 20, against Rice. Bryant and Phil Cutchin went to Houston to scout the game, leaving Carney Laslie to supervise another scrimmage between the varsity and the freshman that afternoon. Neither exercise led to much optimism about the Crimson Tide's opening game.

Against Rice, Paul Dietzel's team was not pressed in winning 26-6 and Cutchin was disappointed that the Tigers showed virtually nothing new. Cannon was Cannon, great as expected, but the coaches were surprised at the ability of his backup, Don Purvis. "All of us were impressed with their terrific team speed," Cutchin told Benny Marshall. "I've never seen anyone treat Rice like that."

To make matters worse, on a rainy Saturday back in Tuscaloosa the Alabama freshmen embarrassed the varsity, tying them 8-8. They scored by running a blocked punt back for a touchdown and then completing a two-point conversion. Laslie was disgusted. "I think the freshmen beat them physically and in every other way," he said. "I didn't see anything good at all except when Pete Reaves hit one lick right toward the end."

Laslie sent the freshmen in and ran the varsity unmercifully. Everyone was fearful that Bryant would schedule punishing practices the next week. Even the freshmen, who might have expected to be happy, were apprehensive. "Everybody was scared to death," Jerry Rich recalled.

At the Bryant home that weekend, Paul Bryant, Jr., remembers some worried faces. If the varsity couldn't beat the freshmen, what chance did they have against LSU? But Bryant decided to forget about the poor scrimmage, and didn't even grade the films.

Things began to look brighter on Sunday. Jerry Claiborne stopped by Don Cochran's home in the married students' quarters on the Northington Campus, and they went to the athletic building to consult with Bryant, Goostree, and Dr. John Sherrill, the team physician.

"They had all these x-rays up there," Cochran said. "It was bad, by Sunday it was really bad . . . Coach Bryant came in, they were standing up there looking at the x-rays . . . and Coach Bryant says, 'Doc, how long's it gonna be before he's ready to play?' And Dr. Sherrill said, 'About a month.' And Coach Bryant said, 'Sheeit.' He turned around and put his arm on my shoulder, the one that was bad, and he said, 'Don, you be ready to practice by Tuesday?' And I said, 'Yessir. Tuesday.'" Fitted with a canvas strap to keep the elbow in place, Cochran was back at work in sweat clothes when promised.

Richard Strum, the running back from Biloxi, was having a good fall. During the summer, working in the oil fields around Citronelle in southern Alabama, he had worn a steel shoe to strengthen his bum knee, and through the first 20 days of practice the joint held up well. The publicity department sent a photo of Strum to the Mobile paper, and it ran along with some others the week before the game. But a freak injury during the last week of practice put Strum's football future in doubt.

"We were running a drill where we were blocking down, and they'd run the play outside," he recalled. "I blocked down, got the dummy from the guy that had it before . . . and then he would run the next play. We were swapping out."

After one rotation, Strum was holding the dummy, listening as Gene

The official team photo of the 1958 team, taken in early September 1958. BACK ROW (L-R): Hootch Collins, Jerre Brannen, Bud Moore, Bill Knight, Don Coleman, Bill Hannah, Chuck Allen, Jerry Spruiell, Buddy Wood, Don Owens, Bobby Jackson, Jim Blevins, Dave Sington, Fred Sington, Baxter Booth, Charlie Gray, Ken Roberts, Bobby Smith, Carl Valletto, Gary White. MIDDLE ROW (L-R): Don Parsons, Sammy Smith, Billy Rains, Don Cochran, Morris Childers, Elliott Moseley, Gary Phillips, Duff Morrison, Donnie Heath, Gooby Stapp, Red Stickney, Tommy White, Ferdy Cruce, Henry O'Steen. FRONT ROW (L-R): Wayne Sims, Charlie Rieves, Mack Wise, Butch Frank, Jim Patton, Gary O'Steen, Bobby Skelton, Dick Strum, Pete Reaves, Allan Mauldin, Marlin Dyess, Walter Sansing, Bobby Boylston. Not in photo: John Paul Poole, Roy Holsomback.

Stallings corrected him on some technique. Then "somebody else blew the damn whistle and I was standing there and they hit me, and I spun around and my damn knee buckled on me." The injury knocked Strum off the traveling squad. Donnie Heath's knee would not get better, and when he tried it again in full gear it betrayed him again. The week before the LSU game, Goostree gave Heath a bus ticket to Birmingham and told him to check into University Hospital for an operation. John Paul Poole was also left at home with a leg injury.

As the LSU game approached, campus enthusiasm for the new Crimson Tide was running high. Presiding at a giant pep rally Thursday night, Bryant introduced his squad, decked out for the first time in crimson blazers and gray trousers. After an early practice and supper the next day, the team boarded buses for the long trip to Mobile.

The bus trip annoyed some people — Dave Sington, elected co-captain along with Bobby Smith, thought it was ironic, given all of Bryant's talk about "going first class." Bryant said his intent was to take a leisurely trip that would have the players arriving around bedtime. Since the team flew on chartered DC-3s on every other trip except to Starkville, Mississippi, it may be that he was concerned about the weather. A hurricane was threatening the east coast around Charleston.

Whatever the reason, the bus trip provided a moment of comic relief. Wayne Sims got stuck in the bathroom. Sims was riding on the second bus, sitting next to Mary Harmon Bryant, and went to the back to use the on-board facilities. Somebody locked the door. "And I couldn't get it open. I would pull that cord . . . feel the bus slowing down, and that went on 15 or 20 minutes," Sims said.

Nobody knew what to do, and what eventually happened is an indication of just how totally Bryant controlled the Alabama program and how everyone deferred to him. Both buses stopped, and as the chatter among the players quieted, Sims could hear the "Big Bopper" making his way down the aisle.

"Hell," the coach growled, "if you can't get out of that little door how do you think you're going to get through LSU's line?" Sims kicked the door open and returned to his seat, his face burning.

ALABAMA THREE DEEP ON SEPTEMBER 15, 1958

	Red	White	Blue
SE	Brannen	Poole	Ronsonet
E	Gray	H. O'Steen	Childers
G	Cochran/F. Sington	Phillips	Pitts
C	Roberts	Blevins/Sims	Moseley/Rutledge
G	F. Sington/Hannah	Campbell	Stutts
T	D. Sington	Reaves/Allen	Holsomback
E	Valletto	Booth	Boylston
QB	Jackson	Patton	G. O'Steen
LH	Morrison	Spruiell	Dyess (off.)
FB	Sansing	Frank/Dyess(off.)	Stickney/Moore (off.)
RH	Cruce	Wise	Stapp

Injured: Rains, Smith, White

CHAPTER TWELVE

Cannon Fodder

No one knew it at the time, of course, but Alabama's first opponent would be the eventual national champions. In his fourth year in Baton Rouge, Paul Dietzel was at the pinnacle of his career, with a deep, experienced team that had better athletes than Alabama at almost every position, plus Billy Cannon.

Cannon was a coach's dream. A football lover since an early age, he had contrived to flunk the ninth grade so he would be bigger when he began high school. And then he had the good fortune to encounter Baton Rouge gym owner Alvin Roy.

Roy was a weight lifter who had introduced a few athletes at Baton Rouge High to weight training. This made Baton Rouge a Louisiana high school powerhouse. Cannon's coach at crosstown Istrouma High had installed his own weight program, with Roy's advice, after Baton Rouge had pummeled his team in 1954.

Roy's methods made a difference for Cannon. By the time he graduated from high school he had reached 193 pounds, held the Louisiana high school record for the 12-pound shot put, and ran the 100-yard dash in 9.7 seconds.

Dietzel knew Bryant well — he had coached under him at Kentucky for two years and his top assistant, Charlie McClendon, had played under the Bear at Kentucky. "Bryant taught me the name of the game is knock," Dietzel said. For his part, Dietzel had warned LSU fans that

Alabama would be tougher. "We'll have to be much better than we were against Rice," he said, "for we're playing a much better football team. A lot of people are going to be shocked when they find out just how good this Alabama team is, and we haven't had the advantage of seeing them play."

LSU had installed a new offense for the season, the wing-T, which was very similar to the single wing, but with the quarterback under center. This meant powerful blocking at the point of attack along with deceptive counter plays and reverses. It was the offense that Forest Evashevski had used very successfully at Iowa.

Cannon, Johnny Robinson, and quarterback Warren Rabb, three-fourths of the starting backfield, were all from Baton Rouge. After being taught the new offense in the spring, the three worked together on their own all summer, perfecting the intricate ball handling needed to make the offense work.

Dietzel had another innovation to unveil in 1958 — a return to platoon football, albeit a bastard version of it.

Most teams had two units that worked out together in practice most of the time and generally played both offense and defense. As practices continued in the fall, Dietzel decided that he had only 16 players who could truly play both ways effectively. His squad was deep, but after the first group, some players excelled on defense, others on offense. So he decided to go with three teams.

He chose his top eleven — with Warren Rabb at quarterback, Cannon and Johnny Robinson at halfback, and Red Brodnax at full-back — and called them the "White" team. This team played both offense and defense, and got most of the playing time.

A second platoon was essentially an offensive unit, but did play defense on occasion. This unit was originally called the "Gold" team, but when a sportswriter misheard Dietzel it became the "Go" team. The third squad — the famous Chinese Bandits — played only on defense. While the names of the teams had not yet been publicized, this was the scheme Dietzel would use against Alabama.

The morning of the game, after breakfast and a team meeting, the

Alabama players were encouraged to take a brief stroll around the Battle House Hotel to stretch their legs. The stroll was taken under the supervision of a coach, and for the interior linemen this was Pat James.

James — never low key — was hyped about the game. Wearing a new suit, he was haranguing the players about football as they walked around a downtown park. Then a pigeon dropped an enormous mess on the lapel of his new suit coat.

The event convulsed the players, many of whom at that point were not fond of the intense and aggressive line coach. "We laughed so much when we got back in my sides were just killing me," Roy Holsomback said. James took a handkerchief and tried to clean off the mess — but never stopped talking about football.

By the time the bus left for Mobile's Ladd Stadium at 4 p.m. that afternoon, things had turned serious. As Butch Frank recalls, the bus was deathly quiet. "Riding there we knew something special was really going to happen," Frank said. "We knew we were tremendously prepared. Nothing scared us. We knew what Marines, Rangers, or anybody like that went through . . . nothing intimidated that group of people. By that time they had absolutely become men."

The game had a zany start. Halfback Duff Morrison had excelled in practice at sailing kickoffs to places in the field where Cannon was not supposed to be. But when the time came for the real thing, Morrison's cleats caught in the long grass and he nearly missed the ball. It trickled only 11 yards hotly pursued by the right side of the Alabama line.

LSU guard Ed McCreedy, a former teammate of Norbie Ronsonet and Richard Strum from Biloxi, was the first man to the ball. McCreedy had spent the summer in the Citronelle oil fields with Strum and Valletto, so he knew them well.*

---

* McCreedy says that Valletto was deathly afraid of snakes and because there were no sanitary facilities in the woods, the big Pennsylvanian would usually climb a tree to answer a call from nature. McCreedy still remembers gleefully the day Strum slipped up behind Valletto and poked him in a sensitive spot with a stick.

"It came to me," McCreedy said. "I recovered and Carl Valletto speared me in the back, must have lifted me about three foot off the ground . . . I turned loose of that ball . . . and then after everybody was piled up, when they started uncovering, I looked and there the ball was right next to me, no one had it, so I just reached over and got it.

"Then Coach Mac (Charlie McClendon) after we changed, said, 'McCreedy, I couldn't believe anybody could take a hit like that and still be able to hang onto that ball like you did.' I didn't have the guts to tell him that . . . I almost indicated . . . they want that ball that damn bad, they can have it . . . but I walked with a stoop for the next two weeks."

McCreedy did take some punishment in the pileup, but the film shows that Valletto arrived late and was not involved.

Sportswriters and fans assumed that Bryant was being audacious with an onside kick. He must have been disgusted: Morrison never kicked off again.

Alabama weathered the early storm, and in the early going was getting the better of the fight. A 62-yard quick-kick by Ferdy Cruce to the LSU 7 set the Tide up a few plays later at their own 50. Then Cruce took a handoff from Jackson, got free on the right side and ran all the way to LSU 25, where a flag flew when Don Purvis speared him out of bounds. It might have been first down inside the 15, but there was another flag back upfield. Fullback Buddy Wesley was caught for holding, and the threat died.

It was at this point that the one event that all of the players remember took place. The bleachers in the South end zone at Ladd Stadium began to sag and then collapsed, spilling fans onto the soggy turf.

The end zone seats, wooden bleachers, were ten years old. They had been inspected before the game and some rotted wood had been replaced. But continuous rain had softened the ground at the base of the stands. Full to overflowing with 1,400 fans, hooting, yelling and stamping their feet, the stands began to buckle. One section of the seats began to slide forward, adding to the stress on the base.

Two Alabama students, Dixon Chandler and Doug Tyler of Prattville were among those in the bleachers. "The crowd was cheering, suddenly it seemed like everybody was stamping their feet . . . the stands began to creak. Dixon and I jumped and landed safely." Not everyone was so fortunate. More than 70 people were injured, and one woman remained in serious condition on Monday. Ambulances were soon screaming their way into the stadium.

This sudden and incongruous event stopped play. "It sounded like somebody with a heavy machine gun," Fred Sington recalled. "Everybody's screaming and yelling, and all of a sudden it was just as quiet as a graveyard . . . ." The game was held up for about ten minutes between the first and second quarters.

Working against the White team defense, Alabama mounted its most successful offensive drive early in the second quarter, moving from its own 20 to its 49. There, on third and two, Bryant sent Gary O'Steen in at quarterback, and the Anniston junior kept for two yards and a first down at the LSU 49. But O'Steen was less successful on the ensuing plays, fumbling a snap on second and 8, and the drive died.

On the next series Alabama got its biggest break, on a play that started badly for the Tide. Cannon took a handoff and raced through an enormous hole on Alabama's left side. Jerre Brannen, the left end, was too far outside to be a factor; Valletto penetrated only to be blasted out of the play by the pulling left guard, Al Dampier. Jack Frayer, LSU's right tackle, crushed the Alabama left guard, Wayne Sims, and Cannon put all of his 200 pounds into high gear. Then, cutting back to the left, he was hit from behind by Butch Frank, and then by Bobby Smith and Duff Morrison. Cannon lost the ball, which slipped up over his shoulder pads and down his back. Morrison grabbed the ball out of the air, escaped a desperate grab by Cannon and took off down the right side of the field with Sims a step or two in front running interference. It looked like a sure touchdown, but Max Fugler, the LSU center, made an impossible leap over Sims's attempt at a block and dumped Morrison out of bounds on the three.

"I made Fugler an All-American that night," Sims said.

In Dietzel's opinion, the next few plays also made the Chinese Bandits. "I knew they were going to score," Dietzel said, "so just to save their morale, I put the Chinese Bandits in . . . our third team. And as I said many times I know that the lights got in their eyes and they slipped because it was muddy down in that area and if the guy had hit the hole he would have scored, but nevertheless they had to kick a field goal on fourth down, the Bandits held them, and from that time on the Bandits had arrived, I mean they thought they were some kind of stuff."

For the Alabama fans, it was a case of what might have been. On the first play after the fumble, from the four, Jackson faked a handoff to Wise and carried himself. Wise would have scored easily had he had the ball but Jackson got nowhere and the next two plays were stuffed. Fred Sington was called on for a field goal try from the 8, and his kick scored the first points for Alabama under Bryant. At the half, the Tide led, 3-0, and there was excitement and hope in the Alabama dressing room.

Both feelings evaporated rapidly in the second half. Dietzel and his staff made some adjustment on defense that shut down Alabama almost completely, and began to use counter plays and reverses not displayed in the win against Rice.

Alabama took the second half kickoff and gained a first down, but stalled.

"I was kicking that night," Jerre Brannen said, "and [Bryant] told me walking back out of the dressing room, 'There's going to be a lot of wind . . . try to keep it low.'" Brannen still remembers the missing end zone seats and the strong wind in his face. "It wasn't a very long punt," he said. It went only 32 yards to the LSU 33, and the Tigers began to assert themselves.

From the LSU 33, Rabb passed to Robinson for 14. Then Robinson, taking a handoff on an inside reverse from Cannon, made a great, ripping run for 10 to the Alabama 43. Two plays later, Cannon got loose behind a Brodnax block, ran out of a tackle by Wesley, and wasn't stopped until Morrison smacked him at the Tide 27.

On the sideline, Pat James could see what was happening. Carl Valletto, playing tackle, was being trapped. "He would run across every time, the end would set back and then block in and then they'd trap Valletto . . . I kept telling him, don't cross the line of scrimmage, look to the inside and see what's going on, but no, he kept going straight across . . . he'd get the shit knocked out of him."

On the next play, a handoff to Cannon, Butch Frank saw Cannon coming through the middle and set himself for the blow: "I had tried to tackle him low, and he was all low," Frank said. "I was supposed to fill the hole in the center when they ran their inside reverse . . . and I filled the hole but I couldn't tackle him, stop him, I went down and he went over . . . and the safety tackled him . . ."

Brushing off Frank, Cannon had exploded up the middle for 20 to the 7. Sington, free in the middle of the field, failed to react in time. "I've looked back on it about a thousand times . . . I just didn't see it. I don't know why I didn't see it. I mean I had a chance, I could have cut Cannon down," Sington said. "I didn't see him until he was past me, but I was there, I should have made the tackle."

On third down, after a 5-yard penalty and two plays that yielded little, Rabb found Robinson at the goal line in the middle of the field, and zinged the ball to him. Frank, defending from the linebacker spot, was a step late and slipped to the ground. Robinson scored, and the conversion made it 7-3.

Alabama went nowhere on its next two possessions, and fended off a field goal attempt by the Tigers. But then LSU began another drive from the Tide 41.

The first play was the inside reverse, handed from Rabb to Robinson to Cannon, who sped past Butch Frank and gained 7. One play later, Robinson slashed from right halfback across left guard and ran 15 yards to the Alabama 21.

The next play, a handoff to Cannon going the other way got only 1. Then, from the 20, Rabb faked to Robinson going across, handed back to Cannon steaming toward right guard from the left wing, and Cannon rambled to the Alabama 11. On the next play, behind a kickout block by Brodnax on Morrison and with the pulling guard Larry Kahlden crushing Butch Frank, Cannon slid into the end zone in the grasp of Bobby Smith. It was the longest touchdown run against Alabama the whole year. The try for the extra point failed.

Alabama did not quit, and on the next series Scooter Dyess got behind the secondary and barely missed reaching a Jackson pass deep in LSU territory. But all was futility after that.

So it was a loss, 13-3, but long after the game was over Alabama fans were excited, milling about the bar and lobby of the Battle House reliving the night and playing "what-if."

It was clearly a different team than the one that had lost 28-0 to LSU the year before, quicker off the ball, more energized, more confident. LSU, with the great Cannon carrying a dozen times for 86 yards, had gained only 182 yards on the ground. On offense, Alabama's best plays were quick-kicks. But the ferocity of the Tide's defensive play held the promise of future success. "That's a hard-hitting bunch of boys we played," Robinson said after the game. "That first one who hit you wasn't too tough, but that second, third, fourth and fifth guy was murder."

Alabama fans were satisfied by the effort, and some coaches might have been satisfied, as well. But Bryant's reaction was different. After the game, he closed the locker room for 35 minutes, and when approached by sportswriters once he emerged, the Alabama coach was not happy. "When you get beat no one can be satisfied," he said, "and around me they better not be satisfied." Asked about injuries, Bryant sent a signal to the team: "Every one of our boys had better have their feelings hurt. When you lose, something better hurt."

After the game, Dietzel boarded the Alabama bus to speak to the Tide players, and predicted the team would eventually win a national championship. But back on campus the following week, the Alabama team learned what practices would be like after a loss.

"They were brutal . . ." Chuck Allen remembered. "We'd gone through the fall, but this was the first time we had really played under the system. There weren't any pats on the back for what a great job we did . . . there was a great concern that we lost, and that was all that mattered. I remember that we had really difficult, hard-ass practices the next week . . . and the reason was that . . . and I remember Coach Bryant saying . . . when you lose, this is the way you practice . . . if you win, it will be different. Every time we lost . . . and we lost four games that year . . . every time we lost it was like spring training all over again . . . ."

Buddy Wesley and Fred Sington both came in for special attention. Wesley, caught for two major penalties including the one that nullified Cruce's long run, was given the ball ten or more consecutive times in a scrimmage, and had to be carried to the dressing room. "I'm going to teach you [not] to get a penalty down there where it hurts," Bryant told him. Sington "caught all kinds of hell" for failing to react in time to Cannon's burst past him on the play that set up LSU's first touchdown. As always, the third team, now known as the "Blue Darters," continued to scrimmage and work on fundamentals. The next opponent, Vanderbilt, was waiting.

OFFENSIVE SUMMARY

(Excerpts from the offensive breakdown for the LSU game. These plays came in the second quarter and led up to the Alabama field goal.)

Series	Situation	Play	Gain	Breakdown
4	1-10-50	27p	3	Butch bust, Sington, Valletto nothing
	2-7-23	C81	7	Brannen late
	1-10-30	3-27opt	5	Sington nothing
	2-5-35	H27	6	Sims nothing
	1-10-41	389	4	Morrison nothing, Jackson nothing
	2-6-44	25	4	OK
	3-2-49	25kp	2	Booth late, F. Sington poor
	1-10-49	C81	2	Booth, Reaves nothing
	2-8-47	P25	1	Ronsonet, O'Steen nothing
	3-9-48	25	1	Reaves
	4-8-47	Punt	35	Reaves, Booth, Fred nothing
5	1-5-5	3-26opt	0	Brannen poor
	2-5-5	P66Q	2	Dyess, Frank poor
	3-3-3	24kp	1	Poor running
	4-2-2	FG	Good	No one cover; Valletto move fast

CHAPTER THIRTEEN

A+ for Effort

Alabama's next opponent was Vanderbilt, and the Commodores were no pushover, having already beaten Missouri and Georgia. Vanderbilt had a very respectable program in those days. Under Art Guepe, the Commodores had won six out of ten and tied two against Alabama teams. Oddsmakers said they were a 3-point favorite.

The Commodores had some quality players — especially a 200-pound halfback named Tom Moore, whom Guepe compared favorably to Cannon and who later had an outstanding professional career; also Rooster Akin, an end who was from Birmingham; and guard George Deiderich, who had earned All-SEC recognition the previous year.

It was a night game at Legion Field in Birmingham. Many fans were still in their cars, stuck in a massive traffic jam outside the stadium, when the game began and they missed an early Alabama threat. On the third play from scrimmage, Bobby Jackson ran an option play to the right, got a nice block from Valletto, and got free. By the time Vandy center Ben Donnell took an angle and caught him, Jackson had gained 33 yards to the Vandy 33. But after Morrison lost 1, Akin ran through a block by Wise to sack Jackson trying to pass, and the threat died.

A Wise interception stopped Vandy's first offensive series, but with Moore pounding into the swarming Alabama defense, the Commodores again threatened after recovering an Alabama fumble at the Tide 43.

The drive started with a pass from quarterback Boyce Smith to halfback Mack Rolfe that gained 11. Among some fits and starts it was Moore for 4, Moore for 5, Moore for 5, Moore catching a pass for 3, Moore for 6, Moore for 3. Jim Butler then carried for 4, and Vandy had a first down at the Alabama 12.

From the sidelines, as Billy Rains recalled it, Bryan sent him into the game saying, "We need a fumble." On the next play. the coaches' defensive summary notes, "Sington and Rains missed tackle for a loss," allowing Rolfe to gain 5 to the Alabama 7. But on the next snap, Smith and Moore bungled a handoff. Rains had penetrated into the middle, and when the pile was unscrambled he was clutching the ball.

Moore — who gained 115 yards in the game — was not finished punishing the Alabama defense. On the next series, he broke free on a delay for 10 yards before finally being stopped by Wise, who took a terrific blow to the face but still managed to bulldog the runner down. Wise broke his nose and bloodied his lip on the play, which earned him little sympathy. "Y'all watch how Wise tackles Moore," the coaches said the next day, reversing the film and showing it over and over.

In the second quarter, fullback Butch Frank, the converted guard, led another Alabama charge inside the Vandy 35. "I had some of the greatest blocking that was done at an Alabama game all year," Frank said. "The holes that were made for me, and if I had been any kind of a back, with those holes . . . I would have scored two or three touchdowns." As it was, Frank gained 12 and then 13 yards on two carries, and O'Steen completed a pass to Baxter Booth for 11. But then Frank fumbled and Deiderich recovered at the Vandy 31.

Moore almost stopped Alabama hearts with a 49-yard kickoff return to start the second half, but an interception by Brannen stopped that threat. The rest of the game was futility. Neither team was able to move the ball consistently. Alabama's punting, by Jerry Spruiell and Stapp, was excellent, and the defense was tenacious. Near the end, Vandy's Smith completed three passes that got the Commodores to the Alabama 18, but time ran out.

Bob Phillips of the *Birmingham Post-Herald* spoke for most Alabama fans when he wrote on Monday that the Tide probably deserved an "A-

Plus for Effort," but the Alabama offense continued to struggle. Vandy outgained Alabama on the ground by 156 to 103, and in the air by 74 to 12. The Tide's passing was horrible — between them, Gary O'Steen and Jackson threw five passes, completed only one and had two intercepted. It was O'Steen's last game at quarterback — and by moving him to halfback, Bryant gained many benefits as the season progressed. "Gary was a bigger, stronger boy than Bobby Jackson . . . you liked your bigger, stronger backs to carry the ball," Phil Cutchin said.

It wasn't until later that Bryant observed that a tie was like "kissing your sister." He was philosophical after the game, and blamed himself for the lack of offense. He took the team back to Tuscaloosa for more tough practices.

CHAPTER FOURTEEN

Passing Parson

Alabama's next game was against Furman, a Baptist school from Greenville, South Carolina, with an enrollment of only 1,350. The Purple Hurricanes were a doormat, but that made little difference to the Alabama players, who were hungry for a win. "The media wasn't nearly as big into it like it is now," Scooter Dyess said. "I didn't know whether Furman was supposed to beat Georgia or South Carolina . . . we approached it just like they were another Tennessee."

Scouting reports for Furman were surprisingly candid. Even the Alabama coaches were hard pressed to build the Purple Hurricanes into any kind of nemesis. They had lost their first two games, 42-6 to Florida State, and 11-8 to George Washington. Furman's quarterback was an ordained minister, Billy Baker, the fifth-ranked passer in the nation in 1957. But the scouting report said that while the passing parson was a "good short and medium passer," he was a poor runner. His play selections were "not particularly good and there seemed to be no game plan of offense." The "defensive line was outcharged most of the time," the scouting report stated, and "Florida State seemed to go wide very easily. Much of the play of both teams, both first and second, was typical of freshmen and sophomores."

Furman was weak, yet it is still surprising by today's standards that the game drew only 17,000 fans. That left 14,000 seats vacant at Denny Stadium.

1959 Corolla

Coach Bryant with Billy Rains during Furman game, 1958.

The walkover began early. On its second possession, Jackson drove the Tide 52 yards in 11 plays, carrying himself twice for 14 yards. With the team apparently stalled at fourth and 1 at the Furman 5, Bryant disdained the field goal. Morrison carried and got a first down at the 2. Jackson scored Alabama's first touchdown of the year on the next play. Fred Sington kicked the extra point.

Alabama scored again almost immediately. Furman fullback Bradley Fowler was swarmed, forcing him to fumble, and Red Stickney got the ball on the 16. On his first offensive play of the season, Bobby Smith faked a running play and floated a pass toward Gooby Stapp, who outran three defenders in the end zone and caught the ball for an easy touchdown. Jap Patton, playing end for this series, kicked the extra point and it was 14-0.

Alabama overwhelmed the Furman offense again after the kickoff, and Gary O'Steen scored his first touchdown of the year on a 61-yard punt return. He made it look easy, running to the right sideline and then cutting back into the middle. Morris Childers, playing in his first game, made the final block on punter Tommy Yates. Patton missed the conversion kick, so it was 20-0, still in the first quarter.

Late in the second quarter, Alabama got three more on a field goal by Pete Reaves after a 14-play drive. On third and 2 from the Furman 21, Valletto was charged with clipping, pushing the Tide back to the 30. Jackson rolled out to pass and ran for 20 to the Hurricane 10, but a delay penalty and a sack of Jackson brought up fourth down at the 17. Reaves's kick was from the 24, the longest Alabama field goal of the year.

Furman scored its only touchdown in the third quarter, the result of a roughing-the-kicker penalty that set them up with a first down at Alabama's 32. Hurricane halfback Ray Nickles got outside the containment twice, once for 9 yards and again for 9 and the touchdown. Furman went for two — and Alabama's first experience against defending that sort of play was successful. Baker was swamped attempting to pass.

Immediately after the kickoff, Gary O'Steen had another moment of glory — catching a 61-yard pass from Bobby Smith for a touchdown. So Smith had thrown only two passes in the season, both for touchdowns.

Alabama had played 36 men in the game, and that was a morale booster for everyone. So was the win. "We saw that what we were doing on the practice field could win football games, and that made all the difference, really," Gary O'Steen said. "If they'd kept on doing like that and we didn't win . . . nobody would have been there. But we said, 'Hey, it may be tough but by golly we're winning ball games now.'"

Injuries, though, continued to be a concern. Gary's elation was tempered by a serious injury to his brother Henry. Rushing on the conversion try after Furman's touchdown, the Anniston end was hit low by a defending back. It was a legal hit, but the knee went out, and O'Steen knew from the pain that the injury was bad. Eventually, it ended his career. Jerre Brannen's knee was badly bruised as well.

Things were no better for Donnie Heath. Returning after his knee operation, Heath had been working with Goostree to rehabilitate the joint. But the knee had become infected, and his weight had dropped below 160 pounds. Heath was lying on the treatment table when Bryant came in. "That infection was eating me alive, and that incision had busted back open and was just oozing," Heath recalled.

"Goddam, Jim, what's wrong with his knee?" Bryant asked Goostree.

"Coach, it's not responding," the trainer replied.

Bryant was abrupt. "You get him in the hospital," he ordered. "And he don't come out until he can walk out."

In the hospital, Heath remembers, he spotted his mother crying. What he didn't know then was that doctors had told her that if the infection persisted, Heath might lose his leg. (The following year, Heath tried the knee again and it lasted about thirty minutes. Fearing a permanent injury, Bryant called him in and told him he was through with contact football.)

The win against Furman was Bryant's first in the stadium that would one day bear his name, and Bryant was elated—as happy to win, he said, "as if we had won the Rose Bowl." But there was no time for rest. Tennessee, the team on Bryant's ballot voted "most wanted to beat," was next in Knoxville.

CHAPTER FIFTEEN

Fumbles & Futility

Bryant was obsessed with beating Tennessee, and practices before games with the Volunteers were always intense. He would talk endlessly about how the Tennessee single wing attack would place pressure on his "little old ends." But Bryant played every game to win. Despite the thinness of their ranks, he and his coaches believed that Alabama had a very good chance to beat the Vols.

Tennessee was rebuilding in 1958. Opening against Auburn on September 27, they had not earned a first down and lost 13-0. The following week, the Vols had come back from an 8-7 deficit to beat Mississippi State in the fourth quarter, 13-8.

On the Saturday before its game with Alabama, while the Tide was toying with Furman, Tennessee had played a tough game against Georgia Tech and lost, 21-7. Since Alabama had virtually ignored Furman in practice, it had the advantage of almost two weeks of preparation against Tennessee formations.

Tennessee had set the standard of excellence for Southern football under General Bob Neyland, the Tennessee athletic director. Neyland's 21-year record as a head coach was 173-31-12, and over the 37-year period he was at Tennessee the school's record was 258-70-18, the best in the nation. In 1958, Neyland protege Bowden Wyatt was in his fourth year as head coach.

Bryant had showed his dedication to beating Tennessee in his own senior year, when he played with a hairline fracture in his leg in a game that Alabama won 25-0. But Bryant-coached teams had fared poorly versus the Volunteers; Bryant's teams had won only once in nine games, dating back to 1946.

At Kentucky, his Wildcats lost four close games and tied one with the Vols between 1946 and 1950. They took a 28-0 drubbing in 1951, and the two teams tied, 14-14, in 1952. Bryant didn't win his first game as a coach against Tennessee until 1952, his last year at Kentucky. That was a 27-21 win, accomplished in the fourth quarter with the help of a blocked punt. As he prepared Alabama to play the Vols in 1958, Bryant was still smarting from the 3-0 defeat Tennessee had handed his Texas A&M team in the Gator Bowl.

Tennessee still utilized the single wing offense, which placed great emphasis on the running skills of the fullback and tailback, and on power blocking from blocking backs and pulling guards. Wyatt, like Neyland before him, abhorred the passing game. Between them, Vol tailbacks Gene Etter and Billy Majors, both sophomores, attempted only 56 passes for the entire year. The two shared the tailback duties about equally. Both were the sons of prominent high school coaches — E. B. (Red) Etter at the Baylor School in Chattanooga and the legendary Shirley Majors, whose five sons all played football.

Tennessee's bread and butter was an off-tackle power play — it was called "12" when run to the strong side — that was designed to put double-team blocks on the tackle, linebacker and end. The tailback took the direct snap, took a few steps to the right, and then headed for the hole where the blocking was concentrated. "It was a powerful play, but there was absolutely no deception," recalled Etter, now coaching at his father's old school.

This play and the reverses or pass/sweeps run by the tailback put tremendous pressure on the defensive ends, who were called upon as the first line of defense. Preparation for these plays was always difficult, and highly physical, as Bryant tried to find someone who could stand up to the onslaught. Morris Childers, the sophomore end from Fairfield, who was in for 47 plays in the Furman game and intercepted a pass, found these drills punishing. "I remember having really bad practices, I just never got in synch and it probably doomed me in Bryant's eyes as a player in the future," he said. "I remember lining up in this drill where they sent two people out to block on one, and the two people that were blocking me — I weighed about 180 — were Billy Neighbors and Billy Rice. Two of the biggest freshmen they had. It was like . . . what the hell do I do now? I think I just tried to crash into them . . . but it got a lot of disapproval . . . it wasn't the thing to do, whatever I did." Childers did not play against Tennessee.

Jerre Brannen, another of the Anniston delegation, who was beginning to make a reputation for himself with Bryant as a hard hitter, had injured his knee and had not expected to make the trip. So he was surprised when Goostree began to give his knee some serious taping before the game.

"What are you putting so much tape on there for?" Brannen asked Goostree. "I don't think I'm going to need that."

"Well, you don't know what will happen, we might have to use even the wounded out there," Goostree replied. Still, Brannen was shocked when Bryant put him in the starting lineup. Unable to move much, he was told by Gene Stallings to just penetrate a little and hold his ground. "You just bury yourself . . . just get down and get a handful of grass and just get low," Stallings told him, and Brannen did the best he could.

Billy Majors, the third of five sons in the remarkable Majors family, proved to be a better runner than the Alabama coaches expected, and he made few mistakes. For additional offense, the Vols depended on their 25-year old fullback Carl Smith, a bruising runner at 6-1, 190.

Alabama's game plan for Tennessee, put together by Pat James, was to minimize mistakes, win the kicking game, and stop the predictable Vol offense. For their own offense, the Tide would keep it simple and hope that a fumble or a poor kick provided a chance to make a short drive for a touchdown or field goal.

On defense, James had concocted a plan to create gaps in the interference and to penetrate the Tennessee offense laterally. In virtually every play from Tennessee's single wing, the blocking back, who lined up right behind the offensive line of scrimmage, would run in the direction of the play. The middle linebackers, generally Don Cochran or Billy Rains, were coached to watch, or "key" on, the direction the blocking back and guards would take after the direct snap to the tailback. While the down linemen occupied the double team blocking at the line of scrimmage, the linebacker was supposed to break into the Vol backfield and make the tackle.

For Rains, it was a difficult assignment. Hampered by his injured back, he had played, but not excelled, against LSU, Vanderbilt, and Furman. He graded poorly against Furman, and was charged with four errors. That sort of performance did not go unnoticed.

It was warm and sunny in Knoxville the third Saturday in October. The game started well for Alabama. The Tide stopped the cautious Volunteers on their first possession. Alabama started at its 32, and after Gary O'Steen gained 3, unveiled its first surprise of the day. O'Steen faked a quick-kick, but the ball went instead to Duff Morrison, who chugged around left end for a first down at the Tide 44.

Alabama was unable to move further, and O'Steen's punt pinned Tennessee deep at their own 14. So far, the game plan was intact. This was the kind of field position Bryant loved. But the tactical advantage did not last — Majors immediately quick-kicked. O'Steen got back to the ball and caught it in the air, but looking for running room to the right, fumbled when hit and Tennessee fullback Carl Smith recovered at the Alabama 47.

That was the first costly fumble, and there were more to come. The remainder of the quarter was played in Alabama territory, and eventually put the Tide in a hole.

Bryant had an unusual ability to see and analyze play on the field from the sidelines.* So it was probably at this point in the game that he began to be dissatisfied with the play of Billy Rains. Even though Tennessee failed to gain a first down in either of the next two series, Rains

---

*He would also get so excited at times that he would try to send in a player who had long ago graduated. So as a sideline coach he also had his weaknesses.

appeared to have a clear shot at Majors, but tackled only air. In the defensive summary compiled from the game film after the game, the reviewing coach's notes said, "Rains should have had for 5 yd. loss." Things would get worse for the senior tackle from Moulton.

Despite Rains's lapses, Tennessee was unable to move the ball. But Wyatt understood field position football, too, and fine punting by Majors kept Alabama backed up. Then, after a short quick-kick by Alabama's Gooby Stapp, Tennessee took advantage of its only pass completion and a big penalty to score its first touchdown.

From the 50, Majors faded and passed to wingback Bobby Sandlin for 9 yards to the 41. Smith then got the Vols their first down with a 3-yard plunge. The next play was the key to the drive. Majors faked a handoff to Smith, faded back to throw, and then took off up the middle — the play was essentially a draw. Rains reacted to the fake, then charged toward Majors, but slipped and fell at the line of scrimmage as the Tennessee tailback skittered by. Majors was tripped and fell at the 32, where he was punished by Pete Reaves on an obvious late hit. The penalty for unnecessary roughness put Tennessee at the Alabama 17 with a first down.

Reaves was no doubt charged with an error when the film was graded, but to the coaches, Rains was also at fault. If he had made the tackle at the line of scrimmage, the penalty would never have happened.

Bryant replaced Rains with Don Cochran, but in three plays Tennessee pounded to another first down on the Alabama 6. Smith got the first 3 on a draw, Majors earned 5 and then 3 more behind the Tennessee power blocking.

From the 6 it was Majors again for 3 and Smith up the gut for 2 to the 1 yard line. On third and goal, Dave Sington and Cochran out-charged the Tennessee blockers, enabling Jim Blevins to snag Smith for no gain. The quarter ended with a classic goal line confrontation, fourth and goal at the Alabama 1. Later in the season, Alabama might have had the confidence and experience to stuff the Vols. But when play resumed, Majors ran play #12, followed his blockers and fell over the goal line at right end. The defensive summary criticized Wayne Sims, Jerre Brannen, and Sington for a "poor charge," and Buddy Wesley for being slow to meet the ball carrier. Carl Valletto was grudgingly given a "fair" on the play. But the most important fact was the scoreboard. After Sammy Burklow's conversion, Tennessee led 7-0.

After a false start, Alabama's offense went to work. O'Steen returned the ensuing kickoff from the Tide 6 to the 33, and would have scored absent a saving tackle by Etter. Ferdy Cruce, who had moved into a starting role on the strength of a good performance against Furman, was in at halfback. He got the ball on first down, was hit at the line and driven backwards. He fumbled and the ball bounced right into the hands of Jackson, who carried it 12 yards to the Alabama 45. Three plays gained only 6 yards, and O'Steen, shrugging off a poor snap, punted dead on the Volunteers' 5.

Tennessee did not care to try its offense so deep in its own territory, and punted on first down. Alabama started at its own 46, and again turned a Cruce fumble into a positive development. On a reverse, Ferdy gained 5 and lost the handle. In the melee, someone kicked the ball and it bounded toward the Tennessee goal line. Bud Moore scooted downfield to recover just ahead of the Tennessee safety. The play was ugly, but it had gained 23 yards, and Alabama had its deepest penetration at the Tennessee 31.

Things looked even more promising after O'Steen slashed for 9 yards to the 22. But then Smith failed to gain on a keeper, and O'Steen was kept short of the first down when the handoff was sloppy and Rains blew a block. At last, when Bobby Smith tried to sneak for the needed yard to the 20, he also fumbled. Tennessee's Sandlin recovered at the 22.

Tennessee had its horns pulled in, and could do nothing on the next two possessions. Then, punting from his 29, Majors had the ball go off the side of his foot and out of bounds on the Tennessee 42. Here was another opportunity, the kind Alabama hoped to exploit.

Smith tried to run and gained a yard. Marlin Dyess, in for O'Steen, gained a couple. Than Smith tried a play called the Utah pass, in which the halfback delayed and then looked for an open spot just across the scrimmage line. The play would have gained big, but the Scooter muffed the catch. The miss brought up fourth down with time in the half running out. Bryant called another pass, and Smith nailed Cruce down the middle. After Majors spun the Tide halfback down, it was first down at the Tennessee 13, with less than two minutes to play in the half.

Then came the play that was fatal to the Alabama drive and eventually to Cruce's career at Alabama. On a simple handoff, he and Smith missed connections and the ball bounced toward Tennessee's Coy Franklin, who wrapped it up, stopping the drive. The half ended two plays later, still 7-0 Tennessee. Alabama had fumbled five times and squandered two scoring chances.

Halftimes under Bryant generally followed a similar pattern. Players would come in, towel off, and then pay attention while assistant coaches described adjustments. Before the team returned to the field, the head coach would normally say a few words, elaborate on a play or two at the blackboard, and send the players back into the fray with some encouraging words. But if things weren't going well, Bryant could be harsh and he was livid over the team's first-half performance in the Tennessee game. The displeasure was general. One account has him telling captain Dave Sington: "You'd better start doing something because you are the captain of the team, and I ain't going to have a non-playing captain. If you don't start playing up to your ability, that's what you're going to be, a non-captain and a non-player." Others got similar encouragement.

Whatever he said, it didn't help matters immediately. Penalties on Alabama's first possession after the second half kickoff pushed the Tide back to its own 15. O'Steen punted, and Majors made the Tide coverage look bad, catching the ball at the Tennessee 44, slipping between Wesley and Rains at the Alabama 45, and running to the Alabama 34 before Roberts could wrap him up. Tennessee got things going from there.

Smith started on a reverse to the left, getting outside of the contain man Charlie Tom Gray, and gaining 9. Then the sky began to fall in on Billy Rains.

First, he managed to sideswipe Majors at the line of scrimmage, but the little tailback shrugged the blow off and got the first down to the Alabama 22. Smith gained 2, was tripped, and then was wrapped up by

Wesley. Majors, pursued by Valletto, was missed by Rains, who was knocked down, got up and got a hand on the tailback but couldn't hold on. Brannen, bum knee and all, finally closed the play for a loss of 2.

In the key play of the game, third and 10 from the 22, Majors again sent Carl Smith on a reverse. Rains took a good angle and penetrated deep. He hit Smith solidly in the right leg, slid to the ground and lost his grip on the runner's ankle. The big fullback kept his balance, left Rains prostrate, and broke past Gray toward the sidelines. He wasn't stopped until he reached the 13. "Rains missed tackle for loss," the coach's defensive summary noted.

Not wrapping up on a tackle was a cardinal sin in Bryant's book, and the play would soon have consequences. Years later, Rains still wondered at his failure to bring Smith down. "I hit him with my head in front of him and he turned . . . and a pain went down my back that was almost . . . I just couldn't stand it," he said. "But anyway, that wasn't an excuse as far as Coach Bryant was concerned . . . I should have made the tackle."

Still, it was fourth down with a yard to go. But on the next play, behind a good Smith block on Brannen, Majors cut inside and slid to a first down at the 10. Tennessee's offense was clicking now, and on the next two plays Rains penetrated far too late to have an impact. First, Smith drove to the 7. Then Majors carried, and as Smith and blocking-back Sadler sealed off Gray, the Tennessee tailback brushed past Wesley at the 4 to make the touchdown. Sammy Burklow kicked the extra point and it was 14-0.

Both teams were hindered by penalties and failed to threaten until Etter led a fresh second unit into the game for Tennessee. Mixing runs by Etter and fullback Neyle Sollee, the Vols drove from the Alabama 44 to the 20, where it was third and 2. Then Cochran and Frank stopped Etter for a loss of 3. On fourth and 5, Morrison smothered wingback Don Stephens after he caught an Etter pass at the 20, and the Tide took over.

On the sidelines, Bryant called his first team together, and according to some accounts, threatened to "kill them all" if they did not score. He sounded serious. Alabama finally began to accomplish something.

First Morrison scrambled for 4, and Jackson ran for a first down on the 30. Morrison gained 3. Then Jackson stepped back to pass and under terrific pressure from Tennessee end Tommy Potts managed to throw to O'Steen, who had sneaked into the pattern from the backfield, at the 40. O'Steen turned upfield and by the time Etter dragged him down the play had gained 41 yards to the Tennessee 26.

Two plays netted nothing. But Jackson's third down pass was complete to Carl Valletto, who leapt between three defenders and clamped his huge hands around the ball for an 11-yard gain to the 16.

As the fourth quarter began, Jackson ran a counter and slithered up the middle for 7. O'Steen gained a yard to the 8, and a third-down run by Jackson gained only 1. On fourth and 1 at the 7, O'Steen took a handoff, was hit at the line of scrimmage, got a push from Jackson and drove forward to the 1. Cruce, vexed at himself for missing a block, pounded the turf in frustration. On the next play, Jackson kept for the touchdown, with Reaves converting, and it was 14-7 with plenty of time left.

Alabama blunted Tennessee's only offensive thrust of the fourth quarter at the Tennessee 46, and the Tide began a drive at its 20 with four minutes remaining.

After missing on first down, Jackson threw a pass toward Dyess across the middle. The little halfback reached high for the ball and then took off for 17 yards to the Alabama 38. Jackson lost 3 trying to pass, but then flipped a pass to Baxter Booth who reached the Alabama 47.

Jackson got the first down on a keeper to the 50, and just missed Booth at the Vol 35. A huge Tennessee rush sacked Jackson back to the Alabama 38, but on the next play the Utah pass worked to Dyess over the middle for 17 yards. That made it fourth and 6 at the Tennessee 45, but there was little time left. Bryant called a desperation play, a pass to Dyess and an immediate lateral to Butch Frank. That much of the play worked, but Tennessee's Sandlin ran right up Scooter's back and leg-whipped Frank down just short of a first down. Coached to fumble the ball forward in such a situation, Butch made an effort to do that, but because he was lying on his back, it amounted to nothing. From there, Majors ran out the clock.

After the game, Bryant was characteristically polite about his opponent. "They hit harder than we did and played tougher football . . . they made less mistakes," he said, and congratulated Wyatt on preparing his team well. But he also let his unhappiness with the team's mistakes show: "We'll never win a game when we draw penalties at the key spots as we did today. If we can't coach better than that, we're whipped before we start. Those infractions killed us, and I'm not complaining about the officiating."

Bryant skipped the usual prayer in the dressing room after the game, but he did not seem unusually glum to Dave Sington, who heard him tell a Gator Bowl official that he thought his team was coming together and they might want to watch closely in the next couple of weeks. Also in the head coach's mind was a drastic remedy for the breakdowns and lapses that had cost the team a victory in Knoxville.

DEFENSIVE SUMMARY

(Excerpts from Defensive Summary prepared by coaches from Tennessee game film on the Sunday after the game. This section covers Tennessee's drive for its second touchdown.)

Situation	Defense	Play	Yds.	Breakdown
		Punt return	22	Very poor coverage by all our middle people
1-10A34	West to North	SWR Rev 39	9	Gray let man outside; Jackson up slow; Blevins blocked
2-1 A25	Rover	SWR TB 7	3	Rains missed tackle for no gain; Blevins and Gray blocked; Blevins good 2nd
1-10 A22	Rover	SWL Rev 36	2	Rains missed tackle for loss; Blevins blocked, Wesley fair
2-8 A20	Rover G's Out	SWR Pass 8 Ran	-2	Valletto had for 7 yard loss
3-10 A22	Rover	SWR Rev 39	9	Rains missed tackle for loss; Gray and Wesley missed tackle; Smith same
4-1 A13	West	SWR TB 6	3	Valletto good charge no 2nd effort; Brannen blocked; Wesley poor
1-10 A10	Rover Goal Line	SWR Rev 37	3	Rains and Sington nothing; Gray too wide; Blevins poor; Wesley good
2-7 A7	Rover Goal Line	SWR TB 7	7 TD	Blevins driven over goal; O'Steen not aggressive; Wesley misses tackle

CHAPTER SIXTEEN

'You've Paid Your Dues'

Back in Tuscaloosa, the evening of the Tennessee game, the
Alabama freshmen were playing Tulane. Arriving after the game
started, Bryant went to Denny Stadium and sat in the stands.
When the game was over — Alabama won, 25-6 — he visited the
dressing room. If the freshmen were expecting a pat on the back, they got
a shock.

Bobby Drake Keith and manager James Beall had stayed in Tuscaloosa to work with the freshmen, and were in the dressing room after the
game. Bryant came in raging, "just went ballistic in there," Beall said.

"By God, we will practice tomorrow morning, you will be here and
the varsity will be here," Bryant told the freshmen.

"I think he was letting off some of the steam that he had and the
disappointment that he had felt at the Tennessee game and the way in
which we played," Keith said. "I don't feel like he thought we should
have lost that game and he was trying to . . . make the point with the
freshmen that things were going to be different . . . from now on and we
wouldn't lose games like that in the future . . ."

There are no records of a practice that Sunday, but several players say
some head-knocking did take place. There is no question that on
Monday there was a long and arduous practice. It was probably on this
day that Bryant called the team around him and read it the riot act.

Bobby Boylston recalled it this way: "He called everybody in . . . and he said, 'I'm going to get some more running in, I don't care if all of you quit. I'm going to have a winning football team and I don't care if I step in everybody's face from here to Washington, D.C.'"

"Listen, I get fired for losing," Butch Frank heard. "They ain't gonna fire me. I'll kill you first."

Baxter Booth remembers that practice well.

"I remember I had to go in the infirmary," Booth said. "I was [the] off end having to go down field and throw [a block], and have a coach pull me back in the huddle and it was just unbelievable. And after practice, we had to repeat that series, so the first team got back out there and ran that same series again and I ended up in the showers, and I was the last man still in the thing, I was dead, drinking water out of my headgear out in the field . . . I crawled in there and the next thing I knew I had passed out."

Two players were not at the drills at all. Bryant, never comfortable with the play of Ferdy Cruce and Billy Rains, had presented the two an ultimatum.

Reporting to the dressing room equipment window to pick up their "baskets" — socks, jock, shoulder pads, all the paraphernalia used in practice — Rains and Cruce were told by the equipment manager that "Coach Bryant has your baskets. You have to go and see him."

The other players, preoccupied with their own problems, stopped for a moment to wonder what was going on, and whispered among themselves about the new turn of events.

In the consultation, according to most of the players who recall hearing about it, Bryant told the two players that they could play on the (nonexistent) B-team if they wished, but they would never play another snap in a game. "I asked Ferdy," Bobby Smith said, " . . . I liked Ferdy and I liked Billy . . . what they told me is that, 'You can play on the B-team . . . or you can just keep your scholarship and not play . . . but you're not going to wear that red shirt on Saturday again.' I still think . . . he was challenging them and they could have said, 'Well, I'll show you.'"

When Rains went to speak to the head coach, he said, "Coach, you know I just can't believe that I'm going to have to fight my way back [to the first team]. I know I didn't have the game that I should have."

Bryant said, "No, Billy, you didn't. You didn't have a good game."

Rains says he told Bryant, "Well, I'm just not physically able to fight my way back."

"You've paid your dues," Bryant said. "Why don't you give it up. If you want to give it up, you've got your scholarship . . . you've paid your dues. Give it up. If that's what you want to do."

Cruce would not agree to talk to me about his meeting. Whatever happened when they met, Bryant told reporters through the publicity office that "Rains and Cruce, after consultation with me, decided to give up football and concentrate on their studies." The story was reported almost without comment in the media. Bob Phillips in the *Birmingham Post-Herald* essentially shrugged his shoulders. The *Moulton Advertiser* expressed the town's continuing support for and belief in Rains. That was about it.

For Rains, enough of a celebrity in his home town to have a photo of himself and his new baby on the front page of the hometown paper, it was a great disappointment and it "almost killed his father," said his wife, Jane. Rains finished out the semester, and then took a job.

Forcing Cruce and Rains off the team was a harsh move, but completely in character for Bryant. It was straightforward to him: play winning football or don't play at all. The move was a reminder for every player that their coach demanded performance at all times and he would not hesitate to bench them, or worse, even in the middle of the season. The players who still remained were with few exceptions the kind Bryant loved and believed in — gritty, dedicated, impervious to pain, quick, generally small, but able to play an entire game of football without being exhausted or even tired. They knew how closely he was watching them.

It was about this time that another promising halfback, Dick Strum, saw his hopes for football glory smashed. Bothered by a circulation problem in his bad knee, Strum fell while doing an agility drill. When he got up he saw Bryant eyeing him. The next day, there was no basket at the equipment window.

Told to go see Bryant, Strum was shown into the head coach's office and was not asked to sit. "I've talked to Dr. Sherrill about you," Bryant said. "If you were to get a hard lick on your knee, you would probably walk with a limp for the rest of your life."*

"Well, Coach, I think it's going to get better," Strum replied.

"No, I don't want you in your later years, if you get your leg hurt . . . and every morning . . . you cuss this school and me." Bryant told Strum he wanted him to stay in school and that his scholarship was good as long as he kept his nose clean.

After Monday's harsh practice, Bryant for the first time eased off of contact work in the ensuing week. It may have been because co-captain Dave Sington had summoned up his courage and told the coach that his teammates were exhausted, or perhaps Bryant realized himself that it was time to back off. In any event, though sarcastic at times about the players' work ethic, Bryant made the remainder of the practice week less strenuous, and he became more optimistic about the team's chances against Mississippi State.

The day before the game, Jerre Brannen ran into Bryant at the athletic building. Brannen was prone to pre-game butterflies and diarrhea and needed a swig of pink Kaopectate, which Goostree kept in large amounts. Bryant spotted him.

"Red, have you got a class?" Bryant asked.

"Nossir, not right now," Brannen replied.

"Well, come on and walk to the drug store with me," Bryant said. Uneasy, as all the players were about being with Bryant alone, Brannen could only agree.

"What do you think we're going to do this weekend?" Bryant asked Brannen.

"Well, Coach, I think we're going to win," Brannen said.

"I don't know if I want to take you," Bryant replied. "I don't want anybody that thinks we can win. I want people who know we can win."

---

*Even as it was, Strum's knee has been a problem for him ever since. Knee operations weren't particularly artful in those days.

Later that day, Bryant found manager Bert Jones packing for the trip to Starkville, and gave him two gift-wrapped boxes to put into the equipment trunk. Jones told Bryant he had "packed him two touch-downs in here," and Bryant beamed.

Mississippi State, coached by Wade Walker, was 3-1 in the season, having lost only to Tennessee. Though its wins were against mediocre opponents, the Maroons were a slight favorite. Wade had a multi-talented quarterback, Billy Stacy, who ran the option to perfection.

The day before the game, Bryant uncharacteristically asked Co-captain Bobby Smith if the thought the team was ready. Smith, who had been impressed with the coach's inspirational talk before the LSU game, suggested that Bryant make another speech. At the pre-game breakfast, Bryant did, recalling Alabama's glory days and reminding the players of the thousands of Tide fans who would be listening to the game on the radio.

The weather in Starkville was cloudy and mild. Stacy ran the option three times on State's first series, but gained only 7. Duff Morrison was charged with holding on the punt return, so Alabama started deep in its own territory. O'Steen immediately remedied that situation: on second down, he quick-kicked over the Maroon secondary, and the ball bounded 62 yards past the line of scrimmage to the 22.

State's Bubber Trammell ran for five yards. But on second and five, Bobby Jackson, playing a close cornerback, penetrated and messed up an option pitch from Stacy. The Mobilian recovered the fumble at the Maroon 28.

Carries by Duff Morrison and O'Steen got a first down at the 15, but the next three plays got only 3 yards. Bryant called on Sington for a field goal attempt. Nearsighted anyway, Sington was unnerved by the open spaces behind the State goal post. "It looked like it was 80 miles away," he said. But with a hold from Dyess, the bulky tackle hit the ball cleanly and Alabama, as it had against LSU, led 3-0.

The lead held up until halftime, thanks to more quick-kicks by O'Steen and Gooby Stapp, and stout defense. State seemed unable to adjust to the quick-kicks. "I always cheated back and over just a little bit,"

O'Steen said. "I can remember one guy saying, 'It's going to be a quick-kick, he's cheated back,' and I hit it right over his head." Midway in the second quarter, Stacy drove the Maroons to the Alabama 21, but on fourth and 2 from the 21, Pete Reaves shot the gap and knocked the quarterback to the ground.

In its opening game, Alabama had allowed LSU to score on its first possession in the second half. Against Mississippi State, the Tide held State without a first down in its first three possessions, and then started a drive for its only touchdown. There were three big plays — an 18-yard run by O'Steen, a 13-yard run by Jackson on a run-pass option, and a touchdown pass from Jackson to Norbie Ronsonet that became the most famous play of that first season.

It was fourth down at the Mississippi State 21. A field goal at that point was of little value and probably impossible anyway. As Bobby Jackson recalled it, Bryant sent Ronsonet into the game with a play.

"You can imagine when Coach Bryant would call one of us to go in," he said. "Norbie wasn't playing that much . . . so he comes in and he's saying, 'Coach says to run . . . .' and he's so excited . . . so I said, 'We'll run 25 or 26 roll weak . . . . It was a play I could either run or throw. I could at least make a first down . . . I told Norbie to run, because he was so excited, 'Norbie, just go straight down field and turn toward the gate.'"

Rolling out, Jackson felt pressure and launched a looping pass toward the end zone. Ronsonet leapt between two defenders in the end zone and clutched the ball. Ecstatic to have caught a touchdown pass in front of so many Mississippians, the Biloxi native staged a mini-demon-stration on his own. "I was just jumping up and down in the end zone running back toward the huddle . . . jumping and waving my hands," he said. Manager Bert Jones had to chase the young end down to get the ball back for the try for the extra point, which was missed because of a poor snap.

The remainder of the game was notable for a couple of incidents that resulted in more playing time for one player, and much less for another.

Tommy White, the sophomore halfback from West Blocton, had

not yet played in a game and was about to accept the fact that he would be redshirted. He had begun to wipe the anti-glare blacking from under his eyes when Bryant spied him. "Come here, Little Buddy," the coach called. "Get in there, hell, I forgot about you." White, playing safety, came up quickly on a trap play and made a career hit. "We butt heads, I cracked my tooth and knocked the guy backwards," he said. "It was one of those things you look at and say, 'Oh, what a lick.'"

"Heyyyy, Little Buddy," Bryant exulted. From then on, White was not forgotten.

Jerre Brannen, quiet and serious off the field and deeply religious, had become a Bryant favorite for the same reason — his willingness, demonstrated against Tennessee, to hit and hit hard. Bryant began to call Brannen his "headhunter." "He told me, if [he] ever went into an alley, he'd take me with him," Brannen said.

Brannen, as defensive left end, was assigned to outside containment against the Maroon option play. But with State backed up inside its five, his aggressiveness got the best of him.

"Stacy stumbled and I thought he was going to fall," Brannen said. "I was going to knock him loose from the ball . . . and he turned as he was falling, threw that ball to the trail back and I think he was just hoping somebody was back there . . . because he knew he was going to get hit . . . and he was going to lose the ball so he just lateraled and the guy was at the right spot . . ."

The pitch went to Bubber Trammell, who ran for 70 yards, all the way to the Alabama 28. It was more than one-fourth of Mississippi State's rushing total for the game, and it burned Bryant up. He yanked Brannen and swore, "Red, you'll never play another down, as long as you're here." In fact, Brannen did play again, but he was never a Bryant favorite after that.

The long run eventually led to Mississippi State's only touchdown. Alabama stopped the immediate threat, but punted to Stacy from inside its 20. Stacy got loose on the return all the way from his 49 to the Alabama 12. On fourth and 4 from the 6, Stacy called a run-pass option, eluded Bobby Smith and Dave Sington and dived into the end zone.

1959 Corolla

Celebrating after the win over Mississippi State (L-R): Dr. Frank Rose, Fred Sington, Norbie Ronsonet, Gary O'Steen, Bobby Jackson. The players were hiding their cigars and cigarettes.

Stacy was hit so hard he had to leave the game —"cold as a wedge" Fred Sington says — and the score came too late to alter the outcome. On the next Mississippi State possession, O'Steen intercepted a pass by Tom Miller, State's second-team quarterback, to complete a day to remember. He had rushed for 60 yards, punted nine times for an average of 45.5 yards, and intercepted a pass. He played the entire second half with a badly bruised rib.

So it was an Alabama win, 9-7, and to Bryant it felt wonderful.* In the dressing room, he found Bert Jones and asked, "Where are those boxes?"

Jones had forgotten. "What boxes?"

"In the trunk, I gave them to you," Bryant said.

---

*The game was Bryant's first SEC win at Alabama. His retelling of the game in *Bear* is entertaining but largely fanciful.

Jones found them. Inside there were cigars and cigarettes, and Bryant passed them out to everyone, even those who didn't smoke. Walter Sansing got sick as a dog, and sat at the front of the bus in case he had to throw up. The elated Bryant insisted that the players sing all the way back to their hotel in Columbus, Mississippi.

CHAPTER SEVENTEEN

'They Can't Do That to Wayne'

Alabama's next opponent, Georgia, was an enigma. Loaded with talent — 12 eventually went into professional football — the Bulldogs had won only two and lost three. In his memoir, *In the Arena,* Pat Dye, a sophomore guard on the team, blames staff squabbles and a negative off-field environment. Wally Butts, the Georgia coach, only 53, was increasingly profligate in his personal life and unable or unwilling to exert the kind of control Bryant insisted on at Alabama. (Ironically, the following year the return of J. B. Whitworth as line coach brought stability to the team, and it won the SEC title.)

Bigger and more experienced than Alabama, Georgia relied on the running of its captain, Theron Sapp, a 200-pound fullback. The Bulldogs had two premier quarterbacks, junior Charlie Britt, and Fran Tarkenton, a sophomore on the brink of greatness. If there was such a thing as a passing team in college football in 1958, Georgia was probably it.

Dye, his brother Nat, a 218-pound senior, and junior center Dave Lloyd at 220 pounds anchored the line. Bobby Walden, the Georgia punter, was leading the nation, which meant that Butts's team was one of the few Alabama opponents that could be expected to compete in that department.

It was to be Homecoming at Tuscaloosa, and Bryant was still tinkering with his lineup. Based on their play against Mississippi State, he elevated Dave Sington and Pete Reaves back to the starting team, and also promoted Gary Phillips, the de facto replacement for Rains, who would start his first game. Jerre Brannen's mistake against Mississippi State had knocked him out of the starting lineup and he ended up playing only five snaps.

Bryant also made a change at fullback, putting another guard, Fred Sington, into that spot. The intent was to use Sington, perhaps the fastest lineman on the team and a lot bigger than Buddy Wesley or Butch Frank, as a blocking back, and to run something similar to the triple option that became such a powerful weapon in subsequent years. Sington and the quarterback, usually Jackson, would read the defensive play of the linebackers and tackles — Sington to determine where to block, and Jackson whether to hand off, keep or pitch.

Butts had been philosophical about dealing with Alabama's quick-kick in pre-game comments — "About all we can do," he said, "is to play them as we do any play. They come out of the double huddle and snap the ball so fast you don't have time to prepare for a kick." In the event, perhaps Butts should have tried harder. Quick-kicks kept the Bulldogs backed up all day, and a 57-yarder by O'Steen, from second and 1 at the Alabama 29, led to Alabama's first touchdown early in the game.

The ball rolled dead on the Georgia 13, and Georgia could not advance. O'Steen returned Walden's 42-yard response to the Georgia 37. From there, with Sington at fullback leading the blocking, Duff Morrison ran a reverse for 14 yards. Jackson, emulating Harry Gilmer, then hit John Paul Poole (starting in front of Brannen) with a jump pass for 9 yards. From second and 1 at the 14, Jackson ran the triple option to the right, was almost collared by two Georgians, and flipped an overhand pitch to O'Steen. It wasn't pretty but it worked — O'Steen was outside the containment and tip-toed down the sideline into the end zone. Sington missed the extra point so it was only 6-0.

Alabama threatened again after a 53-yard quick-kick by Tommy White. Georgia was unable to get its offense going — up in the press box Bobby Luna and Red Drew, who had prepared the scouting report, "called every play before they ever ran it," Luna said. Alabama took over at the Georgia 40, and in four plays had a first down at the Bulldog 26. A Jackson pass to O'Steen and a Morrison run got the ball to the 15, but when Jackson tried the same flip to O'Steen that had earned a touchdown earlier, it was batted in the air and then grabbed by Georgia's Jimmy Vickers. Still frustrated, Georgia barely penetrated Alabama territory in the first half.

But in the third period, led by Britt and Sapp, Georgia pushed Alabama's back to the wall and kept it there.

The Bulldogs took the second half kickoff, and on the first play Britt threw an 11-yard pass to Don Soberdash. From the Georgia 46, Britt faked a pass and handed the ball to Sapp on a draw play. The fullback smashed past both both Morrison and Gary O'Steen and gained 29 yards, all the way to the Alabama 25. Four plays got a first down at the 13, an option play failed, and the Alabama rush spoiled two pass attempts. On fourth and 13 from the 16, Tarkenton replaced Britt but his pass also fell harmless. Threat number one had been stopped.

Before Georgia could blink, O'Steen had quick-kicked for 64 yards and the Bulldogs had to start over again. This time they pushed to the Alabama 31 before Frank, Reaves and Ronsonet stopped a fourth-down thrust and ended threat number two. Almost immediately, a Gooby Stapp quick-kick put the Bulldogs back inside their 40.

Gary O'Steen's star had been glowing, but now he made a mistake that earned him a place in Bryant's doghouse. He fumbled a Walden punt and suddenly Georgia had a first down at the Tide 17. Jackson, a great admirer of O'Steen's then and now, saved him by snatching away a Tarkenton pass lofted toward the end zone. That was the end of threat number three.

Backed up inside its 20, Alabama punted again and Britt brought the return back to the Alabama 32. But on third down, the last play of the third quarter, O'Steen intercepted a Britt pass at the 5. So threat number four was fruitless.

Almost immediately, Alabama was in hot water again, and in Bryant's opinion it was O'Steen's fault. Britt, under little pressure at the Georgia 35, tossed a pass toward end Aaron Box. In coverage, O'Steen played the ball. Box made a circus catch and went racing down the sidelines toward the Alabama goal. Again Jackson, playing safety, made a saving play. Somehow eluding a fleet of blockers, he bumped Box out of bounds at the Alabama 10.

It seemed impossible that Alabama could hold again. Halfback George Guisler got 5 yards and only an extraordinary play by Morrison kept him from scoring. As Benny Marshall put it the next day in the *Birmingham News,* "This was it." The ball went to Guisler again, and Wayne Sims sliced into the backfield and dragged him down at the 10. The coaches' game-film summary said it all: "Sims Great." Sims was given 4 RBIs in the game (but also five errors.)

On third and 10, Britt tried a pass toward Norman King that was batted down by Tommy White. On fourth down, Britt again threw into the end zone toward Box, who got his hands on the ball in a melee with Gray and Frank. After the game, Butts and the Bulldogs contended that the second throw had been caught. But Gray and Frank insist the ball was knocked to the ground. "The ball fell out of his hands," Frank said. "He did not have possession."

Georgia was frustrated, and Alabama sealed the issue by generating a turnover on the Bulldog's next series. The entire line — Valletto, Booth, Hannah, Sims — accounted for a loss of 7 on two plays, and then Ronsonet made his second big play of the season. Britt, under pressure from Valletto, threw toward Gene Littleton but the ball fell short and was grabbed by the lanky Biloxi end. Ronsonet headed west, and reached the Georgia 16 before being knocked out of bounds. On second down, Jackson ran an option for 13 yards and a first down at the 1 and one play later he scored over right tackle. Nobody cared much that his try to circle end for a two-point conversion was fruitless.

Georgia's frustration boiled over on the ensuing kickoff. Bryant instructed Sington to pooch an onside kick, and a big scramble ensued. When Wayne Sims came up with the ball, it was too much for the Georgia players. Jim Blevins was heading back toward the huddle when he saw three Bulldogs "just beating the hell out of Sims."

"I said, 'Why, they can't do that to Wayne,'" Blevins recalled. "I reached down and got one in each hand and was pulling them off . . . and when I did that, the whole Georgia bench emptied."

Bryant, who had stood by in practice when Blevins knocked Johnny Gann's teeth out, hated fights in a football game. He and the other coaches stopped the Alabama reserves at the sidelines, and the big man waded into the fracas. In a short piece he wrote later, Morris Childers said Bryant's topcoat was flopping "like the wings of a giant bird." Somehow, Bill Hannah, who was on the bench, got past the coaches and ran toward the fierce Georgia center, Dave Lloyd. Hannah had been proudly showing off a new face mask with a double bar that was supposed to protect his often-broken nose. Lloyd reached up, pinched the two bars together and broke Hannah's nose again with a single punch.

Blevins was spread-eagled on the ground — "they were just beating the dog crap out of me" — and Valletto had taken on Lloyd. Then Bryant intervened, separating the participants, shouting to Sims about this "bush league shit" and telling Valletto to "get your dumb ass off the field."

Bryant said in *Bear* that he was so mad and ashamed at his team's conduct that "I was shaking." He sent Dave Sington over to the Georgia dressing room to apologize to Butts for his players' conduct. Sington went reluctantly. The players felt that Georgia had started the fight "just because they were getting beat."

The fight did not take the edge off the win for Alabama fans. For the first time since 1954, the Tide had won two straight games and the next opponent, Tulane, looked beatable.

CHAPTER EIGHTEEN

'That's a Little Better'

Tulane had won only two games and lost five, and Alabama was actually favored against them. Yet all week there had been an air of apprehension among the coaching staff. Bryant told business manager B. W. Whittington that he was concerned, and said to the media that he was "more pessimistic about our chances this week than I've been about any game this year."

The game was to be played Friday night, and that week Bobby Jackson asked Bryant if he could take the Saturday after the game off, after the team returned, to usher in a wedding. Jim Lofton, a halfback on the 1957 team, was the person getting married. Bryant, who did not want his players associating with anyone from the losing days, refused. "Bobby, no," Bryant said. "If he wants you to be in his wedding, tell him to change it. We're going to be practicing."

Bobby Drake Keith, assigned to scout Tulane, was also concerned, and not only about the new suit of clothes Bryant promised him as game planner if the Tide won. The Green Wave's quarterback was the redoubtable Richie Petitbon, who became a fine pro player and imaginative defensive coach. Petitbon was leading the SEC in passing and gave nothing away on defense. Eddie Dunn at fullback and the Mason brothers, Claude (Boo) and Tommy, filled out a talented backfield.

Part of Alabama's problem was injuries. Two fullbacks, Buddy Wesley and Butch Frank, were hurting. Wesley had a leg injury and

Frank, speared in the chest by Georgia's Sapp, had developed pneumonia. Second team center Jim Blevins had the flu. Hoping to get him ready in time for the Friday night game, Bryant put Blevins on the train to New Orleans the Thursday before the game.

Walter Sansing, hurt since the Vanderbilt game, was named to start at fullback. Still piqued at Gary O'Steen for mistakes against Georgia, Bryant replaced him in the starting lineup with Tommy White, but O'Steen was too talented to keep on the sidelines and eventually played most of the game. Jerre Brannen, in Dutch with Bryant for allowing the big play at Starkville, was back among the Blue Darters. Wayne Sims's outstanding game against Georgia had earned him back a starting job.

The night before the game several players, among them Fred Sington, slipped out to the French Quarter and into a strip joint where the lead ecdysiast was called Willie (the Cat) Christine. The Cat offered a signed picture to anyone in the audience who could meow the loudest. The Alabama players were trying to look inconspicuous in their crimson blazers, but won the meowing contest. Sington took the signed picture — it said, "I had a great time with you in New Orleans" — and later arranged for Red Stickney's girl friend to find it.

Tulane justified Bryant's premonitions early in the game. On the second play from scrimmage, Jackson fumbled on an option play and Tulane recovered on the Alabama 29. On third down, Petitbon faded back to pass, spotted an open lane and spurted up the middle for a first down at the 14. On the next play, Ken Roberts was offside and from first and 5 at the 9, a sneak by Petitbon and three blasts by Dunn earned the touchdown. The point after went wide.

This was a better Alabama offense and it would soon show. But a rare fumble by the reliable Duff Morrison stopped the first Tide thrust. On a pitch from Jackson he gained 7 into Tulane territory when adversity struck. "I go around left end," Morrison recalled, adopting the present tense favored by baseball players. "I get past the halfback, the safety's rotated over, I go to cut back on the safety, and I'm changing hands with the ball, watching him, and this off-side tackle hits me and the ball says, 'ptuoo,' it falls to the ground." Tulane recovered.

Bryant benched Morrison briefly, but he was back in on defense soon and intercepted a Petitbon pass, setting Alabama up at the Green Wave 38. But two passes by Jackson went incomplete, and then he was sacked.

Alabama wasn't done. The Tide had gained field position when O'Steen punted out of bounds at the Tulane 6. Two plays later, Scooter Dyess, little used on defense, was in the right place when Petitbon overthrew Tommy Mason and the little halfback snagged an interception at the Tulane 23.

Jackson called a pass play, but when Morrison made a great block on the corner, he pulled the ball down and ran to the 16. On second and 3, the Tide came out in their double huddle and shifted into an unbalanced line. Dyess went in motion from right halfback, and someone 'twitched' — the offensive summary says it was Baxter Booth or Wayne Sims, or both, but the film doesn't clearly show who moved. When Jackson threw a pass to O'Steen in the left flank and Gary eluded Petitbon and scored, the play was called back.* On the next play, Jackson had Dyess wide open in the end zone but threw short and Petitbon made an easy interception.

The half ended 6-0, Tulane, and Bryant was steaming. Arriving at the shabby dressing room, he found the door either locked or jammed and kicked it open. It didn't help matters when he found that his towel and the chalk he demanded be waiting for him at every halftime were not there. Bert Jones, responsible for such things and hearing the coach rave, was back in the showers and started out to brave the storm. Jerry Claiborne grabbed him by the seat of the pants. "Don't go out there," he said, and Jones didn't.

The first person on Bryant's mind was Carl Valletto. Late in the half, playing defensive end right in front of the Alabama bench, the big Pennsylvanian had first lined up too tight and let Petitbon outside on an option, and then too wide and missed a tackle on Dunn. "Where is that

---

* Rumors persist even today that one of the officials had placed a bet on Tulane and that there was something fishy about this call. There's nothing on the film, at least, to confirm or deny that.

goddam Valentino," the coach growled. Valletto, seated at the coach's feet, had his helmet on and raised a finger reluctantly. Bryant still didn't see him, and when he eventually did find him, as the team headed back out to the field, it was too late to do more than grumble at the big tackle.

Early in the second quarter, a rare Alabama error in the kicking game led to a second Tulane touchdown. Blevins's snap to Gooby Stapp on a fourth-down punt was high and wide, and it took a valiant effort to get the ball away at all. The punt was good for only a yard to the Alabama 39, and Petitbon took immediate advantage of some miscommunication between Valletto and Bud Moore.

"Carl was playing left defensive tackle and I was playing left defensive end," Moore recalled. "We ran this wide tackle six defense, called 'North,' where the defensive end would drop halfway off and split the difference between the flanker back and the tackle or tight end . . ."

Tulane was putting a man in motion and cracking back to trap Valletto. Blocking below the knees was legal then, and Valletto was not enjoying the punishment.

"They started that motion, and I called 'off,'" Moore said, "and Valletto turns around hollering at me . . . 'don't call "off," don't call "off"' . . . they snap the ball and run a handoff."

Freed by the indecision in the Alabama line, Tulane fullback Eddie Dunn went pounding past Valletto all the way to the Alabama 16. Moore, angry at himself and Valletto, trailed the play and took out his frustration on Dunn. Unfortunately, he arrived too late and penalty flags flew. Mortified, Moore bent his forehead to the turf like a Muslim at prayer. "I wanted to crawl under that grass, because I knew the camera was on me . . . I knew Coach Bryant was going to kill me." If the foul had happened a year later, Tulane would have had a first down at the 8, half the distance to the goal line, and Alabama's defense would have had a chance. But in 1958, it was a 15-yard penalty all the way to the 1-yard line. Petitbon immediately sneaked into the end zone and the PAT made it 13-0.

Something about being behind by two touchdowns seemed to energize the Alabama offense. Or possibly it was Alabama's superior

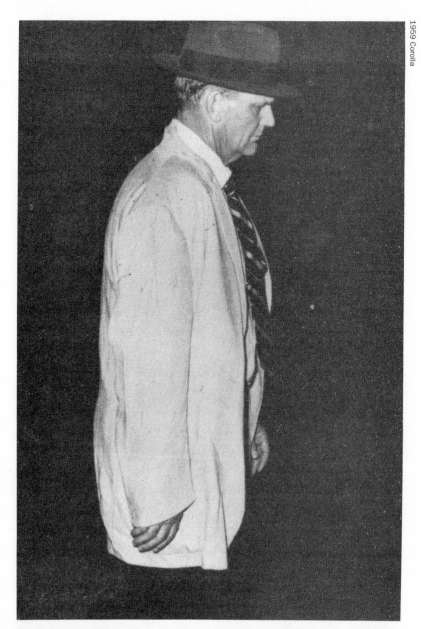

Bryant after the loss to Tulane. Practices the next week were especially tough.

conditioning coming into play. Whatever the impetus, the Tide took the kickoff and drove for a touchdown.

Mack Wise, playing more now with Cruce gone and probably because Morrison had fumbled, returned the kickoff to the 31. Jackson then took over. He ran the keeper and slipped free for 18 yards to the Alabama 49. A penalty nullified a third-down run to the Tulane 39, but then Jackson threw a pass to Tommy White who slipped a tackle and made it to Tulane's 43. On fourth and 2, Sansing got a push in the rump from Jackson and earned the first down at the 40. Immediately, Jackson ran for 23 more before Petitbon collared him. Five more running plays, the last by Jackson from the 1, earned a touchdown, and Sington's conversion made it 13-7.

As the game neared its end, Alabama started another drive. Bryant had replaced Jackson, who despite his fumble had had a brilliant game, with Bobby Smith. "He said, 'Go in there and throw,'" Smith remembered. Smith did, completing a delay pass to Marlin Dyess that carried for 37 yards to the Tulane 22.

On the sidelines Bryant had Jackson ready, called to him, then changed his mind. Alf Van Hoose, in the *Birmingham News,* said there were no more timeouts. Dennis Smitherman, in the *Mobile Press,* said Jackson had used up his eligibility. Jackson remembers nothing about that, nor does Smith.

So Bryant stayed with Smith, and he ran "a little old pass I made a bad pitch on, Scooter would have scored standing up," Smith recalled. "It was an option type thing where you jump up and throw it . . . to the end, or if he's not open you come down and a pitch it to the tailback. If I had made a good pitch he would have scored." As it was the play gained 5 yards, and two carries by Wise got a first down at the 11.

There was still opportunity and time to seize it. But Smith was sacked, losing 8; he threw an incomplete pass, and then completed one to Charlie Tom Gray for 11 yards to the Tulane 8. It was fourth and 7. Trying to run to his left and throw, Smith dropped the ball, picked it up and tossed up a prayer that fell harmlessly short of the end zone. Petitbon ran out the clock in three plays.

The game was a terrific disappointment to Bobby Drake Keith. "I was very upset," he said. "I was angry at Coach Bryant, really . . . the coaching on the field was not like what he was up to."

Bryant himself was very disappointed and blamed the penalties: "We had a lot of effort in the second half," he told the media, "but if we can't do better than make silly penalties, we ought to get beat."

Bryant had planned to allow the team some time in the French Quarter after the game. As Fred Sington remembers it, the players were standing in line to get their meal money from Coach Laslie when Bryant came in.

"Coach Laslie, what are you doing," he asked.

"I'm giving them their meal money," he said.

"Damn, that's all they came down here for, and they played that way, too," Bryant said. "All right, you've got 2 o'clock permission, but nobody better miss bed check."

The team had not had a head-knocking workout since the ones after the loss to Tennessee. Fred Sington had a feeling that things were going to change. "I guess about 12:30 . . . I told some of them . . . 'I think I'm going back to the hotel, for some reason I just don't feel comfortable about this situation.'"

At 5 a.m., phones rang in the players' rooms. By 7:15 they were flying back to Tuscaloosa. Buses were waiting at the airport to take them directly to the athletic building. By early Saturday afternoon, they were at football practice.

IF YOU WANT TO START an argument, just ask an Alabama player from 1958 exactly what happened the week after the Tulane game. Some say it was the roughest week of practice of the entire season. Others say that Bryant scared them into believing he was going to "kill" them, and then took it easy.

It seems to have been a little of both. Though the written record is sketchy, the following version seems most likely.

After being flown back to Tuscaloosa so precipitously, and taken to the practice field, the players feared a punishing practice. But, as Bobby

Smith remembered, "It was Saturday, and everybody else is scouting or something. So we go in and draw out equipment, and it's sweats. I couldn't believe it. He didn't mention the Tulane game . . . we went out in sweats and he showed us some things we were going to do against Georgia Tech, a few new wrinkles."

On Sunday, according to Marlin Dyess, the players were still apprehensive. Bryant called all the players and coaches to a meeting in Foster Auditorium. "Probably after we'd been there ten minutes or so, not knowing what to expect, in street clothes . . . so we hear him, plop, plop, we hear him walking. He comes in . . . he says, 'I want you to go out and get your sweat clothes and helmets, let's go out and run a little bit, loosen up.'"

On one of those days, Bryant threw out a carrot, telling the players that if they beat Georgia Tech, he would allow them to trade four tickets to the Memphis State game for four to the Auburn game. That would mean a total of eight tickets for the Auburn game — once sold, a source of needed Christmas money.

On Monday afternoon, Bryant took out the stick.

Monday was lab day, so practice always started late. Once it did, around 5 o'clock, it was a return to the bloodlettings of the spring and early fall. Alf Van Hoose wrote in the *Birmingham News* that Alabama "yesterday and early last night in Denny Stadium went back to fundamental blocking and tackling." "I don't remember anyone carrying a football," Wayne Sims said. "All we did was just head-on-head blocking and one-on-one blocking." As Don Parsons remembered, "We had some 1 x 6 or 1 x 8 boards . . . for each pair of us, and you'd straddle those things, they were maybe 7 or 8 feet long, and one of you got on each end, and you just hit like a couple of groundhogs until one came off the end . . . and then you got up and did it again . . . that's all I remember doing all week long."

But it was what happened the next day that most of the players remember.

It was Tuesday, November 11, the 52nd recorded practice since September 1. There was nothing particularly unusual about the schedule, which called for 20 minutes toward the end of the day for the first two teams to go "full speed" against Tech goal-line formations for 20 minutes, divided between offense and defense.

But when the Red team went on defense, things did not go so well.

"Gene Stallings had the scout team," Bud Moore said, "and he said, 'Okay, it's second and 6 on the right hash mark, 6-yard line, this is what Georgia Tech's going to run.' And they run an option and score. Everybody, all the coaches, all the players, look up at the tower.

"Stallings comes back and says, 'Okay, same situation, second and 6 on the right hash mark, 6-yard line.' They run the same play and score again. That time, the chain starts rattling on the tower . . . all of the coaches start getting a little tighter and jerking us around, hollering."

The third time, the play scored again.

Bobby Jackson picks up the story.

"Gary [O'Steen] and I were on the right side, on defense, he was inside and I was outside, we were playing a 6-5 . . . Gary and I are over here [opposite the play], so we weren't concerned. They scored. They moved the ball back to the 10. I looked up and Coach Bryant was coming down, Coach Claiborne was in charge of this drill, so I said, 'Coach, Coach Bryant is yelling at you.' He didn't hear. Well, Coach Bryant, and I think it was Gary Phillips he first picked up, the guard, [he] just picked him off the ground and started yelling, 'line it up, line it up.' I was still hanging back, heck, they didn't score on us, they scored on the other side."

In Bryant's opinion, football was a team game and the freshmen were scoring on everybody out there.

Ken Roberts remembers the drill well.

"He was behind us," Roberts said, "and he started grabbing up people and started grabbing up freshmen and having one-on-one tackling practice right there. He was livid. 'You guys can't tackle, you're not hitting, you're not doing anything . . .'"

Bryant was still unhappy about Jackson's request to miss practice for a wedding. "Where's Jackson? He's been goofing off all week," the coach yelled.

As Jackson came forward, Bryant singled out freshman Benny Parrish, a huge lineman, and "we had the darndest tackling practice you ever saw," Moore said. The first person assigned to tackle Parrish was Jackson, and Jackson put him on his back. "Jackson hit old Parrish right up under the chin . . . it was not vicious but it was the best one Jackson ever hit the whole time he was in school," Moore said. "Everybody was surprised," Jackson recalled.

It was "just head on tackling, one-on-one for about two licks apiece," Roberts said. When it was over, "they gave the freshmen the ball on the 6-yard line and they were [pushed back to] the 10; and they gave them the ball on the four and four plays later they were back . . . and gave them the ball on the 2 and we stopped them on the 2, and one time they ended up back on the 20, trying to score from the 2.

"And then he looked at us and . . . kinda sneered at us and said, 'That's a little better, go on in.'"

CHAPTER NINETEEN

'Tech Will Quit'

T he head coach of Alabama's next opponent, Bobby Dodd of Georgia Tech, did not conduct a goal-line drill like the one Bryant staged at Alabama that week. Dodd didn't believe much in contact work during the season. And although Dodd did have a tall tower from which he watched his talented athletes practice, it would have been completely out of character for him to descend from it in a rush to become involved in a drill.

Dodd and Bryant were still good friends in 1958. Dodd, Bryant says in *Bear*, helped him install the T-formation at Kentucky, and gave him the Georgia Tech play book. And it was Dodd who invented the wheel-about quick-kick that Alabama had used to such advantage. A few years later, Dodd was grateful when Bryant used his reserves in the fourth quarter of a 28-14 win that might have been much worse. In later years, and especially after the Holt-Graning incident in 1961, relations between the two men became strained. Certainly, the contrast in their approach to football is stark.

Bryant's felt that "regardless of its ability, if a team wallows around all week playing drop the handkerchief and the players don't think tough or live tough, how can they be tough on Saturday?" Dodd, in his book *Bobby Dodd on Football,* says it's wise to "sometimes break up practices with touch football games, volleyball games with a football over the crossbar, foot races, punting games, touch pass scrimmages, etc."

Georgia Tech was an obvious favorite. The game was at Grant Field, Tech's home ground, and Tech had beaten Tulane and Tennessee, teams that had beaten Alabama. Tech had tied the defending national champions, Auburn, 7-7. The Engineers' record was 5-2-1, with only Alabama and Georgia left to play. Dodd and his team were thinking Gator Bowl. The Atlanta papers were almost smug in their belief in the superiority of the Tech team, which was both bigger and faster than Alabama.

Gene Stallings, assigned to scout Tech, told the players that this was "the best football team you have played this year." Three players from Alabama — center Maxie Baughan from Bessemer, halfback Cal James (Fob's brother) from Lanett, and Floyd Faucette from Brent — were prominent in the Tech lineup. Faucette, very agile for his 190 pounds, had run 54 yards for a touchdown against Clemson the week before the Alabama game. But the Alabama coaches thought Tech was vulnerable.

In a meeting with the players, Chuck Allen said, Stallings "went through the game plan and . . . went down the roster of players . . . and every player on their team was bigger, faster and better than we were." But Stallings finished his report this way. "I'm going to tell you how to win this game," he said. "Georgia Tech will quit. Sometime during the ball game they will quit. It may be early, it may be late, but there'll be a time that they'll quit."

In the game plan, one "wrinkle" the coaches had installed was a counter trap play designed to take advantage of the aggressiveness of the Tech line. During the week, Mack Wise, who had graded 81 on 16 offensive plays against Tulane, ran the play again and again.

On his television show following the Tulane game, Bryant had said that if the team could win two out of three of its remaining games, it would "deserve a place in heaven." Then, early in the week, captain Bobby Smith got a letter with an Atlanta postmark. In the envelope was a small powder puff and a short, sassy note — something to the effect of "don't forget your powder puffs when you come to Atlanta, girls." Smith put it on the bulletin board, and the next day there was another similar one beside it. No one knows who sent them but they didn't hurt the Crimson Tide's determination.

Things could not have been more perfect when Jesse Outlar wrote in his column Saturday morning in the *Atlanta Constitution* that "a team without superior speed is apt to spend a long afternoon at Grant Field." Outlar predicted that Tech would win easily, 21-0, and Bryant made sure every Alabama player had a copy of the clipping before the pre-game meeting.

As Fred Sington remembers it, when the Alabama players returned to the dressing room after their preliminary workouts, Bryant did not come in.

"Coach Bryant doesn't show up," Sington said. "He's not there. And the officials come in and say, 'We've gotta have the captains, three minutes until toss of the coin.' And they walk out, and about that time Coach Bryant walks in and he says, 'Captains, if we win the toss, take the wind.' There was a wind blowing North to South. 'If we win the toss, take the wind, if they win the toss, take the wind, we want them to have the football.' And he got up to go out and . . . he said, 'Wait a minute. Gentlemen,' he said, 'I want to tell you one thing. You lose this football game and you'll think last week was a piece of cake.'"

Then Bryant collared Mack Wise, who had practiced on the Red team all week, and who had been told he would start the game. "If we start on defense, I'll let Morrison start," he said. Wise, pumped to the gills, was crushed.

What he missed was one of the great quarters of football in Alabama history.

Alabama won the toss, took the wind and kicked off. By the time Ronnie Lewis was stopped at the 20, three Alabama players were hurt. Dave Sington got kicked in the knee; Don Cochran, pushed over backward, strained his back; and Walter Sansing twisted his bum knee.

Jim Goostree came onto the field and told Cochran: "Y'all are going to have to decide who's going out." Cochran stayed in the game. Both Sington and Sansing were taken off, but Sington soon returned and all three played almost the entire game.

Georgia Tech's James ran twice, gaining 6 and then losing 3 when he dropped the ball, was missed by Baxter Booth, but struck by Cochran.

Then Tech had its first disaster. On a sweep, Tech's right halfback, Frank Nix, let a pitchout from Fred Braselton slip through his hands. He picked the ball up and eluded a hard-charging Norbie Ronsonet, but then lost it for good when caught by Gary Phillips and Dave Sington. Booth came out of the pileup with the ball at the Tech 21.

Alabama immediately went to the trap it had specially prepared for the game. Morrison slashed for 8, and then for 10 to the Tech 3. O'Steen got 2, and Jackson, as Morrison recalled, "ran a 24 dive and he didn't hand off and I knocked the safety down and he stepped into the end zone . . . stood up for a touchdown." Jackson also benefited from surging blocks by Cochran and Sington. Pete Reaves, replacing the injured Fred Sington, kicked the extra point, and the Tide led, 7-0.

Alabama kicked off, and Morrison, the sprint man on the kickoff, eluded a "big joker" and unloaded on Faucette who got up yelling, "Whose man was that, whose man was that?" Tech had replaced Braselton with Walter Howard, and he got the Engineers a first down in three plays. But on third and 6 from the Tech 34, Howard floated a pass toward halfback Joe DeLany that soared high. Morrison, behind the play, picked the ball off around midfield and raced back to the Tech 15. When an offside penalty stalled the drive, Bryant again called on Reaves. The kick went straight through, and Alabama led 10-0 with just seven minutes gone in the quarter.

Alabama kicked off again, and went to its second team on defense, but it didn't help Tech, whose nightmare continued. On second and 9 from the Tech 21, Howard fumbled the snap and Butch Frank dived in to dig the ball out. With Bobby Smith at quarterback, two plays failed to gain and Alabama was penalized back to the 26 when O'Steen moved before the snap. It looked as if this time Tech would hold. But Bryant reinserted Jackson, who slid to the right to pass, got a block from O'Steen that got him as far as the 10 and then another one from little Dyess that gained him 3 more. One play later, he went wide again in the other direction, juked the Tech defenders, and stepped inside the flag for the touchdown. The extra point by Reaves made it 17-0.

The score did not seem credible. Late arrivals at Grant Field, laughing uneasily, assumed the scoreboard was in error. Benny Marshall got this note from an editor watching the ticker: "Alabama-Tech first period score comes 17-0. That correct?"

As the game continued, the Alabama players' awe of Bryant grew. His rampage during the goal line drills of the previous Tuesday began to look like precognition. Alabama was fighting for its life in the same goal line defenses he had emphasized.

The first crisis came early in the second quarter when O'Steen fumbled a fair catch and Tech recovered at the Tide 14. On fourth and 2, Braselton lofted a pass toward Jerome Green in the end zone. Bobby Smith made the defensive play of his career, leaping at the goal line to snag the ball with one hand and running out to the Alabama 34.

Soon, the Engineers began another drive, and with a mixture of passes and strong running by Faucette and Lester Simerville arrived at the Alabama 7 with a first down. Alabama went into its goal line defense, and stopped Simerville after a yard. On second and 6, Pete Reaves penetrated to hit Howard early, and Faucette had to dive on his pitchout, losing 2. Then it was Cochran's turn, chasing Howard and batting his pass away behind the line. On fourth down, it was Smith again, breaking up a pass in the end zone.

At halftime, Sington and Sansing had their knees taped. When the players were seated around the dressing room, Bryant went to each player and reached out to shake hands, looking directly into their eyes: "I want the best you can give," he said, with great intensity, "the very best you can give."

When he reached Mack Wise, who still had not played, he pulled back his hand.

The best was required almost immediately when the same situation that Alabama had taken advantage of in the first quarter occurred in reverse. On the second play of the second half, Jackson fumbled and Tech had the ball at the Alabama 27.

In three plays, including a 15-yard run by Faucette, it was first down at the 2. There would be many legendary goal line stands in Bryant's history at Alabama. This was one of the best.

Faucette got the first carry, the same play that had just gained 15, and got only 1. Howard tried to sneak left, and was short by inches. "The ball was so close to the goal line that the goal line was under my wrist," Ken Roberts remembered. "The only things that were out of the end zone were my hands."

Tech tried fullback Marvin Tibbetts, and O'Steen and Wesley stopped him short. On a fourth down sneak by Howard, the defensive summary said only "GREAT." Alabama took over at the 3.

O'Steen punted out, and on its next thrust Tech finally scratched out a touchdown behind the running of Cal James. The touchdown itself was fluky — a third-down fumble by James, perhaps intentional, that rolled into the end zone and was covered by tackle Billy Shaw. Braselton passed to Gerald Burch for a two-point conversion, and it was 17-8.

Tech failed in three plays on its next possession, and Morrison intercepted a pass on third and 25 when they got the ball back again. It was early in the fourth quarter by then, and the Alabama offense consumed some time when Jackson ran for 11 and then tossed a pass to Jerre Brannen for 11 more. When the drive died at the 21, Tech tried two passes that failed, and then ran a draw to the fullback. Roberts, playing perhaps his finest game, had the defensive assignment. "I can remember thinking, your brain just working like mad, thinking . . . if I miss him, we're in trouble . . . they told you a hundred times, keep your eyes open and your head up and get down, and I can remember just focusing in and in and in, watching this guy coming and looking at the numbers, because when you tackle somebody . . . you can't look at heads, you look at the numbers, they go where the guy is going . . ." Roberts stuffed the play.

Desperate, Tech tried to pass again from deep within its own territory. When Wesley intercepted a pass by Braselton and returned it to the 14, fans of the Ramblin' Wreck headed for the aisles. Alabama ran seven plays and failed to score on fourth and 2, but no one cared. Alabama had won four games, as many as it had in the three previous years, and no win could have been sweeter. Bryant presented the game ball to Pete Reaves, for his outstanding defensive play and for the field goal. Flying home to Tuscaloosa, the head coach led the singing.

Everyone took part but Cochran, who rode home on the floor of the DC-3, flat on his painfully sore back.

The following week, manager Bert Jones found a note asking him to see Coach Bryant. In the coach's office, Bryant said, "Do the players know we have a chance to go to a bowl game? How would they feel about going to a bowl game?"

Jones was unprepared. "Are you kidding?" he asked.

The response did not suit Bryant. "I didn't call your ass in here to joke with you," he said. "I want you to tell me what the players feel about going to a bowl game."

"Coach, it's the furthest thing from their minds," Jones told Bryant. "They're just trying to survive. One more day."

"That's what I need to know," Bryant said, and Jones was dismissed.

Coaches Grading Sheet after the Georgia Tech Game

	OFFENSE							DEFENSE						
	Plays	Plus	Minus	U	%	RBI	Error	Plays	Plus	Minus	U	%	RBI	Error
Roberts	39	19	11	9	63		1	54	13	10	31	57		3
Blevins	14	9	5		64		1	21	3	6	12	33		1
O'Steen	42	16	5	21	62			50	5	4	40	50		1
White	11	6	2	3	75		1	14			14			
Sington, D.	41	18	14	9	56			61	18	11	32	62	2	
Allen	17	6	5	6	54			22	8	5	9	61		
Reaves	21	9	4	8	69	1		48	15	12	21	56	1	
Hannah	23	4	11	8	23			21	12	4	5	75		
Ronsonet	27	12	9	6	57			45	12	7	26	63		
Brannen	32	14	10	8	58		2	33	5	3	25	62		1
Cochran	38	25	12	2	67			51	36	7	9	85	4	
Parsons	15	7	7	1	50			16	8	5	3	61		
Phillips	32	20	7	5	74		3	43	20	12	11	62	1	
Sims	17	8	8	1	50		1	36	13	10	13	56	2	1
Booth	36	14	11	11	56		1	53	15	4	35	79	2	1
Gray	24	9	9	6	50		2	30	7	4	21	64		1
Sansing	12	5	2	5	71			17	7	5	5	58		2
Wesley	40	10	5	25	67		2	56	18	14	24	56	1	2
Frank	6	1	1	4	50		1	8	3	4	1	43	1	
Jackson	40	29	11	0	73	2	1	44	3	2	39	60		1
Smith	13	7	6	0	54			18	3	2	13	60	2	
Morrison	37	14	5	19	74			45	11	5	29	69	3	
Dyess	11	6	3	2	66			2	-	-	2	-		
Stapp	2	1	0	0	100			19	2	1	16	66		
Valletto	12	3	3	6	50			9	5	1	3	83		

Plus: Completed assignment

Minus: Failed in assisgnment

U: Not involved in play

% = (plus) divided by (plus+minus)

RBI: Caused something good to happen (from baseball's "run batted in")

Error: Caused something bad to happen (from baseball's fielding mistake)

CHAPTER TWENTY

A Winning Season

I t is a time-honored tradition in college football to schedule a patsy the week before a big game. In 1958, there was a new opponent, Memphis State.

The Tigers had a rookie coach, Billy (Spook) Murphy, and had been no better than mediocre during the season, winning four and losing four. The defeats were to Ole Miss, Tennessee Tech, Southern Mississippi and The Citadel, an undistinguished lot. That did not prevent the Alabama coaches from pointing out that State had beaten Chattanooga, and that Chattanooga had beaten Tennessee and that Tennessee had beaten Alabama.

As it turned out, the Tigers did not have a chance. The Alabama scouts had noticed a weakness in the secondary, and had a plan to take advantage of it.

Alabama received the opening kickoff, and Bryant told Bobby Jackson: "If you get the ball past the 35, fake a counter and throw to Scooter." The runback got only to the 32, but Jackson decided that was close enough.

"I faked to the halfback and pulled up, stepped back . . . I hung it," Jackson said. Dyess was way behind the secondary, and he had to stop and wait for the ball to arrive. Once it did, he was off. It was a 69-yard touchdown play, the longest of the season. Pete Reaves try for the extra point was blocked, but Alabama led 6-0 only seconds into the game.

198

Gooby Stapp's punting set up a second Alabama touchdown in the second quarter, backing State up inside its 10. O'Steen returned the ensuing punt to the Tiger 38. Penalties were a problem for Alabama all day, and one here nullified an 18-yard pass completion by Jackson to O'Steen. But the two tried it again on the next play, and O'Steen reached the State 24. Dyess gained 6, and then Jackson faked a hand off up the middle and got free. He ran into a mass of bodies around the goal line, but forced his way in for a touchdown.

Reaves came in to try the extra point, but on the sidelines Bryant had given his instructions: "Run it," he said. The team had practiced a fake kick, in which the holder was supposed to pull the ball away and run for the corner. But by the time the play was called, Alabama had dithered for too long and got a penalty for delay of game.

Jackson didn't think the fake kick would work from the 8. "Pete, take your kicking tee and flank to the right," he directed, and called an option. "Lord have mercy, what have I done," Jackson thought, knowing that Bryant would blister him if he failed. But the play worked. Jackson scored, it was 14-0, and there it remained.

Memphis State gained only 140 yards all day, and never got inside the Alabama 17. The Tide had twice as many yards, not too bad when you consider that they were mindful of Auburn scouts and displayed nothing new offensively. Still, the State defense was frustrating to Bryant, who berated Ken Roberts roundly on the sidelines.

"They had a linebacker, and he was good . . . we couldn't block this guy all day long," Roberts said. "Coach Bryant was mad at me because I was supposed to block him, but I couldn't get to him, the guards were pinching down on the center. When that happens, the guard is supposed to come through and pick the linebacker up. We weren't doing that and Coach Bryant was absolutely livid . . . this guy was making every tackle from sideline to sideline and I can remember Coach Bryant on the sideline saying, 'Y'all can't block that so-and-so, he's better than any football player we've got. I'd swap him for any of you guys.' I mean he was livid."

After the game, Bryant said he thought Memphis State was "better prepared than we were," but the win was precious. It was the first time since 1953 that Alabama had won as many as five games and it assured a winning season no matter what happened against Auburn.

There was a party for the team at the Stafford Hotel after the game, hosted by a tuxedo-clad Bryant and a happy Mary Harmon. Bobby Smith had suggested to the coach that the players would appreciate having a place to go and enjoy themselves together in a more restrained atmosphere than that offered on fraternity row. Bryant thought it was a good idea, and he told Smith that he thought that he could get Guy Lombardo's orchestra to play. "Talk to some of the players and see if they like that," he told Smith. It took all of Smith's diplomatic skills to tell Bryant a few days later that Guy Lombardo was not exactly, well, making any hit records just then. "Coach Bryant just died laughing," Smith said. He got a band that suited the players better, using the money accumulated in the "profanity fund" to cover the costs.

Practices the following week were placid by Bryant standards. The Red team spent some time trying to perfect a trick play, called the Bum-a-rooski, that the head coach thought might work against the aggressive Auburn defense. Conceived by Bryant's old Texas chum Bum Phillips, the play was designed for the speed of Scooter Dyess and a fake quick-kick.

In the Alabama quick-kick, the center snapped the ball through the quarterback's legs directly to the halfback. In the Bum-a-rooski, the snap went instead to the fullback. While the halfback whirled and pretended to kick, the fullback slipped the ball between the legs to Dyess, who sidled up right behind the left tackle in what was supposed to look like a blocking position. Scooter was directed to wait a count or two while the defense reacted to the fake, and then light out for the end zone. In practice, the play looked good.

CHAPTER TWENTY -ONE

' . . . That Close'

I t seems strange, but before 1958 no Paul Bryant team had ever played Auburn and Bryant himself had never suited up against the Tigers. There's little doubt that in his first year at Alabama Bryant still regarded Tennessee as his major personal rival. "He didn't like Auburn, but he knew domination of Auburn was the key to steady improvement," Fred Sington, Jr., said. "But he hated Tennessee. Hated 'em."

If Bryant did not yet hate Auburn with the requisite ferocity, he understood the intensity of the cross-state rivalry. A win would have been a sensational achievement that brought with it a significant bowl bid, either the Gator or Cotton Bowl. Auburn, after all, was ranked second in the nation after winning the national championship in the previous year. The Tigers were riding the crest of success under Ralph (Shug) Jordan.

An Auburn alumnus and D-Day veteran, Jordan had been a tonic for Auburn football. Hired in 1951, he took over a team that had not had a winning season in 17 years. His first team beat favored Vanderbilt in its opening game and went 5-5. Between 1954 and the Alabama game in 1958, Jordan's teams had won 41, lost only 6, and tied once. Entering the game against Alabama, the Tigers had not lost a game since the middle of 1956 — 22 consecutive games.

In the series with Alabama, resumed in 1948, Auburn held a 12-9-1 lead. Alabama had scored only one touchdown against Auburn in the last four years, and had lost four straight. Yet everything on the Plains was not rosy. The Tigers were on probation as a result of the infamous Don Fuell case and therefore ineligible for a bowl game. It had not helped that the only blemish on the 1958 schedule was a tie with Georgia Tech, whose coach, Bobby Dodd, made no bones about having turned Auburn in to the NCAA over the recruiting of Fuell.

Auburn had excellent athletes, and it had a lot of them. At quarterback, left-handed Lloyd Nix had led 19 consecutive wins and had never started in a losing game. Nix had a sore shoulder and was not expected to play much. His backup, stork-like Richard Wood, looked awkward but was an effective passer. Auburn was deep at halfback. Senior Tommy Lorino was ending a great career with over 1,400 career yards rushing, but was suffering from a dislocated shoulder. Jimmy Laster had scored three times on pass plays of over 40 yards. Halfback Bobby Lauder, the best athlete to come out of Foley until Snake Stabler came along, had caught a 44-yard touchdown pass and had run 20 yards for another TD. Little Jimmy Pettus was quick off the ball.

Guard Zeke Smith and center Jackie Burkett would both make All-American in 1958. Senior end Jerry Wilson was All-SEC. And there were more — Ken Rice, an All-American in 1959, at 245 pounds; tackle Teddy Foret, end Bobby Wasden, fullbacks Jimmy Reynolds and Ed Dyas. In the line, Auburn outweighed Alabama by 25 pounds a man, and they had six tackles who each played about the same amount of time. Not surprisingly, having had their way with Alabama for so long, the Auburn players and coaches were somewhat complacent about the game. "You know when you beat a team over the years, you just feel like you own them," Lorino, now in the office equipment business in Birmingham, said.

Game day was bright and sunny, but the field was sloppy from rain the previous week and from high school activity. Every seat at Legion Field — 44,000 — was filled.

Alabama received the kickoff, and tried the Bum-a-rooski in its first series. On third and 9, Roberts snapped directly to Wesley, who slipped the ball to Dyess and peeled off to the right with everybody else. Dyess, crouched behind Dave Sington, waited for a count, and then ran. But Auburn end Mike Simmons had stayed home, and he swatted the Scooter to the ground before he had gained a yard. "If Dyess had waited one second longer, we'd of scored on the play," Dave Sington said. "The guy just didn't run by fast enough."

So much for trick plays.

Auburn's kicking game, perhaps the only area of the game in which the Tigers were thought to be inferior, led to an Auburn touchdown. Lorino's punt from midfield went out of bounds on the Alabama 3, and when Alabama quick-kicked a few downs later, Auburn began to move from its 47.

Two plays gained 4, and Nix ran for 8 and a first down at the Alabama 43, reinjuring his shoulder. The gawky Wood replaced him and he immediately handed to Pettus, playing more on offense because of the injury to Lorino. He gained 16 up the middle when Wesley took the wrong angle and got blocked. A Wood pass to Leo Sexton covered 15 and reached the Alabama 9 with a first down. On third and 3, Wood drew O'Steen toward the middle with play action and flipped the ball to Pettus wide open on the left side in the end zone. Dyas converted, and it was 7-0 with only half the first quarter gone.

Alabama's aggressive defense created three turnovers and kept Auburn bottled up for most of the quarter, but the Tide was unable to make the opportunities count. The most serious threat came after a Nix fumble.

On the first play of the quarter, the left-hander ran wide to pass, but was forced deep by Baxter Booth and Cochran and lost the ball on a fumble to Dave Sington. Almost immediately, Jackson employed the little delay pass that Auburn had not prepared for. As Drake Keith described it, the line would "hold one side and the other side was a draw, you let them through and . . . just put it out there . . . almost like a screen/draw type of thing." Morrison caught this one, reaching the Auburn 21, and then O'Steen ran for 7 more to the Tiger 14.

Jerry Wilson, the big end from Birmingham, spoiled things after that, penetrating to force a wild pitchout by Jackson that lost 6 and then sacking the quarterback for a loss of 12 to the 33. There was no one on either team who could kick a 50-yard field goal, so O'Steen punted into the end zone.

Later, another delay pass from Jackson to Morrison got the Tide 20 yards to the Auburn 34, but Baxter Booth couldn't handle a Jackson pass on fourth and 5 and the ball went over. Late in the quarter, an interception by O'Steen and then another by Bobby Smith on a ball tipped by O'Steen frustrated Auburn's offense. At the half it was 7-0.

Auburn scored again near the end of the third period, again taking advantage of a Lorino punt that forced Alabama back to its 1-yard line. But it wasn't easy.

After Stapp punted out to the Auburn 42, Auburn drove to a first down deep in Alabama territory, keyed by a 17-yard burst by Pettus and a tremendous catch by Lauder on an 18-yard rifle shot from Wood. It was first down at the Tide 2, and another chance for the first team to practice the lessons learned after the Tulane game. Dyas dug out a yard. Lauder failed to gain. Wood again tried the fullback but didn't penetrate. Finally, Wood flipped a pass toward Pettus that fell incomplete, and Alabama had held.

Stapp again punted, this time to the Alabama 39, and this time Auburn wouldn't be denied. The big play was a 24-yard pass from Wood to Joe Leichtnam that reached the Tide 13. Then 6 yards by Pettus and 6 more by Nix got a first down on the one, and finally Reynolds bulled over Wesley into the end zone. The conversion made it 14-0, and as it had in the losses to Tennessee and Tulane, Alabama had fallen two touchdowns behind.

Again, the two touchdown deficit seemed to be a signal to the Alabama offense and the Tide controlled the fourth quarter. Part of the reason was Alabama's superior conditioning, which began to take effect despite Auburn's greater depth. Part of it was chicanery that took Jerry Wilson out of the game.

First, Alabama gained better field position when Dyess returned the kickoff following the touchdown to the Alabama 36. A few plays later, Walter Sansing broke free over the middle.

Sansing, whose injured knee had been a constant worry, had been running well, and on this play he believes he could have scored. "I remember breaking into the open, and there was one guy between me and the goal," he said. "I made one little move and that knee . . . nobody even touched me. It sounded like you broke a chicken leg or something." Sansing had gained 17 and Alabama had a first down at the Auburn 22. A pass to Marlin Dyess gained 5 more, but then a holding penalty stalled the drive, and O'Steen went back to punt.

Alabama had been employing a "whirlwind" on Wilson, using the end and then a linebacker to prevent him from peeling back and blocking on the Tiger punt return. "As soon as the end hit him, the linebacker would get up and hit him again," said Ken Roberts.

On this play, according to Roberts, Baxter Booth did more than just hit Wilson. "Baxter had his shoulders into his waist and was kinda holding him at the line of scrimmage," Roberts said.

"Oh, this is great, Baxter's got him set up," Roberts thought.

"I went across to hit him," he said, "and missed him, so when I missed him, I backed up and hit him with an elbow across the head. And Baxter's holding him and he is just screaming."

Soon Wilson, naturally combative anyway, fought back. "He went ballistic," Roberts said, "he just jumped straight up in the air . . . and he took a swing at me, and that's what the official saw, and threw him out of the ball game." The loss was a blow to Auburn's defense: "He was a great defensive end," Lorino said, "there was no way they were going to get anything going on that side of the field, there was no way, with him in the game."

Backed up by the 15-yard penalty, Auburn punted and Alabama began to move. Red Stickney had replaced Sansing, and he and O'Steen gained a first down in three plays to the Auburn 31.

Jackson again called the delay pass, and slipping past Haywood Worrick, Dyess gained 16 to the Auburn 15. Then it was Stickney in the middle for 6 to the 9.

Alabama had a play called the Special 8, a fake trap up the middle and a quick pitch to Dyess, and Jackson had already called the play when a messenger came from Bryant with the same call. With Wilson out, the play worked to perfection and Dyess scored easily in the right corner.

Bryant decided to go for two. Jackson sprinted out to the right where Wilson would have been, and got immediate pursuit. Then he spotted Gary O'Steen who, coming from left halfback, had found no one to block and was idling alone in the end zone. Jackson pitched him the ball, and as Benny Marshall wrote it the next day in the *Birmingham News,* "suddenly the whole complexion of the wintry afternoon had changed."

Auburn did not fold. First they claimed an onside kick by Stickney and then Nix ran three option plays, gaining 6, 6 and 16 yards and a first down at the Alabama 28. But on the fourth try, Nix got pressure from Carl Valletto and Lorino fumbled after taking a pitchout.

A few minutes earlier, Don Cochran had felt the strings in his shoulder pads break. Waving his hands, Cochran signaled the coaches and yelled to trainer Jim Goostree that he needed to come out to repair his equipment. Goostree ignored him. There was no way Alabama could spare Cochran at this point. So now Cochran recovered the football, and Alabama had the ball and a chance to win with 3:56 to go.

Stickney took a handoff, fumbled, recovered, and gained 3 yards. Again Jackson found Dyess on the little delay pass, and the play went for 17. The two ran the play again, this time for only 4, and the little halfback was shaken up. Mack Wise replaced Dyess and caught another Jackson pass for a first down at the Tiger 42.

From there, on third and 9, Alabama ran the play that for ever after was the catch that might have been. Perhaps hopeful that the short passing game had brought the Auburn secondary up, Bryant sent Jerry Spruiell in with a long pass play.

"I remember being so anxious and nervous about the play that I slipped coming off the line," Spruiell said. "I finally got down in the end zone, it seemed like forever for the play to develop. Bobby Jackson was scrambling to keep from being sacked and finally he got it off."

Astride the 50, Jackson threw the ball as far as he could. Defending, Lamar Rawson had let Spruiell get behind him near the goal line. A classic photo by Robert Adams from the *Birmingham News* the next day

Jerry Spruiell (l) leaps for a pass in the end zone against Auburn. Lamar Rawson tipped the ball and it fell incomplete.

showed both players fully extended, Rawson's left hand in the path of the ball, Spruiell reaching with both hands.

"It was a long high lob," Spruiell said, "and we were kinda jostling one another for position . . . the ball was coming down and we both went up . . . I believe he tipped it, because I believe the ball hit me just on the inside of my left forearm."

As Jackson remembered, "It wasn't his fault, Lord have mercy . . . he

Bobby Jackson watches the final minutes of the Auburn game.

was cold . . . he had no way of catching the ball . . . but it was that close." As Spruiell fell to the ground, the ball seemed to follow him down and a hush fell over the entire crowd until Auburn fans saw the ball rolling free.

That wasn't quite the end. Jackson ran the delay pass again, to Wise, and got the first down at the Auburn 28 with a minute and a half left. But from there, frustration set in. Jackson was sacked and then penalized. He completed another short pass to Wise and was penalized again for grounding the ball to stop the clock. On fourth down, he missed on a pass to Charlie Tom Gray, and Auburn had won.

In the dressing room after the game, a disconsolate Jerry Spruiell was sitting on a bench near his locker. Bryant squatted down in front of the young end and put his hand on his knee. "You tried," he said. "There'll be another day."

Bryant spoke to the players quietly and said he was proud of them. "You played as hard as I believe you could, and we came awfully close," he said. "I'll make one vow. It will be the last time we lose to those sonsabitches ever again." In fact, Auburn did not score a touchdown on Alabama for four years and won only once in the next ten years.

Having threatened, chastised, berated, challenged, belittled and driven his players unmercifully for 11 months, Bryant was solicitous and perhaps even grateful to his seniors after the Auburn game. Told at the beginning that they would have to be twice as good as anyone else to play, eight seniors had stuck it out and become the foundation of the first Alabama winning season in their careers. Five — Bobby Jackson, Dave Sington, Baxter Booth, Charlie Tom Gray, and Ken Roberts — had started against Auburn. The remaining three — John Paul Poole, Pete Reaves, and Bobby Smith — had played often and contributed often.

Bryant invited all eight to appear on his television show the Sunday after the Auburn game, awkwardly asking them questions about their memories and their plans. Their college careers were over, and he wrote each of them a check for $50 as pay for the TV appearance, saying "It's time you earned some money." Later, he and Mary Harmon served them steak and shrimp at a party at their home.

The loss to Auburn had ended any chance at a major bowl. But back in Louisville, a group of businessmen had put together enough money to sponsor the first Bluegrass Bowl, and they wanted Alabama. Bryant, his Kentucky ties still strong, was thinking about it. At an impromptu press conference Saturday night at the Pick-Bankhead Hotel in Birmingham, he told the media that "the players have already voted to accept an invitation if offered."

Nobody remembers much about a vote, and the players were divided. Many were hoping fervently that the team would stay home, feeling that Bryant would use the extra practice to prepare for the next year. "We sweated it out," said Charlie Gray, who was engaged to be married on December 20 and had no wish to be practicing football.

Finally, Bryant called Dave Sington and Bobby Smith and told them his decision. The bowl organizers had declined to provide the players a jacket or a watch, he said, and Bryant felt that "if they're not going to treat the players right, there's no sense going up there." Furthermore, the opponent was going to be Florida State and Alabama would "have to work on those formations and everything." So Alabama stayed home for the only time in Bryant's career at the Capstone.

"The first beer I ever drank in my life," Gray said, "was Monday when we got the word . . . A bunch of us decided to celebrate. Tuscaloosa was a dry county, the nearest place you could go was a honky-tonk down at Knoxville, at a place called Nick's, down toward Eutaw, just over the Greene County line."

"I think that was the biggest celebration we had," Mack Wise said.

DESPITE MISSING A BOWL GAME, Bryant had exceeded almost everyone's expectations but his own. Still, he must have not been completely unhappy when he reflected on his accomplishments in his first year at Alabama.

His strategic approach to the season had been masterful. Lacking skilled offensive athletes, he had played the most conservative offense imaginable, and placed his bets on defense. His use of the kicking game, especially the quick-kick, had been brilliant. Alabama had given up more yards rushing and more yards passing than its opponents. But with its manic defensive intensity, the Tide had not yielded a touchdown play longer than 11 yards. No opponent had scored more than 14 points and the biggest margin of loss was by 10 points to LSU, the national champions.

Bryant's intolerance for mistakes and turnovers was a major factor in the team's relative success. In Whitworth's final year, Alabama quarterbacks had 17 passes intercepted. Bryant's first team lost only 8 passes to interception, and his defenders had taken away 18. The total turnover ratio, 33:18 in favor of opponents under Whitworth in 1957, improved to 31:18 in favor of Alabama under Bryant.

There were other accomplishments. Bryant had started to make improvements in the University's neglected athletic facilities. Ultimately, he would turn the Alabama infrastructure into a showplace, and a real asset in recruiting.

Winning five games was not the most important thing. Indeed, the team might have won more games had Bryant shown more patience with some of the young men who were slow to adapt to his approach. But then he wouldn't have been who he was. It is true that some individuals had suffered, and that some had been treated unfairly. So what. Through example, consistency and an uncompromising emphasis on his basic principles, Bryant had excised the drift and malaise that had plagued the Alabama program.

The turnaround was complete.

EPILOGUE

Alabama football teams under Bryant continued to improve in 1959 and 1960. Younger, more talented athletes were coming aboard, but a number of players from the group who first encountered Bryant in that fateful meeting in December 1957 made significant contributions in those seasons.

Bobby Skelton returned to the team in 1959, and sharing time with sophomore Pat Trammell, threw touchdown passes in wins over Houston, Chatttanooga, Mississippi State, Tulane and Auburn in a 7-1-2 season. Fred Sington, invited back by Bryant solely as a place kicking specialist under liberalized substitution rules, kicked winning field goals against Houston and Georgia Tech but missed one that would have broken a 7-7 tie with Tennessee. Duff Morrison intercepted a pass against Memphis State that led to a touchdown, and Tommy White, playing regularly at halfback, got off an 81-yard punt, fifth longest in Alabama history, in the same game.

Against Auburn, Skelton's pass went to Marlin Dyess, co-captain that year with Jim Blevins. Jerry Claiborne had spotted a weakness in the Auburn defense and designed a play that put Dyess at split end, one-on-one with a defensive back, when the Tigers ran a certain defense. In the second quarter, with Alabama leading 3-0, Auburn left the flank unguarded. Skelton flipped the ball to Dyess, and the little halfback streaked by the coverage for a 39-yard touchdown — a fitting cap to his career. Gary O'Steen, moved to fullback, was the team's second leading ground gainer and primary punter. Gooby Stapp also punted and played some at quarterback.

Invited to the inaugural Liberty Bowl at the end of the 1959 season, the Alabama seniors were unenthusiastic. As Wayne Sims remembered it, "We didn't have but seven or eight seniors and he called us in and wanted to know if we wanted to go to a bowl game . . . . It's my recollection that we voted not to go to a bowl game . . . the next day it says in the paper, 'Bama seniors choose Liberty Bowl.'"

Bryant called the players back into a meeting, Sims says, and told the players, "I know you didn't want to go but the school needs it, our recruiting program needs it, so we're going up north, we're going to play the Yankees, they're big, they're slow and they don't like to hit."

"So . . . I was going to go up there and show those folks how a country boy from Columbiana could [play] . . . because Coach Bryant had done told me they were big, slow and didn't like to hit.

"Damn, they snapped that ball on the first drive and I got up about 15 yards down the field looking out the earhole, grass everywhere. Walked over there to the huddle and told Blevins, 'Blevins, he's lied to us again.' They liked to beat us to death . . . they only beat us 7-0 but they physically whipped us all over the field . . . they did me, I guess everybody else was getting the same treatment . . ." *

In 1960, with a dozen players left from the 1958 team, Alabama went 8-1-2, losing only to Tennessee and tying Texas, 3-3, in the Bluebonnet Bowl. The season highlight was the 16-15 comeback win over Georgia Tech, and again Bobby Skelton played a big part, leading the drive for a second touchdown and passing the team into position for Richard O'Dell's winning field goal.

Only Jap Patton, Jack Rutledge and Duff Morrison, all redshirted in previous seasons, appeared on the roster of the 1961 team that went 11-0 and allowed only 25 points to be scored against it all year. By then, Bryant's Alabama program was in full bloom, flush with quality athletes — such as Pat Trammell, Mike Fracchia, and Lee Roy Jordan — and imbued with the kind of spirit the coach demanded.

---

*After the season, Sims had an offer to play professional football and stopped by to ask Bryant if he thought Sims was good enough. "Wayne, no," he said. "You wouldn't have played for me if I'da had anybody."

In the years that followed the Bryant record grew and his legend burgeoned. But the years were not without controversy.

In 1961, Alabama linebacker Darwin Holt, protecting a punt receiver, caught Georgia Tech halfback Chick Graning with a forearm. The blow fractured Graning's cheek bones, broke out several teeth, and knocked him unconscious. The incident blew into a cause celebré. Georgia newspaper writers accused Bryant of teaching brutal football.

The following October, Furman Bisher, sports editor of the *Atlanta Journal,* repeated the charge of brutality in an article in the *Saturday Evening Post,* and Bryant sued for libel. The next spring, an even more sensational article appeared in the *Post,* accusing Bryant and Wally Butts, then athletic director at Georgia, of conspiring to fix the opening game of the 1962 season.

Bryant again sued, and when the case went to trial, skewered the ill-prepared defense offered by the publisher. James Kirby, whose book *Fumble* gives a full and revealing account of the entire scandal, said that Bryant was "the single most awesome figure this writer has ever seen in a courtroom, including lawyers and judges." Bryant won the suit, eventually settling for $300,000.

While immensely painful to Bryant, the scandal caused barely a ripple in Alabama's football success. The Tide won national championships in 1964 and 1965, and went undefeated in 1966, when Notre Dame won the title. There were some lesser years — Alabama won only six games in both 1969 and 1970 — but Bryant displayed his resiliency by turning to the wishbone offense and winning another national championship in 1973. Two more national titles came in 1978 and 1979. By the time he retired after the 1982 season, Bryant had coached 232 Alabama victories, against only 46 losses.

Bryant often cracked that he would probably "croak in a week" if he quit coaching. As it was, he lived less than a month after the final win over Illinois. Worn out by the years of stress, the smoking, and the whisky, he collapsed on January 25, 1983. The next day he died at Druid City Hospital. State Police estimated that 100,000 people lined the highway between Tuscaloosa and Birmingham as the funeral cortege passed.

You can get a great many answers from associates and former players about what made Bryant successful, but in the end, like all great men, he was a man of such complexity and inner contradiction that he defies easy analysis. Jim Goostree, who worked for Bryant for more than 30 years, subscribes to the theory (attributed to Furman Bisher) that "Paul Bryant was a man of many moods . . . he could turn them off and on in a matter of seconds; he was a Jekyll and Hyde." It would not be hard to use Bryant's own words from his autobiography to indict him for being reckless with the well-being, both physical and emotional, of the young men he first met in December 1957. But, paradoxically, by far most of the young men who first encountered him then believe that by enduring the ordeal they gained a sense of self-esteem that has served them well throughout their lives. "After we grew up to a degree," Bud Moore said, "we realized that he was doing for us. At the time we questioned it, of course . . . a lot of good players, or average players like myself, thought about quitting, even talked about it . . . I wouldn't take anything in the world for it . . . because that struck the match that allowed me to go and do some things I wouldn't have been capable of doing. I'd probably have been back in Bug Tussle on my daddy's farm."

"There was more to him than just a slave driver," Gary Phillips observed. "He made you respect yourself and in so doing you respected him."

Those who stayed developed a growing sense of pride that they had been present at the beginning of Bryant's remarkable career at Alabama. "I feel especially gifted," Red Stickney said, " . . . like it was a dream that made my whole life . . . Alabama's been so much a part of me . . . to this day, people say, 'You played for Coach Bryant,' and . . . you're proud of it, it gives you dignity . . ."

The distinction of simply having been there was impressive to others, as well. Richard Strum was with an army general one night in St. Louis and ran into Gene Stallings, then coaching the St. Louis Cardinals. Strum introduced Stallings to the general, who was impressed when Stallings said, "Listen, the guys that started in '58 were the toughest sons of bitches that ever walked on a football field . . . let me tell you, I was in

College Station when Coach Bryant came to Texas A&M, and I went
through hell, but let me tell you, the hell that I went through plus what
these guys went through, we put it on these guys, we were sent there to
run people off . . . the guys that were there at the end of that spring . . . they
did well, they were tough."

Among those who did not complete that first season, conversely,
there are many who still reproach themselves for what they have come to
believe was a mistake, even a failure of character, at a critical time in their
young lives. It is not an exaggeration to say that some of them have spent
the rest of their lives trying to come to terms with this failure and
continue striving to rise above it. Danny Wilbanks, who became a
dentist, got a degree of satisfaction when he ran into Bryant at an
Alabama alumni function. "He looked at me, like 'Well, I'll be damned,'
because Coach Bryant thought if you didn't stick . . . you would never
amount to a hell of a lot . . ."

It would, no doubt, require a strong sense of self-confidence to be a
Bryant detractor in the state of Alabama, and perhaps this accounts for
the fact that, even among those who quit or who were "run off" in that
first season, there are many who now profess admiration for their coach.
But there is something impressive, nonetheless, in what seems to be
genuine affection among these "lost" players for this man who had
treated them so callously.

"That has haunted me all my life, quitting," Sammy Smith said.
" . . . so now when I undertake something I think very carefully about it,
I say if I'm going to do this, I'm not going to quit."

Danny Wilbanks says, "Coach Bryant has always been my hero."
Billy Rains says that he regarded the coach as a "second father." But there
are others, no doubt, who simply hold their tongues in the face of the
reverence accorded the legendary coach.

That Bryant mellowed in his later years is indisputable. When Bud
Moore came back as an assistant coach in 1972, Bryant quickly made it
clear to him saying, "You can't coach these boys today like I coached
you." Jack Rutledge said that Bryant, sometime in the '70s, told all of his
coaches, "Don't put your hands on them any more, because if you do,

I'm going to be on the players' side." Bryant "felt he had done wrong . . . he knew he had made some mistakes by pushing a lot of these athletes too hard," Rutledge said. When Buck Burns finished law school, Bryant wrote him a warm letter of congratulations — perhaps a sort of atonement.

The players who had stuck it out and played through the pain and sacrifice of that year, even those who never rose above the Blue Darters, earned Bryant's lasting respect, and whenever he encountered one in later years he seemed genuinely glad to see them. He always remembered their names and asked how they were doing, and if Bryant made a speech where one was known, he would never fail to mention him kindly. Jasper Best, who was redshirted in 1958 and never played in a game, took his four-year-old son by Bryant's office one day, and was surprised when the coach remembered his name and home town. Bryant would go out of his way to help with a small loan or to intercede with a fellow coach, a principal, or a potential employer for a job. When Marlin Dyess, always a Bryant favorite, had a heart attack in 1982, Bryant broke away from practice before the season's opening game to call him in the hospital.

Stopping by to see the coach many years later, Bobby Jackson, still uncomfortable in his presence, was amazed when Bryant came over and put his arms around him. "Bobby Jackson, how are you doing . . . . I haven't hugged you in a long time," the old Bear said.

Jackson could not help thinking, "Coach, you ain't never hugged me." But he was touched, nonetheless.

Where They Are Now

CHUCK ALLEN is a senior bank officer in Birmingham.

SAM BAILEY remained at Alabama until 1988, serving at various times as assistant head coach and assistant athletic director. Bailey died in 1990.

JAMES BEALL is president of the Farmers and Merchants Bank of Centre.

JASPER BEST works for Scapa Pressed Fabrics. He lives in Ashford.

JIM BLEVINS works for Roadway Express in Huntsville.

BAXTER BOOTH is an insurance agent in Huntsville.

BOBBY BOYLSTON is an account executive with Interstate/Johnson Lane, an Atlanta investment firm

JERRY BRANNEN is a sales representative for Duck Head clothing in Gainesville, Florida. His son, Jay, lettered for Alabama in 1993.

JOE CAMPBELL is assistant headmaster at Brentood Academy in Nashville, Tennessee.

MORRIS CHILDERS and his partners run a marketing firm in Birmingham.

JERRY CLAIBORNE became head coach at the University of Kentucky. Now retired from coaching, and he lives in Lexington, Kentucky.

DON COCHRAN is in the home construction business in Pinson.

MERRILL (HOOTCHMAN) COLLINS died in 1968, at the age of 80, three years before the first black football player played at Alabama.

FERDY CRUCE transferred to Northeast Louisiana, where he averaged 4.4 yards a carry as a halfback in 1960. He lives in Florence.

PHIL CUTCHIN became head coach at Oklahoma State, and then became a stock broker. He is retired and lives in Afton, Oklahoma.

BENNY DEMPSEY lives in Montgomery. He is a sales representative with AAA Cooper Transportation.

MARLIN (SCOOTER) DYESS owns a commercial and industrial construction firm in Montgomery.

BUTCH FRANK is a cardiologist in Atlanta.

JOHNNY (RED) GANN builds homes in Huntsville.

JIM GOOSTREE retired in 1983. He lives in Tuscaloosa.

CHARLIE GRAY is a bank consultant. He lives in Birmingham.

BILL HANNAH died in a plane crash in 1971, on a recruiting trip for Cal State–Fullerton.

DONALD HEATH continued to work out in practice as a backup center. Bryant honored his scholarship, and he earned a letter without playing in a game. He is production manager for Goodyear Tire and Rubber in Gadsden.

ROY HOLSOMBACK is a retired high school principal. He lives in Mt. Olive.

DODD HOLT earned a law degree but does not practice. He is semi-retired in Cullman.

BOBBY JACKSON played professional football for the Philadelphia Eagles and Chicago Bears. He is an account manager for a radio station in Mobile.

PAT JAMES coached at Alabama until 1964. He runs a barbecue restaurant in Birmingham.

BERT JONES sells Jostens class rings and graduation supplies. He helped design and produce all of Alabama's national championship rings and SEC championship rings. He lives in Tuscaloosa.

DRAKE KEITH stayed in coaching until the mid-'60s, when he went into business. He is president of Arkansas Power and Light Company in Little Rock, Arkansas.

BOBBY LUNA went back to pro football in 1960, and then went into the construction business. He lives in College Grove, Tennessee.

BILL KNIGHT is managing partner of Burr & Forman, a Birmingham law firm.

BUD MOORE became a coach and eventually head coach at the University of Kansas. He raises cattle, horses and bird dogs in Catherine, Alabama, and runs a beer distributorship in Pensacola, Florida.

DUFF MORRISON runs a janitorial and painting company in Birmingham. His son Tim also played at Alabama. Duff lives in Pell City.

ELLIOTT MOSELEY died in an automobile accident in 1971.

GARY O'STEEN's three daughters attended the University on Bryant scholarships. He lives in Anniston.

HENRY O'STEEN went into law enforcement, first as a state trooper and then with the Federal Bureau of Alcohol, Tobacco and Firearms. He now works for the U.S. State Department in Washington, D.C.

DON PARSONS was redshirted, re-injured his neck in practice before the 1959 season, and left the team. He returned in 1960, won a spot, and then re-injured his neck again. He lives in Houston, Texas.

JAP PATTON practices law in Tuscumbia and lives in Sheffield.

GARY PHILLIPS is a retired orthopedic surgeon. He lives in Montgomery and Baker, Florida.

DAN PITTS owns three convenience stores in Ft. Payne.

JOHN PAUL POOLE is a nuclear engineer in Bay City, Texas.

DEE POWELL is a development director at Auburn University.

BILLY RAINS stayed in school until January 1959. Then he took a job with Commercial Credit Corporation, where he worked for 33 years. Now retired, he lives in Moulton.

PETE REAVES works for a manufacturer of gas and oil well equipment. He lives in Houston, Texas.

JERRY RICH is an Allstate agent in Carollton, Georgia.

CHARLIE RIEVES transferred to the University of Houston. In his junior year, he was the team's leading ground scorer. He lives in Houston.

KEN ROBERTS is a retired engineer in Birmingham. His son played at Alabama under Bryant and Ray Perkins.

NORBIE RONSONET is president of an automobile dealership in Lake City, Florida.

JACK RUTLEDGE was redshirted, and played on the 1961 National Championship team. He is academic counselor and director of Bryant Hall at the University of Alabama.

WALTER SANSING is a sales representative for Alabama Institutional Foods in Tuscaloosa.

WAYNE SIMS and his partners manufacture mobile homes in Boaz.

FRED SINGTON JR. earned a law degree at Alabama. He is administrative assistant to the mayor of Gadsden.

DAVID SINGTON is in the travel business in Huntsville.

ROBERT SKELTON is an NFL official and a project manager with the Alabama Development Office in Montgomery.

BOBBY SMITH is a middle school principal in Shalimar, Florida.

SAMMY SMITH went into the army and retired as a Lieutenant Colonel. He lives in Lacey Spring.

JERRY SPRUIELL went into the Army, flew rescue helicopters in

Vietnam, and retired as a full colonel. He works for the Georgia State Board of Pardons and Paroles in Atlanta.

GENE STALLINGS is head football coach at the University of Alabama.

LAURIEN (GOOBY) STAPP is retired. He lives in Dover, Tennessee.

RED STICKNEY coaches high school football in Virginia Beach, Virginia.

RICHARD STRUM is a retired Navy commander. He has a home in Honduras.

RUSSELL STUTTS is in the investment business in Birmingham.

CARL VALLETTO's son David played for Alabama in 1983 and 1984. Carl, an insurance adjustor, lives in Woodland Hills, California.

BUDDY WESLEY runs a construction company in Talladega.

GARY WHITE retired as associate athletic director at the University of Alabama and is now a consultant to the athletic department.

TOMMY WHITE is director of adult education for the Pickens County Board of Education and is an SEC official.

DANNY WILBANKS finished his senior year and went to dental school. He is a dentist in Tallassee.

MACK WISE manufactures and distributes fishing tackle in Luverne.

Game Boxes and Statistics

LSU 13, Alabama 3 — September 27, 1958
Ladd Stadium, Mobile, Alabama. Attendance: 34,000.

	Alabama	LSU
First downs	7	17
Yards rushing	104	182
Yards passing	0	73
Passing	3-0	13 - 6
Passes int'd by	0	0
Punting	8 - 43	7 -36.5
Fumbles lost	1	1
Yards penalized	60	75

Score by quarters:

Louisiana State	0	0	7	6	—	13
Alabama	0	3	0	0	—	3

Alabama — FG Singon 19.
LSU — Robinson 9 pass from Rabb (Davis kick).
LSU — Cannon 11 run (kick failed).

ALABAMA (3): Left ends — Brannen, Ronsonet, Moore. Left tackles — Valletto, Booth. Left guards — Sims, Hannah. Centers — Roberts, Blevins. Right guards — Cochran, F. Singon, Rains. Right tackles — D. Singon, Reaves, Allen. Right ends — Gray, H. O'Steen. Quarterbacks — Jackson, G. O'Steen, Smith. Left halfbacks — Dyess, Morrison, Spruiell. Right halfbacks — Wise, Cruce. Fullbacks — Frank, Wesley, Sansing.

LSU (13): Left ends — Hendrix, McClain, Bourgeois. Left tackles — LeBlanc, McCarty, Branch. Left guards — Kahlden, Fournet, Lott. Centers — Fugler, Langan. Right guards — McCreedy, Dampier, Fournet. Right tackles — Strange, Bergeron, Leopard. Right ends — Norwood, Mangham, Kinchen. Quarterbacks — Rabb, Matherne. Left halfbacks — Cannon, Purvis. Right halfbacks — Robinson, Daye, Roberts. Fullbacks — Brodnax, Davis.

223

Vanderbilt 0, Alabama 0 — October 4, 1958

Legion Field, Birmingham, Alabama. Attendance: 36,000.

	Alabama	Vanderbilt
First downs	6	14
Yards rushing	103	156
Yards passing	12	64
Passes	1 -5	8 - 15
Passes int'd by	2	2
Punts	9 - 38.1	9 - 32.3
Fumbles lost	2	2
Yards penalized	30	25

VANDERBILT (0): Left ends — Hilley, Riggs. Left tackles — Redmond, Cobb. Left guards — Deiderich, D. Thompson. Centers — Bonnell, Bates. Right guards — Grover, Hughes, Dudley. Right tackles — Wagner, Wildman. Right ends — Kin, Burnham, Miller. Quarterbacks — B. Smith, McKee. Left halfbacks — Rolfe, Ray. Right halfbacks — Moore, Hagewood, McCall. Fullbacks — Butler, P. Thompson, Bulkeley.

ALABAMA (0): Left ends — Brannen, Ronsonet, Moore, Poole. Left tackles — Valletto, Booth. Left guards — Sims, Phillips. Centers — Roberts, Blevins. Right guards — Cochran, Parsons, Hannah, Rains. Right tackles — D. Sington, Holsomback, Allen, F. Sington. Right ends — Gray, H. O'Steen. Quarterbacks — Jackson, G. O'Steen, Smith. Left halfbacks — Morrison, Spruiell. Right halfbacks — Wise, Dyess, Stapp, Cruce. Fullbacks — Sansing, Wesley, Frank.

Alabama 29, Furman 6 — October 11, 1958

Denny Stadium, Tuscaloosa, Alabama. Attendance: 17,000.

	Furman	Alabama
First downs	10	12
Yards rushing	149	183
Yards passing	39	75
Passes	3-10	2 - 4
Passes int'd by	0	2
Punts	7 - 32.0	6 - 42.3
Fumbles lost	1	0
Yards penalilzed	45	100

Score by quarters:

Furman	0	0	6	0	—	6
Alabama	20	3	6	0	—	29

Alabama — Jackson 2 run (F. Sington kick).
Alabama — Stapp 14 pass from Smith (Patton kick).
Alabama — O'Steen 44 punt return (Patton kick failed).
Alabama — Reaves, field goal, 24.
Furman — Nickles 9 run (pass failed).
Alabama — O'Steen 61 pass from Smith (Cruce kick failed).

FURMAN (6): Left ends — Siminiski, Stewart, Newnan. Left tackles — Boroff, Alkin. Left guards — Harrison, Belskis. Center — Walton. Right guard — Ingrum. Right tackles — Markofski, Oliff. Right ends — Avery, mery. Quarterbacks — Baker, Taylor. Left halfbacks — Nickles, Fowler, Yale. Right halfbacks — Gay, Edwards, Morrison. Fullbacks — Horton, Sampson.

ALABAMA (29): Left ends — Brannen, Moore. Left tackles — Valletto, Booth, Reaves. Left guards — Sims, Phillips, Holsomback, Rains. Centers — Roberts, Blevins, Moseley. Right guards — Cochran, Rains, F. Sington. Right tackles — D. Sington, Allen, Hannah, Boylston. Right ends — Gray, H. O'Steen, Childers. Quarterbacks — Jackson, Smith, Patton. Left halfbacks — Spruiell, Dyess, O'Steen, White, Cruce. Right halfbacks — Morrison, Dyess, Stapp, Wise, Cruce. Fullbacks — Frank, Stickney.

Tennessee 14, Alabama 7 — October 18, 1958

Shields-Watkins Field, Knoxville, Tennessee. Attendance: 34,000.

	Alabama	Tennessee
First downs	10	8
Yards rushing	98	131
Yards passing	129	12
Passes	7 - 10	2 - 4
Passes int'd by	0	0
Punts	9 - 37.5	10 - 35.6
Fumbles lost	3	0
Yards penalized	75	30

Score by quarters:

Alabama	0	0	0	7	—	7
Tennessee	0	7	7	0	—	14

Tennessee — Majors 1 plunge (Burklow kick).
Tennessee — Majors 6 run (Burklow kick).
Alabama — Jackson 1 plunge (Reaves kick).

ALABAMA (7). Left ends — Brannen, Moore. Left tackles — Valletto, Booth, Reaves. Left guards — Sims, Phillips, Holsomback. Centers — Roberts, Blevins. Right guards — Cochran, Rains. Right tackles — D. Sington, Hannah. Right ends — Gray. Quarterback — Jackson, Smith. Left halfbacks — Cruce, Spruiell, Dyess. Right halfbacks — Morrison, Stapp. Fullbacks — Wesley, Stapp.

TENNESSEE (14). Left ends — LaSorsa, Leake. Left tackles — Shafer, Jackson. Left guards — Urbano, Schultz, Lukowski. Centers — Brant, Ditnore, Husband. Right guards — Franklin, Patterson. Right tackles — Schaffer, Shields, Krause. Right ends — M. Armstrong, Letner. Blocking back — Sadler, Cartwright. Tailbacks — Majors, Etter. Wingbacks — Sandlin, Stephens, Burklow. Fullbacks — Smith, Sollee.

Alabama 9, Mississippi State 7 — October 25, 1958

Scott Field, Starkville, Mississippi. Attendance: 26,000.

	Alabama	MSU
First downs	8	10
Yards rushing	142	234
Yards passing	44	22
Passes	4 - 5	3 - 10
Passes int'd by	1	0
Punts	11 - 46.6	9 - 38.6
Fumbles lost	0	1
Yards penalized	60	15

Score by quarters:

Alabama	3	0	6	0	—	9
Mississippi State	0	0	0	7	—	7

Alabama — Sington, field goal, 12.
Alabama — Ronsonet, 21 pass from Jackson. (kick failed).
Mississippi State — Stacy, 6 run. (Tribble kick).

ALABAMA (9): Left ends — Brannen, Moore, Ronsonet. Left tackles — Booth, Valletto, Reaves. Left guards — Sims, Phillips. Centers — Blevins, Roberts. Right guards — Cochran, Hannah, F. Sington. Right tackles — Hannah, D. Sington, Allen. Right ends — Gray, Poole. Quarterbacks — Jackson, Smith, Patton. Left halfbacks — O'Steen, Dyess. Right halfbacks — Morrison, Dyess, Stapp, Wise. Fullbacks — Wesley, Frank.

MISSISSIPPI STATE (7): Left ends — Blake, Neaves. Left tackles — Tribble, M. Smith. Left guards — Benson, Daniels, Hodges. Centers — Potete, Goode. Right guards — Kennedy, Mangum, Rushing. Right tackles — Suggs, Irby, Clements. Right ends — White, Brooks. Quarterbacks — Stacy, Miller. Left halfbacks — Trammell, Daniel, Collins. Right halfbacks — Peterson, Bates, Shute. Fullbacks — Batte, Skipper, Shroenrock.

Alabama 12, Georgia 0 — November 1, 1958

Denny Stadium, Tuscaloosa, Alabama. Attendance: 28,000.

	Georgia	Alabama
First downs	14	7
Yards rushing	179	126
Yards passing	112	16
Passes	6 - 20	3 - 3
Passes int'd by	0	4
Punts	8 - 35	12 - 43.7
Fumbles lost	1	1
Yards penalized	20	10

Score by quarters:

Georgia	0	0	0	0	—	0
Alabama	6	0	0	6	—	12

Alabama — O'Steen 14 run (kick failed).
Alabama — Jackson 1 run (run failed).

GEORGIA (0): Left ends — Vickers, Kick. Left tackles — Lancaster, Gunnels, Leeburn. Left guards — Roland, P. Dye. Centers — Lloyd, F. Ashe. Right guards — Anderson, Ramsey. Right tackles — N. Dye, Hansesn, Lawrence. Right ends — Kelly, Herron, Box. Quarterbacks — Britt, Tarkenton, Lewis, Paris. Left halfbaccks — Guisler, Brown, Walden. Right halfbacks — Soberdash, Littleton, Towns. Fullbacks — Sapp, Lucas.

ALABAMA (12): Left ends — Poole, Brannen, Ronsonet, Moore. Left tackles — Reaves, Valletto. Left guards — Phillips, Sims. Centers — Roberts, Blevins. Right guards — Cochran, Hannah. Right tackles — D. Sington, Allen. Right ends — Gray, Booth. Quarterbacks — Jackson, Smith, Patton. Left halfbacks, O'Steen, Dyess. Right halfbacks — Morrison, Stapp. Fullbacks — Wesley, F. Sington, Frank.

Tulane 13, Alabama 7 — November 7, 1958

Sugar Bowl Stadium, New Orleans, Louisiana. Attendance: 35,000.

	Alabama	Tulane
First downs	10	11
Yards rushing	170	155
Yards passing	64	41
Passing	3-14	6 - 13
Passes int'd by	2	1
Punts	8 -35.1	6 - 36
Fumbles lost	2	1
Yards penalized	45	10

Score by quarters:

Alabama	0	0	7	0	—	7
Tulane	6	0	7	0	—	13

Tulane — Dunn 1 run (Kisner kick failed).
Tulane — Petitbon, 1 run (Kisner kick).
Alabama — Jackson 1 run (Sington kick).

ALABAMA (7): Left ends — Ronsonet, Moore, Brannen. Left tackles — Reaves, Valletto. Left guards — Sims, Phillips. Centers — Roberts, Blevins. Right guards — Cochran, Hannah, Holsomback. Right tackles — D. Sington, Allen. Right ends — Booth, Gray. Quarterbacks — Jackson, Smith. Left halfbacks —O'Steen, Dyess, White. Right halfbacks — Morrison, Stapp, Wise. Fullbacks — Sansing, Wesley, F. Sington.

TULANE (13): Left ends — Brabham, Abadie. Left tackles — LeSage, Ridgway. Left guards — DiVietro, Cosse; Centers — Jones, Painter. Right guards — Clements, Blount, Guillot. Right tackles — D. Egan, Darre, Klick. Right ends — Young, McLean. Quarterbacks — Petitbon, Nugent. Left halfbacks — Kisner, Colon. Right halfbacks — C. Mason, T. Mason. Fullbacks — Dunn, McClellan, Andrews.

Alabama 17, Georgia Tech 8 — November 15, 1958
Grant Field, Atlanta, Georgia. Attendance: 44,726.

	Alabama	Georgia Tech
First downs	6	15
Yards rushing	124	173
Yards passing	10	102
Passes	1 - 2	9 - 22
Pass int'd by	4	0
Punts	6 - 35.8	3 - 39.3
Fumbles lost	2	2
Yards penalized	10	35

Score by quarters:

Alabama	17	0	0	0	—	17
Georgia Tech	0	0	8	0	—	8

Alabama — Jackson 1 run (Reaves kick).
Alabama — FG Reaves 19.
Alabama — Jackson 5 run (Reaves kick).
Georgia Tech — Shaw 7 run (Burch pass from Braselton).

ALABAMA (17): Left ends — Ronsonet, Poole, Brannen, Moore. Left tackles — Reaves, Valletto, Boylston. Left guards — Phillips, Sims. Centers — Roberts, Mosely, Rutledge. Right guards — Cochran, Parsons, Holsomback. Right tackles — D. Sington, Hannah, Allen. Right ends — Booth, Gray, Childers. Quarterbacks — Jackson, Smith, Patton. Left halfbacks — O'Steen, Dyess, White. Right halfbacks — Morrison, Stapp, Wise. Fullbacks — Sansing, Wesley, Frank.

GEORGIA TECH (8): Left ends — Rudolph, Green, Murphy. Left tackles — Deese, Shaw, Lasch. Left guards — Watkins, Tye. Centers — Baughan, D. Smith. Right guards — Goodrie, Reed. Right tackles — Mason, Thomas. Right ends, T. Rose, Burch. Quarterbacks — Howard, Braselton. Left halflbacks — Faucette, James, Logan. Right halfbacks — Delany, Nix, Wells. Fullbacks — Tibbetts, Lewis, Fonts, Simerville.

Alabama 14, Memphis State 0 — November 22, 1958

Denny Stadium, Tuscaloosa, Alabama. Attendance: 26,500.

	Memphis State	Alabama
First downs	7	11
Yards rushing	106	208
Yards passing	34	85
Passes	6 - 14	2 - 11
Passes int'd by	1	1
Punts	11 - 33.6	10 - 33.8
Fumbles lost	2	2
Yards penalized	60	85

Score by quarters:

Memphis State	0	0	0	0	—	0
Alabama	6	8	0	0	—	14

Alabama — Dyess 68 pass from Jackson (kick failed).
Alabama — Jackson 18 run (Jackson run).

MEMPHIS STATE (0): Left ends — Sterlin, Coffee. Left tackles — Armstrong, Hudson, H. Jenson. Left guards — Hathcock, Buckner, Self. Centers — Taylor, Tirey, Lott, Bibbs. Right guards — Randolph, Mathews, Adragna. Right tackles — McKinnon, Heathcott, Owen. Right ends — Lee, Liss. Quarterbacks — Buoni, Wright, Hearn. Left halfbacks — Wimpee, Lovelace, Cole. Right halfbacks — Steadley, Reese, Brooks. Fullbacks — Lyles, Parrish, Loyd.

ALABAMA (14): Left ends — Poole, Moore, Brannen, Ronsonet. Left tackles — Reaves, Hannah, Valletto. Left guards — Phillips, Sims, Pitts. Centers — Roberts, Blevins, Mosely. Right guards — Cochran, Parsons, Stutts. Right tackles — Allen , Holsomback. Right ends — Booth, Gray, Childers. Quarterbacks — Jackson, Smith, Patton. Left halfbacks — O'Steen, White, Spruiell. Right halfbacks — Dyess, Morrison, Stapp, Wise. Fullbacks — Wesley, Frank, Stickney.

Auburn 14, Alabama 8 — November 29, 1958
Legion Field, Birmingham, Alabama. Attendance: 44,000.

	Auburn	Alabama
First downs	13	12
Yards rushing	174	92
Passes	6 - 11	13 -22
Yards passing	86	132
Passes int'd by	0	2
Punts	4 - 34	9 - 30
Fumbles lost	2	0
Yards penalized	55	65

Score by quarters:

Auburn	7	0	0	7	—	14
Alabama	0	0	0	8	—	8

Auburn — Pettus 3 pass from Wood (Dyas kick).
Auburn — Reynolds, 1 run (Wilson kick).
Alabama — Dyess 9 run (O'Steen pass from Jackson).

AUBURN (14): Left ends — Wilson, Wasden. Left tackles —Foret, Myers, Paduch. Left guards — Smith, Warrick, Putman. Centers — Burkett, Ricketts. Right guards — LaRussa, Clapp, Braswell. Right tackles — Wester, Jeffery, Rice. Right ends — Simmons, Sexton, Leichtnam. Quarterbacks — Nix, Wood. Left halfbacks — Lorino, Pettus, Laster. Right halfbacks — Rawson, Lauder. Fullbacks — Reynolds, Dyas.

ALABAMA (8): Left ends — Poole, Moore, Brannen, Spruiell. Left tackles — Reaves, Valletto. Left Guards — Phillps, Sims. Centers — Roberts, Blevins. Right guards — Cochran, Hannah. Right tackles — Allen, D. Sington. Right ends — Booth, Gray. Quarterbacks — Jackson, Smith. Left Halfbacks — G. O'Steen, Dyess, White. Right halfbacks — Morrison, Stapp, Wise. Fullbacks — Wesley, Stickney, Sansing, Frank.

Index

Occurrences of football players' names in the statistical game summaries on pages 223-232 are not included in this index.